Too Much Tuscan Wine

by Dario Castagno
with Robert Rodi

Copyright © 2008 by Dario Castagno and Robert Rodi

© Copyright 2008 Dario Castagno / Robert Rodi
Sketchs by: Monica Minucci
Layout and phototypesetting: Bernard & Co, Siena
Printed by: Ciani Artigrafiche, Colle Val d'Elsa SI
May 2008

ISBN: 978-88-901102-4-5

Wine makes you feel the way
you should feel without a wine

Contents

Author's note 7

1 The proposal 13

2 Chasing after memory .19

3 Encounter on a hillside 27

4 Reverie 33

5 At the office 37

6 Things misheard, things overheard 41

7 Doctor's orders 49

8 The rise of the wine 55

9 Addio Umberto 59

10 From the renaissance to modern times 63

11 The final truss (part one) 69

12 The final truss (part two) 83

13 The final truss (conclusion) 91

14 Out and about 95

15 Suddently, Elio 99

16 The birth of Andrea 105

17 The tennis experiment 113

18 Well oiled 125

19 The fruit of the labors 135

20 Una giornata particolare 143

21 In vino veritas 153

22 Crappy new year 165

23 The poolio 183

24 Requiem 199

25 The importance of being on time 215

26 The bolshevik 227

27 he madre of them all 243

28 Mimì 261

Ringraziamenti 280

uthor's note

The well-known American author Don DeLillo, whose Italian parents emigrated to the US before he was born, once wrote "Authors drink too much because they are so often alone with their weighty thoughts, and this exacts a toll: writing is like a disease".

The events that have marked my personal development, combined with an amazing series of flukes and happenstances, have combined to determine the unusual course of my life and made it possible for me to live in my own marvelous world, but alone.

I wouldn't define my current situation as the result of conscious choices, but as the inevitable end of a long, winding path — one that I hadn't exactly planned, but which was probably sketched out somewhere in the deep recesses of my subconscious.

Ironically for one so solitary, I've often been described as a "people person" who seeks out and enjoys the company of others. Irrefutable proof of this would seem to be my embarking on a career as a tour guide at the end of the 1980s; I made a profession of sharing with others the passion I feel for the land on which I live, and of providing the proper context for appreciating the bounty of historical, artistic and oenological beauties the Chianti area offers.

Please forgive me if I point with pride to my success. The numbers alone are confirmation; I've had the good fortune to accompany some thousands of tourists over my fifteen years in the field. What's more, the vast majority were sent to me by friends, relatives and acquaintances whom I had previously encountered —word of mouth being the most efficient and satisfying of all agencies, a dense, nearly infinite cobweb of correspondence and contacts that expands like an oil stain; an inexhaustible font of priceless value.

It was indeed a pleasure as well as an honor to share day by day the traditions of my hills with the enthusiastic and the curious. Without doubt the most significant remuneration, from a purely human point of view, was being able to meet such an astonishing variety of wonderful people from all over the world; their singularity and capacity to surprise kept me alert and engaged and gave me the strength to continue in my activity almost non-stop for a decade and a half.

Alas, however, this magic spell was shattered after the publication of my first book. It became apparent that many tourists were booking my services less to discover the secrets of Chianti than to discover the secrets of Dario Castagno. Unwilling to play the role of celebrity, especially at the expense of the countryside I love so much, my will to continue as a tour guide began to fade. My spiel, which had always been in part improvisation, became rote, a series of phrases that issued from my mouth: but not from my heart.

I hadn't become a tour guide by chance, or alternatively by some carefully calibrated plan for success; it had been purely a matter of profound interior desire. I've always believed in listening as the best means of judging the world; now, listening to myself, I realized I no longer had anything worth saying. Painful as it was, I knew the era of Dario the guide had irretrievably concluded.

The official excuse to end the activity soon followed. As a consequence of the remarkable tourist boom Chianti now enjoys, the local authorities decided to regulate (rightly so) the tour-guide profession. In the last few years, new laws have been enacted to safeguard tourists and guarantee them quality service, and today whoever desires to become a guide is obliged to take special courses and pass examinations in order to obtain the required license.

My innate pride and rebelliousness prevented me from doing this; I refused to solicit permission to practice a profession that I had, in Chianti, practically invented. And considering that my appetite for the job had waned while my literary career waxed, I decided to give way to a new generation. That way I could still offer tours but delegate the task of conducting them to newer and fresher guides.

This all occurred between Winter 2004 and Spring 2005, when I returned from my first U.S. book tour (for *Too Much Tuscan Sun*). I rewarded myself with a breather — or maybe it would be better defined as a hiatus in which to consider reordering my life. In defiance of my sudden fame I decided to dedicate the rest of the tourist season entirely all to myself. I purchased a second-hand racing bike and spent days immersed in what I consider my natural habitat: cycling in solitude for thousands of miles, as I did in my teenage years with my scooter. I discovered once again the euphoria of that carefree period of my adolescence when I would aimlessly stooge around without any particular destination, seeking only strong and unknown sensations.

Oddly enough, these rediscovered feelings enticed me to encounter people again, and I began experimenting with a new formula that I consider a sort of logical evolution of my original profession.

Today I limit myself to small gatherings that I hold in the splendid medieval structure of the Relais Borgo Scopeto. There I welcome old friends and former clients as well as new faces, most of whom come as fans of my books specifically to make my acquaintance. Many drive themselves to my door; others include me as a stop while touring Chianti with another guide. Either way, I again have the pleasure of spreading my love for the area by narrating anecdotes, lecturing on the history of the area, and enumerating its curiosities — a labor that often extends into lunch and a bottle (very often more) of Chianti Classico.

This third volume completes the trilogy of memoirs of my Chianti life and times; I undertook it in 2006 and completed it in 2007. Unlike the first two, it was conceived more by chance than by design, and was prompted entirely by a third party — whose remarkable story will unfold in the pages ahead of you. But once I began setting down these new stories — of my life-long and often wildly eventful relationship with this region's incomparable wine — I felt a welling of desire to honor my subject; it became a subtext to my daily, solitary life, from which I drew much more than the satisfaction of a job well done, as you will soon discover in these pages.

For those readers who enter this book after having read my first two, my wish is that you will be able to detect and appreciate the different state of mind in which I wrote them. *Too Much Tuscan Sun* is a light-hearted look back from a happy vantage point in my life; *A Day in Tuscany* springs forth from the melancholy of having been abandoned by a companion I loved dearly. Now comes *Too Much Tuscan Wine,* which brings about a rebirth, both of my spirit and of my connection to Chianti. Obviously the common theme uniting all three is the love I feel for this territory, for its beautiful, picturesque natives both past and present, and — especially in this case —for its most famous product. The wine!

Salute
Dario Castagno

To Mimì

1

THE PROPOSAL

Saturday, November 11, 7 a.m.

My wake-up call is all-natural. I'm roused by the sun as it ascends behind the eastern hills of Chianti. Its insistent rays penetrate my bedroom window and ripple over me, and I allow them to stroke my face gently for a few luxurious moments. Then I slowly open my eyes and watch as the light expands to take possession of the entire room. The sudden brightness warms the egg-yolk hued paint with which I recently adorned the walls, and brightens the cool green of the ficus plants in their terracotta vases at the foot of my brass bed.

It's been many years since I stopped closing the shutters at night; in my opinion, it would be unforgivable to block out the spectacular show nature offers us daily. True, observing the sunrise each morning is a bit like attending the same theatrical performance every day. The crucial difference is that the performance I enjoy varies wildly with regard to the temperature, the level of humidity, the disposition of the clouds and an infinite number of other imperceptible, ambient factors that can never be truly identical to the scene as it was played the previous day. So while each new sunrise might initially seem repetitive, it is in fact never predictable — and let me add an element unusual in today's society: it never asks for anything in exchange.

Still half asleep, I slip out of bed and head to the window. Despite the fresh, fizzy morning air I lean out, the better to take in the view of the valley below. As always, it has been swallowed by a thick layer of fog, which will melt away as soon as this first glorious burst of sun reaches it. In the meantime, from the mountains of mist there emerge only the uppermost tips of the ancient towers scattered across the countryside; with a bit of imagination it can seem as if a freakishly high tide has taken possession of the entire valley. Some million years ago, when the Tyrrhenian Sea used to lap against these very hills, this is what Chianti might have looked like. I nurture this fantasy, toy with it as I sway between lingering sleep and the sweet torpor of waking.

This, then, is the serene, refreshing way my mornings almost always begin.

Today, however . . .

My head, as I crane my neck through the window, feels as heavy as concrete, like it might snap off my neck and fall; it bobbles, it throbs, each chirp of a bird resounds like thunder in my ears. My eyes refuse to focus; they well up with tears, as though the fresh air were laced with mustard gas. My mouth puckers and parches; it still holds the acid flavor of the wine I drank in such epic quantities last night, at an assembly in nearby Siena of the Noble *contrada* of the *Bruco* — my beloved Caterpillar district.

I try to recall the specifics of what happened. As is usually the case at such gatherings, after the conclusion of the agenda and the closing comments by the *Rettore*, I stopped to exchange a few words and to drink a few *gottini* (shots) with my Caterpillar comrades. As always, we punctuated our drinking with several rounds of songs and hymns dedicated to the glory of our *contrada* — glory which surrounded us, physically, there in the Caterpillar's headquarters, hung with the effigies, banners and photos of the victorious horses and riders who had triumphed in past Palios — those enduring, immortal bareback horse races that each July and August are the highlights of the Sienese calendar. And so, between bursts of lyric and bottles of Tuscan red, we paid homage to our heritage deep into the night.

And then what happened? . . . I remember eventually making my way to my car, and becoming aware that I was slightly staggering — no doubt due to the copious amounts of wine coursing through my veins. I accordingly decided it would be best to return home via an anti-breathalyzer route I've perfected over the years. It amounts to a longer distance, but has the essential advantage that its nearly complete isolation neatly evades any possibility of encountering any police. The snag, alas, is that en route I'm obliged to pass in front of Albert's *osteria* — in whose window last night I spotted a dim light filtering through the half-closed rolling shutter. It had been a while since I'd seen Alberto, so I reasoned it would be rude not to stop in for a quick hello. I pulled up and parked in the small square in front of the restaurant.

Alberto, I now recall, had just finished cleaning up, his staff had gone home, and all the chairs but one had been stacked on the tables for the night. Alberto himself was seated casually and alone, puffing on a cigar and pouring himself a glass of Morellino di Scansano from a bottle he'd just opened. As soon as I passed beneath the partially lowered metal shutter — with my head dangling behind me and my torso curved back as though I were doing the limbo — he invited me to join him, and fetched me a glass which he proceeded to fill up to the brim.

As we drank, we discussed the new American Center that Siena's basketball team had purchased for its upcoming season, which we agreed could only result in the squad's decisive leap in quality. Eventually, having exhausted the subject of defense tactics and strategies, we switched to more substantial topics for the second bottle; and by the third we were avidly solving global warming, eliminating Third World starvation, and forging brilliant solutions to the murderous conflicts that beset the Middle East.

When finally I reached home and lay my head upon the pillow, the blue readout on the alarm clock proclaimed that it was 3.47 a.m.

Now that I've recalled all this, I feel quite justified in having a ringing headache, a furred mouth and — I imagine — the kind of breath one might have after swallowing the corpse of a decomposed sewage rat who died of dysentery.

As I don't want to feel guilty, I decide to don as penance a heavy woolen poncho I purchased in Guatemala and which has been hanging on my poplar cloak hanger ever since. Then I drag my sluggish body to the small office next to the bedroom to check my e-mail — after the performance of which duty, I promise myself, I will return to bed and hope that Morpheus, the Greek god of sleep, will readmit me to his realm of dreams.

I turn on the computer and the 56K modem. With my bloodshot eyes — "the eyes of a sailor' as we say in Italian — I stare at the monitor as it slowly downloads 224 new messages. My heart sinks at the sheer volume of them.

With a bit of difficulty (due to my numb, unresponsive fingers) I manage to identify the spam, first deleting any correspondence offering me cheap Viagra and Cialis. Then I abolish the invitations to websites where I'm assured I can see photos of Paris Hilton or Posh Spice naked. Finally I eradicate all the notifications of the many lotteries I've won overnight, and two urgent pleas from fake relatives of fake monarchs of fake African nations offering me millions of fake dollars in exchange for all my financial passwords and the free use of my bank account.

I've always taken it for granted that anyone who spends time on-line must receive this kind of spam daily. Otherwise — if this were really the fruit of research by expert marketers who have studied the habits and attitudes of my Internet usage and tailored their messages accordingly — I would have to be classified as a perpetually impotent sex maniac, who is also utterly guileless. (While I may confidently deny the former, I admit to being a little wary about being the latter.)

After having banished all the annoyances to the trash, there are nine mails left, six of which comprise fan mail for my previous books, which is always very welcome. As usual, the writers ask for tips for their upcoming trips to Tuscany and ask hopefully if they might meet me during their stay.

Another email seems at first to be such a fan letter, but turns out to be rather the opposite. It's from a woman who read my first book in anticipation of coming to Tuscany and found it "a binful of garbage" and me "a pretentious son of a bitch." Perhaps unsurprisingly, she does not ask to meet me.

Then there's a message from an old friend from New Jersey who needs a supply of my extra-virgin olive oil as a Christmas gift for a friend.

Then, finally, I reach the last — but as it turns out, far from least — e-mail, sent to me by a literary agent in America. I open it and read with curiosity:

From: Mia Lane
To: Dario Castagno
Subject: A proposal for you

Dear Mr Castagno,
Buongiorno! I've been commissioned to write you on behalf of an established publisher in Los Angeles who is interested in a professional collaboration with you. They will be producing a series of books dedicated to the great wines of the world. We've already hired a number of authors who live in the most prestigious wine-making regions, and having read and enjoyed the style and personality of your previous books on the Chianti region,

I'm convinced that you would be perfect for this endeavor. If you are interested in this proposal, let me know and I will respond with more specifics.
I look forward hearing from you.

Best Regards
Mia Lane

A book based on wine. . . ? That could be a very interesting undertaking. But . . . where could I possibly begin? Not with history — too heavy; nor with an attempt to describe the qualities that make the wine great — too lofty. Facts and figures on consumption and export? . . . Too dry. But if not these, then what? . . . With a subject as enduring, complex, and culturally weighty as this, it's almost impossible to come up with an appropriate introduction. Especially with a hangover.

I resolve to consider the problem of the first chapter later, when I've had a chance to recover. I'm sure *something* will come to me. Meanwhile, I turn off the computer, shrug off the poncho, and return to the enveloping warmth of the blankets.

2

CHASING AFTER MEMORY

I awaken again, in midmorning; the sense of nausea has abated almost entirely. I can even enjoy a light brunch. While I'm rinsing the dishes under the tap, I feel a sudden impulse to go for a long run in the woods, the better to complete my recovery.

I slip on my running shoes, a pair of shorts and a sweatshirt, and head enthusiastically out the door; it's a splendid, crisp autumn day, very inviting for open-air activities. Running, for me, isn't just a way to cleanse my body of its accumulated toxins; it's also an essential element to clearing my head of its own detritus. It's not uncommon that, while jogging alone in the countryside, I'll be struck by sudden, unexpected bursts of inspiration — ideas for passages and reflections that I'll set down on paper later, in the company of an honest red table wine, either seated on my terrace or, in the colder season, before the crackling hearth.

Today I have the literary proposal to meditate on as I run. I can't wait to be immersed in my element, the physical exertion flooding me with bright, white consciousness and helping me evaluate whether I'm willing — or able — to fulfill the publisher's request.

I turn the ignition key of my old Fiat and as soon as the engine snarls to life, I flip the stereo to Radio Toscana Classica — and am just in time to hear a broadcast of *Qual occhio al mondo* from Puccini's *Tosca*, performed by the immortal Maria Callas and the great tenor Giuseppe di Stefano. Minutes later, after the duet has reached its crescendo, I park the vehicle on a rough dirt road close to an ancient, abandoned village.

I often set off on my runs from this time-haunted hamlet, whose last few inhabitants departed about ten years ago, and which in the intervening years has become ever more tumbledown. The ruin comprises a series of crumbling houses that form the central nucleus, gathered around an ample courtyard in the center of which stands an old red brick well. On one side, there is a small, rather anonymous chapel whose tiled but leaking roof has now been taken over by a colony of squabs, that make an incessant clamor with the beating of their wings.

I set out by jumping over a rusty chain (and the NO TRESPASSING sign that hangs from it — a message, I decided long ago, that does not apply to me). My usual path unfolds itself before me, taking me through an uncultivated field on whose borders sit two scruffy barns choked with farm equipment and mud-caked tractors, now languishing in mournful disuse.

Eventually the path leads me into a dark oak forest. The air becomes thick and humid, and the soft, damp ground on either side of me is covered with lichens and mushrooms. I leave my footprints amidst a number of others — impressions of the hooves of deer, stag and wild boar. Occasionally I come across an elegant, black-and-white striped quill that once belonged to one of the indigenous porcupines.

I manage to keep a regular pace while I withdraw farther into my head, digging through my memories to recall how, during my childhood, wine was always a protagonist in my life — even when I lived in England, that chill, northerly island nearly barren from vines or any kind of viniculture.

My father studied oenology and became a wine merchant, and devoted his life to educating the British in the time-honored traditions of Bacchus's noble nectar. Over the course of two decades he imported millions of cases of Italian wine and distributed them to all corners of the United Kingdom.

My arrival, which took place in a clinic in Wimbledon, was I'm sure greeted with a rousing *brindisi*. My father must have been very proud that both my brother (now himself a renowned oenologist) and I both made our debuts together with historical vintages of one of the greatest Italian wines produced in his native Piedmont: the Barolo.

I continue steadily along the path, taking in the intense, fungal odor of decomposing leaves; then the dense vegetation suddenly clears, and I find myself again under an immaculate blue sky. Like magic, the air becomes dry and cool again, and the sun splashes boldly over the roof of a splendid colonial house that is sadly mired in drear abandonment. One of its ancient walls is surmounted by a crooked old fig tree which during its season still generously produces an abundance of ripe, juicy fruits. I've officially appointed this venerable edifice the house of my dreams;

alas, it's not for sale. But if one day the owner should put it on the market, I would do my level best to meet his price.

I try to maintain a robust respiratory cadence, inhaling through my nostrils and exhaling through my mouth; and in the meantime I reorder the memories of my remote childhood, trying to recall my very first experiences with wine.

My mother is from Tuscany, the only other region in Italy that can compete, in terms of quality wine production, with Piedmont. The union of a Piedmontese man and a Tuscan woman must therefore produce children inclined to oenophilia. And so it is not by chance that, despite spending my first few years in England, the names of the major grape varieties grown in my parents' homeland were among the first words I ever learned: Sangiovese and Nebbiolo.

I start to feel the first waves of fatigue; my sweat glands are now in full production and my sweatshirt grows damp with dark, spreading stains at the armpits. I hold my pace while keeping a close eye on the ground before me, in case I encounter one of the poisonous vipers whose habit at this time of year is to lie coiled in the sun. Timid by nature, the vipers keep out of sight in the warm summer months; but as the weather cools they grow slow and stupid, and it's not uncommon to stumble across one as it soaks up the final rays of life-giving sunlight before slinking into hibernation.

The tight path now abruptly becomes a steep descent, until it transforms itself into a sort of scree that ends at the foot of the valley, close to a small lake where a large heron, disturbed by my presence, takes flight — brushing the tips of its wings against the surface of the water. There are no wild boar today, however; and this is one of the places where it's not at all unusual to stumble across an entire herd pausing to quench its thirst. Fearsome beasts, they're usually indifferent to my presence, acknowledging me with no more than a slight raise of their furry heads.

I re-enter the woods, following the course of a small torrent that in the summer months dries up completely; then gradually the path begins ascending, coming before yet a third abandoned farmhouse, whose main entrance is no longer visible; the door has been swallowed by ravenous nature, all but erasing it from view.

This building is not as attractive as the classic colonial houses of Chianti because its otherwise typical stone walls have been covered with an anemic coat of white paint by the last farmers to live here, back in the Seventies. Obviously they were attempting to whitewash any trace of their peasant heritage.

When, as a child, I accompanied my father to his distribution warehouse in north London, I found it great fun to roam around the immense yard. I would climb up the pallets, where thousands of cases of wine, from all over the Italian peninsula, were stacked. In no time the names of Italian wines and their producers became very familiar to me, and while my friends swapped football cards I would amuse myself by collecting and gluing the wine labels of the suppliers of Italvini, Ltd. in a special album.

I'm about halfway through the run; I recognize the untended olive grove that surrounds the farmhouse and whose trees urgently need trimming. The perimeter of the property is enclosed in a series of blackberry bushes and brooms that host entire families of pheasants, which now, at my approach, take off in terror, squawking loudly.

A bit further ahead I pass a rundown, desolate barn that until recent times was used to raise turkeys. The path now clambers uphill again. My breathing becomes labored and irregular, and I grind my teeth with the effort. After having skirted the olive grove, the path dips into a wood of chestnut and poplar. Even here my way is blocked by a rusty metal chain — which, alas, I can no longer pass over with a single, agile vault as was my habit in bygone years, but must slow down to an easy trot, then swing one leg at a time over it.

During the early years of my life, in London, I would spend my days doing all the things a typical English kid would do. The cornerstone of my nutrition, for instance, was fish fingers and mashed potatoes. But on Sunday I became Italian, as all the family snapped temporarily back to its roots. After mass the fish fingers were replaced by fresh pasta prepared by mamma, and my papà would open a bottle of red from which both my brother and I were allowed a watered down half-glass.

I'm now on a wider country lane that is traversable only by off-road vehicles, and which will take me back to the hamlet I originally departed from. I pass a fourth farmhouse, this one perched atop a hill and thus exposed to heavy winds; its wooden beams have given way, allowing the roof to fall in. If you look closely, you can find a marble engraving on one of the outer walls which depicts a bundle of sticks; this is the fasces, symbol of Fascism, and was undoubtedly placed here sometime in the Thirties.

The property is surrounded by a well manicured vineyard of Sangiovese whose dangling bunches of grapes, in October, release a sweet-smelling musk into the autumn air. I circle the ruin, after which I only have a few more miles more to tackle — and these the toughest.

My family usually traveled to Italy during the Easter school break, to visit our relatives. The first stop was always Alba in Piedmont, home of my paternal grandparents; then we would descend to Tuscany to see my other *nonna,* who was widowed when my mother was a teenager.

My Piedmontese *nonni* were of the old stamp. Of modest farming origins, they spoke in their local dialect, so that I had difficulty understanding them. Nonna Clelia had snow-white skin and sky blue eyes, dressed very soberly, and would spend entire days preparing delicious homemade *agnolotti* and *taglierini* pasta which she served on Easter Sunday to the entire family, gathered together at her long wooden table. She never, ever mixed her wines, and would justify this resolve with an old proverb in her dialect: *Bianc e nei fa ballà pè trei;* literally, "Red and white make you dance for three."

Nonno Bino was a man of rigid posture and proud demeanor, who often sported an elegant gray felt hat that covered his almost completely bald head. His cheeks were hollow and his wrists had prominent veins that branched out like tributaries across his bony, calloused hands. Despite our difficulties communicating, his company amused me, and I well remember the time I accompanied him in his ancient, mouse-gray Fiat 600 to purchase fruit and cheese at the markets in nearby villages. He was very much respected and was frequently stopped by people hailing him with warm, even excited greetings, and with whom he would exchange a few words — always in dialect. He suffered from major health problems and as a result walked with a very pronounced limp, but he was extremely strong and vigorous, and never said no to a glass of *vin bun* (good wine, in his dialect). He had been too young to fight in the First World War and slightly too old to be called to duty for the second. But it's doubtful he would have made a good soldier; he didn't respond well to authority. For instance, after his street was designated a One Way thoroughfare, he stubbornly ignored the sign and continued driving in whichever direction suited him at the time. I will always associate the intense flavors of the Barolo, Barbaresco and Barbera, and all the other great Piedmontese wines, with the proud, ancient faces of my *nonni*.

Now the uphill path reaches its maximum inclination, and my thigh muscles harden during the tremendous climb. The road is bordered on both sides by old limestone walls, no longer tended so that, alas, at every rainfall they lose a few more chunks and crumble further into ruin. In the slits in between the bricks live a number of bright green lizards, insects, and small scorpions. I don't see any today; but I barely look — my heart is now pounding its fastest as I approach the summit.

I take a big gulp of air as I reach the top, where I allow myself a moment of rest. Now I face an expanse of less demanding level ground before beginning the final downhill run.

After the Piedmont visit my parents would drive us down to Tuscany, the land of Brunello, Nobile and Chianti wines — and of my other grandmother. Her husband, my grandfather, was killed in a plane crash when he was a colonel in the Italian air force. He was also a renowned journalist, so his death made national headlines. I still possess the newspaper clippings, as well as other heirlooms from his past. I also recently discovered that all I need to do is to enter his name on any Internet search engine, and an impressive number of listings of articles will come up.

My *nonna* — who required that we address her as *grand-maman* in the French manner — lived alone with the memories of *grand-papa* in an elegant residence that had once been a hotel in the center of Florence. More than a residence, it was a kind of mausoleum where she had accumulated many rooms' worth of objects (some might say junk) that had once belonged to her seven brothers and sisters, who were all deceased. My brother's and my favorite pastime was to explore these rooms, climbing the stacks of furniture, sometimes exploring boxes that contained photos, books and personal tokens, or paging through the precious stamp and coin collections. Despite living alone, my *nonna* seemed quite contented, even serene. She was in this way a contrast to my bustling, busy Piedmontese *nonni;* you could tell she came from an aristocratic background. She would often wear very colorful dresses with fine jewelry, and she loved spoiling us. In her house, wine wasn't the main topic of conversation, but even so, the traditional Tuscan straw flask was an unfailing presence on the table at mealtimes.

I've almost reached the end of the run; I make a final push for a sprint to the finish line. In all, I've covered about eight miles, and as usual nowhere along the way did I see another human being.

I stop to rest, leaning obliquely with my head low and my open palms against the wall of the chapel, out of whose cracks protrude tiny twigs of wild caper plants. I try to catch my breath and, still gasping and soaked in my own sweat, plop onto the driver's seat of my Fiat and return home.

As usual, despite the fatigue, I keep smiling — a habit adopted the day I was seated on the porch of a bar, sipping red wine with my elderly friend Fosco, now long gone. While I was listening attentively to his pearls of wisdom, a man in jogging gear raced passed us. The old man clucked in disdain and remarked that he could never comprehend why people ran; it certainly didn't appear to be fun, because they always had such a sour expression stamped on their faces. At that very moment I decided to prove him wrong. Now each time I jog I grin as wide as I can. It isn't difficult.

During the short drive I dab my sweat away with an old towel, then tie it around my neck. I choose Radio Siena, which is now broadcasting some rather amusing Italian hip-hop.

As I've concluded my run, I try to wrap up my early wine memories with a recollection of my very first taste. Like most children I didn't find the experience a pleasant one; the consistency was far too intense, too complex, for my undeveloped palate, so much so that I had a momentary fear it wouldn't flow down my throat, but would stick there. I did, however, appreciate the bouquet, in the same way that I liked the heady aromas of the wooden barrels impregnated with must, the odor of the mould that sweated out of stone walls in the cellars, and the scent of the cardboard boxes stacked in my fathers warehouse. At that age, I even liked setting my nose on the rims of glasses left empty at the table by grownups.

The turning point occurred in my teens, during the period in which my friends and I used to bum around the Chianti hills, seeking abandoned farmhouses on our scooters. To stay warm, we purchased wine in bulk from a local farmer whose surname was Mecacci; in fact ever since that time, Mecacci has been my private name for any house wine that has no label. We would indiscriminately slug down this wine directly from the bottles, following the local saying *"Chi beve al boccale beve quanto gli pare"* ("He who drinks directly from the bottle drinks as much as he wants"), passing it back and forth as we roasted sausages and red meats directly on the embers in the old farmhouses' ancient hearths.

Our taste buds, as if by magic, gradually started to distinguish different flavors and to perceive subtle complexities; and we began to realize that the wine, which we took for granted, was going to play a decisive role in defining the quality of our adult lives.

Back home I take a shower, and afterwards, as I'm happy, I decide to pour myself a healthy serving of Mecacci. I raise my glass and wonder to whom I should toast; then I realize, I've been toasting them all morning, in my memory: my parents, my nonni, my brother, Fosco, my teenage friends. I drink now to them all, not for the first time, and certainly not for the last.

3

ENCOUNTER ON A HILLSIDE

Despite the long run I feel compelled to go back outdoors. I decide to walk up to my office while continuing to consider the literary agent's proposal.

Impulsively I grab a leather rucksack and fill it with a notebook, a pen, a few sugar cubes, and a bottle of Mecacci; after which I pause to down a healthy *gotto* (shot), in accordance with the proverb: *Non ti mettere in cammino se la bocca non sa di vino* ("Don't start out on a walk if your mouth doesn't taste of wine").

The late-autumn days have been growing progressively shorter, but the sun, while it's out, is unusually warm, even a few hours before sunset. As I commence climbing some nearby hills I take in the breathtaking vistas. The heat of the day has by now completely dissolved the mist at the bottom of the valleys, so thoroughly eliminating the early-morning "ocean effect" that it's difficult to recall that this dreamlike phenomenon ever existed.

Whenever I find myself immersed in this much beauty, I make a vain effort to put into words the stirring emotions the Chianti landscape instills in me. Alas, nothing does them justice; my soul swells, I am enraptured and ecstatic, my mind is stimulated by a thousand creative flourishes; and yet to say as much is to render it all suddenly quotidian — a cliché.

Leaving language behind with the other inadequacies of civilization, I continue my climb, cutting through the uncultivated fields with my head high and my arms open wide, extending the tips of my fingers in an attempt to graze the tops of the towering grass as it ripples to and fro in the soft winds. In my wake I leave an improvised path, set down by trampling heels; but no other traveler will follow it, for in mere moments the shafts will spring back up as though I'd never been there, erasing any trace of my passage.

I pay my usual visit to the nearby stable and am greeted by the two fine steeds, who trot towards me across the corral. I return the greeting with an energetic rub of their noses and a sugar cube each. While they chew on the sweets, I notice that, unusually for this time of year, I can still hear the clamor of cicadas and see a few colorful butterflies hovering in the air.

Halfway up the hill I notice an impressive, brand-new, fully accessorized beige camper van with a Milan license plate. A rather noisy family has descended from it and taken possession of a dusty clearing where a few courageous tufts of grass have managed to survive.

At a glance, I guess the parents to be in their early forties; they're beneath a large tarpaulin, reclining on some striped wooden deck chairs and sipping German beers directly from the bottle, while puffing at cigarettes between sips. They seem to have been here a while, given the quantity of yellowed butts strewn unattractively across the ground. Their two overweight teenagers occupy themselves at a distance.

I have no desire to disturb these people, so I slip quietly behind the camper, thus evading their notice. Several yards on I decide to rest for a moment on a large, flat rock and admire once more the majestic view, which never fails to reveal some surprising new facet despite the countless times I've studied it from this very spot. I have to squint because I'm facing the sun. The gentle southwest wind soon dries the sweat on my skin, which sets me scratching insistently at my two-day beard. To divert myself with a more pleasant activity, I take the bottle from my sack, pull out the cork, and I drink like a suckling infant: giving credence to the old farmers' saying, *Il vino è la poppa dei vecchi* ("The wine bottle is the old man's teat").

I listen with scant interest to the quarrel of the two teenagers, which seems to be about nothing in particular. When their carping at each other finally dies down, I turn to look at them. The girl, who appears to be the elder, is dipping some French fries in a pinkish sauce that she squeezes from an aluminum tube. Her hair is a bright, copper red tied in a ponytail, and she sports a pale blue T-shirt that exposes her midriff; a tiny ring pierces her navel. Her belly is too bloated to render the piercing erotic, and the elastic of her metallic-green G-string has ridden up past her low-waist hip-hop jeans, which are identical to those worn by her brother. Turning to him, I see that his childish face is sprouting its first, tentative beard; I can easily imagine him spending hours before a mirror, shaping it lovingly with a Gilette blade. To avoid his sister's droning complaints, he has inserted some

28

stereo earbuds and sat down to amuse himself with a Gameboy. His face is utterly neutral — it bears nothing even close to a recognizable human expression — and this is odd, because the volume of his iPod is so high you'd think it would have him writhing in agony; I can hear its booming, hypnotic rhythms all the way over on my rock. Suddenly I can't tear my eyes away from these people — maybe because they give off such an aura of sadness and futility. They seem tragically and hopelessly wrapped up in themselves, completely insensible to the glorious panorama of nature that surrounds them.

My attention is recaptured by the parents, who have now moved inside the camper and turned on the TV. The glow of the cathode-ray tube attracts a swarm of tiny flies and other insects. The parents are following a quiz show, interrupted, continuously, it seems, by shrill commercials, presented by an extremely popular entertainer who was recently elected as a positive role model for our modern times. (Perhaps I should have cast a vote.)

The father returns outside to answer his cell phone, and begins gesticulating wildly, his hands darting up repeatedly towards the oblivious blue sky. He's arguing, abusing his caller with an astonishingly vast repertoire of insults. Then his wife — a brittle, attractive type, the kind of woman who frequents all the most prestigious restaurants but doesn't actually eat — joins him outside, because her own phone has started ringing. She talks as loudly as her husband, all the while sucking staccato puffs from a cigarette that hangs precariously from her lips; it droops but never drops, and she never bothers to tap off the ashes.

This picture of the family — physically together, but each member utterly isolated in his or her own little world — is now completed by the daughter, who begins sending text messages from her phone, her fingers moving as quickly over the keypad as her brother's are over his Gameboy.

I raise my bottle and take a second swig, this time turning to view the wavy outlines of the hills on the horizon. But almost immediately a tiny, yellow ladybug distracts me; it's climbing with great difficulty over the hairs of my forearm, causing a very faint and pleasant tickle. I observe the little maculated creature for an short spell as it tries to plough its way through what must seem a dense jungle, and eventually I doze off, with my back against an old empty tree trunk that during the summer had hosted a swarm of honeybees and their enormous communal hive . . .

My *pennichella* is interrupted by a raucous voice with a very pronounced Milanese accent. My eyes flutter back open and find before me the imposing figure of the owner of the camper. His gray shirt is soaked with sweat and is hanging unbuttoned, revealing a mass of thick, curly, ink-black chest hair. Hitching up his baggy khaki shorts, he moves in closer, his large feet slapping against the turf in his crimson rubber flip flops. His acrid body odor reaches me before he does.

"Hey, buddy," he says, taking off his expensive sunglasses and drying pearls of sweat from his forehead with a checked handkerchief; "I need to check my email. Is there by any chance an Internet coffee down in the village?"

"Nope," I reply with a slight shake of my head. I'm still not fully awake, and rather alarmed by his sudden invasion of my private space. "But if you like," I add, trying to be friendly, "you can use mine, I live just down there." I point towards my house in the valley below.

"Mmm," he says, looking more than a little reluctant. "No thanks, I don't want to disturb you."

"Not at all. If you like, we can go right now."

He pauses to consider this for a few moments, during which I prepare to get up and lead him to my house. But to my amazement, he sits down next to me instead — after first sweeping the dust from the rock with the side of his hand.

"It can wait till tomorrow," he says, apparently deciding that nothing is so crucial as to require him to intermingle with the locals. He brushes his hands together to rid them of dust.

We look into each other's eyes and hold the gaze for several moments, as though we're having some kind of silent duel. Then he lowers his gaze and asks if I'm not bored, living in this isolated spot, so far from the cities, from the civilized world. It seems incomprehensible to him that anyone could be happy here. For instance, don't I miss going to the theatre?

I look towards the hills while I try to frame an appropriate reply. With the exception of the pageant the kids put on every Christmas, no, as a matter of fact there is no theatre in the village. But does that seem to me a loss? As I continue reflecting on his question, I instinctively offer him my bottle of wine, but he refuses it with a look of disgust. I feel like asking him if he is aware that *what* he is actually rejecting, the ancients refered to as *il sangue della terra* ("The earth's blood") and more recently Mario Soldati as *la poesia della terra* ("The soil's poetry") His pedantic air, his insistence on pointing out how far he is from his natural place, his arrogant gestures, and his lofty upper-class northern accent have stirred up in me a number of senti-ments, none of them positive. I'm not willing to engage in a debate with someone whose mind is already made up, so I limit myself to observing his pale skin, his soft cheeks, and his dull, exhausted eyes which resemble those of a frozen hake on a fish stall in the discount supermarkets; and it occurs to me that we are not only from different worlds, but are vastly different men.

I ask him, more out of politeness than interest, what he's doing here. Proudly he explains that he and his family have come down from Milan to attend the wedding of his boss's daughter. This boss hired a castle for the ceremony, which I am given to understand was quite lavish and spectacular, and now the family are on their way back to Milan.

"Frankly I can't wait to get back," he says with a shudder. "These wide-open spaces make me feel panicky. I feel sorry for you people who have to spend your entire lives in these godfor-saken outposts, without ever having the opportunity to do any-thing constructive with your lives, and no access to all those conveniences and privileges we have in the city.".

I take a deep breath and tell him yes, I agree with him; I'll have to seriously consider moving to Milan. It's what he wants to hear, after all, and the only thing I could possibly say that he wouldn't immediately dismiss. When I stand up to go, I ask him if he often goes to the theatre.

"As a matter of fact it's years since I last went," he says as he lights up another cigarette. He takes a puff, then purses his lips and releases a puff of smoke, still completely immune to the aching beauty all around him. As I have nothing at all in com-mon with this deep-frozen slice of fish, I conclude our meeting with a curt goodbye. I take a final swig of Mecacci, place the bottle back in the leather rucksack, and continue my climb to the apex of the hill, heading towards my office.

REVERIE

It's perhaps inevitable that my run-in with the unhappy Milanese family stays in my thoughts long after I've left them. I can't get over their tense, pallid looks or the father's bloated, benumbed countenance — all in such contrast to the bracing vitality of the wilderness that surrounded them, wilderness they seemed positively eager to dismiss. Sadly, I conclude that they might well be representative of the Italian family in the new millennium.

Possibly the father was trying to provoke me when he said he felt pity for me; well, if that was the case, he succeeded; in fact I'm provoked into a thorough comparison of our very different worlds.

I reflect on how fortunate I am to be the owner of a bedroom window that looks out onto the lush Chianti hills and valleys, a sort of living painting of inestimable value and endless variety, not reproducible by even the most talented of forgers. Then I try to imagine *his* neighborhood in some squalid development somewhere around Milan, piled together without any organizing harmony. When he opens his window, what would he see? The dull, tick-colored façade of another apartment block, inert and invulnerable, that will never change with the seasons or alter a jot from its present granite graceless.

He probably has scant contact with his neighbors and may not even have made the acquaintance of any of the people who pass him daily in their airtight common corridor, and with whom he rides the claustrophobic elevator. I'd be willing to bet he can't name a single other resident on his own floor.

My village certainly isn't a hub of nonstop activity, but at least I never feel alone there; I can always go to its medieval central piazza and without fail find a friendly resident to chat with. I can spend hours at the local bar or under the acacia tree, or anywhere else the elderly villagers liked to congregate, and listen to a thousand tales of lives past and present, narrated by genuine storytellers with bright, generous souls.

I feel so privileged to be able to do, on a whim, just what I've done this morning: slip on my sneakers and run through the majestic, uncontaminated woods, breathe in the heady scents peculiar to the season, and listen to the crunch of fallen leaves beneath my feet. I shrink from imagining a life in which I had no opportunity to open my mouth to the sky and let pristine rainwater fill it to the teeth, or brush against the foliage and come away with my arms dampened by the dew. In a large city I'd be left gasping in air vitiated by "progress," and being stained by polluted downpours.

When I'm out running, immersed in the silence of the Chianti hills, it's not uncommon to come across a range of wild animals as they go quietly about their business. The only evidence of wildlife my city friend would encounter is the pigeon dung spattered across the windshield of his car. What must it be like, never to be awakened by the sunlight streaming through the shutters and dancing on your forehead? Even if he did have a window accessible to the morning light, he'd have to keep it bolted with the blinds down, to keep out the din of traffic, the roar of the crowds and the burglars. In such a life, a window is more a liability than a convenience; I wonder why they bother having them at all.

My own soundtrack alters according to seasons, from the deafening silence of the winter snowfalls and the clamor of the cicadas in the summer, to the cries of the swallows that plunge headlong from the skies in daring pursuit of fat, juicy insects. At night I fall asleep to the unending lament of the horned owl, the big bass burps of the frogs by the creek, and the furious sizzle of the crickets. If I want to lie awake for awhile, I can watch the glow of fireflies, blinking and winking and filling the night with magic. In most cities it's second nature to lock yourself in after dark; here I have no problem leaving the keys in the front door all night.

During the summer I spend my free days diving into crystal-clear springs, where bright fish and colorful crabs run riot. I'd think twice about even touching the contaminated "water" that runs through the average city.

I ask myself if my Milanese friend has ever stopped to enjoy the splendor of a rainbow shimmering over the hills after a violent thunderstorm.

During the appropriate seasons I go out hunting for mushrooms, chestnuts, wild strawberries, arbutus and more. I seek out truffles with my old friend Gosto and his dog Lalla, without ever having to get into my car. I wonder what my friend pays for truffles in Milan? And I ask myself if he has ever walked through a wheat field that's just been harvested . . . collected wild fruits in a burlap bag . . . or suffered indigestion after eating too many grapes picked directly off the vine. Certainly he's never filled his lungs with the powerful perfume of olives that have just been pressed for their precious extra-virgin oil in a stone mill. He will never have returned home after a solitary stroll in the fields with a collection of wild herbs to sweeten a salad, or merely picked a bunch of wildflowers and given them lovingly to his wife. These are the simple acts and gestures that make each day worth living; they are, I think, the very essence of a life well spent.

Having considered the many ways in which I'm so manifestly lucky, I realize that it's another good excuse for a toast. I raise the bottle, salute the open countryside around me, and take a long and loving swig.

5

AT THE OFFICE

Some time has now passed since my encounter with the Milanese family, and I find myself seated beneath a splendid oak tree at whose base the local council has placed a comfortable wooden table. This is where I regularly come to write or take notes, and accordingly I have christened it *"Il mio ufficio"* — my office.

I've regained my equilibrium after my reflections, and now I really feel like getting something down on paper; my head is once again clear, my thoughts free and light. Suddenly I recall a quote — attributed, I believe, to Baudelaire: "The art of writing originates from unhappiness." I couldn't disagree more.

I decide to sit on the side of the table facing south, from which vantage point I can see where the Chianti hills, thick with luxuriant oak, suddenly give way to the arid but no less evocative lunar landscapes of the Crete. When the days are particularly clear, like today, it's possible to catch sight of the peak of Monte Amiata, which borders on the Lazio region to the south of Tuscany. If I shift my view to the east, just a few meters below I can see my beloved village, with the hills just beyond, and further back the Apennine mountains that border on another of Tuscany's neighboring regions, Emilia-Romagna.

Looking west, I spot my city, Siena, and the fresh young woods of the Montagnola; and further on, the so-called metal hills, rich both in mines and in geysers spewing from underground fumaroles. On exceptionally clear days, one might be lucky enough to spot the snowy peaks of the Abetone mountains.

To the north, my view is blocked by the oak tree's immense trunk, home to a seeming infinity of tiny creatures (who, unfortunately, seem to long for better housing, judging by the way in which they seem continually to creep onto my notepad, into my hair, onto my rucksack). But if I get up and walk around the tree, I can see the medieval towers of San Gimignano, the ancient, hardy walls of Monteriggioni, and — less felicitously

— the yellow clump of smog that marks Florence's location in the far distance.

It seems to me I live in a kind of fairy tale, a dream that I fell into thirty-odd years ago and from which, unlike Sleeping Beauty, I hope never to awaken. The moment that happens would almost certainly mean my time in this world has ended. Possibly this is why I'm an atheist; I can't believe there is a "better life" beyond the paradise in which I already live.

But enough idle thought; it's time to do some work. I take out my notepad and start to consider how to reply to Mia Lane.

I've already written two books detailing my life and experiences in Chianti — encompassing both the halcyon days of my youth, and my years as a professional tour guide, escorting a variety of characters through the beauties of this countryside and its environs. Still, the idea of undertaking a third literary effort is enticing.

My first book was something of a lark, written to pass the time before the fireplace during a long winter, and inspired by some of my zanier clients. Imagine my amazement when it was not only published, but became a kind of cult hit, bringing me undreamed of attention and drastically changing my life.

The second book was a logical consequence of the first, but was conceived and structured much more carefully than its predecessor — and with the anxious awareness that I now had an army of readers, as well a literary agency and a publishing house, whose high expectations I had to meet.

The "real" writers whom I've had the good fortune to encounter (and among whose number I will never be able to place myself) have often told me that in fact it's the third book that can make or break one's career. If it's a success, then your legitimacy is complete and official; but if it's savaged by the critics, or fails to sell, then you sink back into the obscurity from whence you rose; and climbing back up again is all but impossible.

In addition, I have to consider the bounty of technical, oenological material that already proliferates on the bookshelves — exhaustive volumes by wine experts and luminaries with whom I would be embarrassed to be compared or in competition.

However . . . if Mia Lane is looking for something less specialized — an appreciation by someone whose daily life has been substantially enriched by the fruit of the grape — perhaps placed in a rough historical context, balanced by observations and proverbs on the subject — why, then, I definitely feel up to the task.

I fact, how can I refuse it ? I live in a place that gives its name to one of the most famous wines on the planet; the address of my house is Via del Grappolo — literally, Bunch of Grapes Lane — and my immediate neighbors live on Vine Street, Wine Road, and thoroughfares named Chianti Classico and Black Rooster (the latter being the symbol of the consortium that controls the quality of our local wine). What's more, the local village feast is dedicated to the grape harvest; and the sole source of income in the area is wine production. I'm surrounded by illustrious wineries and a myriad of tiny producers who provide work to the entire village, composed of about three hundred souls.

I feel a shiver of doubt; does all this really make me an authority? Well, if I met someone who lived on Hops Street, between Malt Road and Draught Avenue and whose home and community were ringed by breweries, I'd take what he said about beer as gospel.

By these various means I convince myself to return home and respond in the affirmative to Mia Lane's e-mail. Then I'll go to the village to celebrate the initiation of my third book at the local bar, where I hope to find some good company and — why not? — some inspiration for my new work.

I want to raise my bottle in another brief toast — but find I can't; alas, the Mecacci is empty.

I pack up my notebook and shoulder my sack, and start on a different route home so that I don't again run into the family with the camper.

6

THINGS MISHEARD,
THINGS OVERHEARD

My high hopes of finding good company to celebrate my new project are dashed as soon as I enter the bar. The place is virtually empty. There are only two regulars, one of whom is Giulio, a reclusive old-timer bent over his wooden cane and drinking wine from a very large glass. In the village, they laughingly say of him that the more he drinks, the more he shrinks. I remember the first time I heard this said of him; I hadn't yet met him, and I imagined he was like one of the colorful grotesques created by the Colombian novelist Gabriel Garcia Márquez — and in truth he might well have sprung from that Nobel prize winner's pen.

The other patron in the bar is Orazio (Italian for Horatio), who is closer to my age, and who works as a laborer in one of the local vineyards. Unlike Giulio, Orazio is extremely talkative, though his company would be vastly more enjoyable if he kept his mouth shut. He's what we call a *brav'uomo* — a man who wears his emotions on his sleeve. In the village he's well loved because of his innocent, almost childlike nature. Like many others, he appeared about ten years ago from some tiny, remote *paesiello* deep in the poverty-wracked southern peninsula in search of a job. He lives alone and works as hard as a mule. Physically he's diminutive, stocky, and plump with short yet amazingly muscular arms. His belly dangles far over the fly of his jeans, and is so swollen that he resembles some drowned beast fished from the Amazon River. More than once, when observing anew the stubby upper limbs nature has inflicted on him, I've asked myself how he manages to reach his penis when he's having a piss. (Maybe his penis is unusually long and can meet the arms halfway.) His hands are enormous, with fingers like plump wild-boar sausages, and since he refuses to wear gloves when working they're permanently stained by the must and the wine that have penetrated his pores daily during the thirty or so years he's been working in the vineyards.

But what's most arresting about Orazio is the curious shape of his skull, which looks almost Neanderthal, larger and more flattened than those belonging to the Homo Sapiens who have been masters of the planet for the last eon or so. His cheekbones are extremely pronounced, his eyebrows dense and hairy, his forehead low. As if all this wasn't enough, he has two tiny black sunken eyes separated by a wide, squashed nose. His beard covers most of his face, obliging him to shave all the way up to the orbits of his eyes, and its thickness is such that he must have to take a razor to it more than once a day. In short, he looks uncannily like the "missing link" anthropologists have been searching for to plug the gap in the evolutionary record; certainly good old Charles Darwin would have been keen to meet him.

Poor Orazio — his brutish appearance is so at odds with the sweetness of his character. Yet he's saddled with another handicap: he has trouble putting together a coherent sentence, and requires no small amount of time to relate even the simplest anecdote. When he speaks extemporaneously, his words flounder and overlap, and in no time his original thought gets lost in a maze of stuttering pauses and embarrassed silences. Even worse, when he does manage to spit out his story, he does so literally — launching tiny bullets of saliva laced with his favorite snack, *ciaccino* a Tuscan specialty stuffed with mortadella.

For all these reasons, Orazio isn't quite the kind of brilliant, witty companion I'm seeking today; but it's too late, he's seen me, I can't duck out of the bar again. I order a glass of Chianti Classico Oliviera and take a seat some distance away, thinking perhaps he won't target me. But alas, he immediately starts up:

"Have you seen . . . no, I mean, you know where he . . . mmm, do you know who I'm talking about? . . . I mean Franceschino. I think? . . . No, no, the one who works for . . . what's his name? Come on, you know, help me, he used to live at . . . at . . ." (Here he pauses, his eyes roll back in his head and he stares at the ceiling.) "Ooohhh . . . who are we talking about? . . . You must know . . . Oh, yes, he used to live close to the truck driver that was married to . . . What? . . . You never heard of him? No, you have . . . ehh, what's her name, help me . . . the wife, that's who!" (He snaps his fingers to hurry himself on, and bites his lip.) "Her father was Sicilian. No, from Calabria, or maybe . . . Is she from Apuglia? . . . Yes, you do know her, she's had an accident along that road, remember . . . ?"

At this point I don't know who his original story is about, this woman or the man she may or may not be married to. But there's no stopping Orazio as he haltingly lurches on:.

"No . . . hang on a sec . . . wait." (He rubs his palm over his forehead, as though massaging his brain. "The road that connects the town . . . named . . . it's close to that other town . . . what's it called?" (A brief pause as he reaches down and adjust his lower parts.) "No, wait, actually it wasn't that road, it was that other one . . . where those two horny sisters live? . . . Yes, I'm sure you know one of them personally . . . don't you?" (A full stop as he digs something out of his nose.)

. . . And so on for another twenty minutes, an incredible length of time when you consider that all of this was his way of telling me that the night before he'd gone for a pizza in Radda in Chianti. God knows how long it would have taken if he also tried to tell me what kind he ordered. But that's Orazio, take him or leave him.

I decide to leave him, after having emptied my third glass. I deposit the empty goblet on the wooden counter and avoid the crumbs of minced *ciaccino* on the bar's floor as I make my way back to the street. I'm relieved Orazio doesn't follow me outside, because he isn't able to do two things contemporaneously, such as walking and conversing, and so it would have taken me another half hour to cover the few yards that separate the bar from the village square where he lived.

By now it's time for dinner and I haven't had any luck with my impromptu celebration. I think about returning home and cooking something; then I remember that the refrigerator is empty — unless I can make a meal of a dried-up lemon and a jar of mayonnaise past its expiration date. And since I live alone, there's no possibility of being surprised at finding the table set, a crackling fire in the hearth, and a wine decanter filled by a girlfriend who's been eagerly awaiting me. Well, no use dwelling on it . . .

I pass in front of the village restaurant and my eyes catch sight of an inviting fireplace, and what appear to be some juicy steaks ready to be roasted on its embers.

On the spot, I decide to dine her, and I enter. Here, then, is the advantage of being single; since there's no one awaiting me at home, there's no one to disappoint by being late — or, worse, no one whose permission I need to ask.

The proprietor greets me and the waiter accompanies me to my table. As I settle in I see that the place is still empty but for a pair of older women who are seated a few tables away, busily leafing through their menus. It only takes a glance to peg them as American. They're both dressed rather garishly, and their makeup seems to have been applied with the liberal use of a bricklayer's trowel. The lady wearing the flashiest jewellery reminds me a little of the Queen Mother; she sports a voluminous hairdo with conspicuous purple highlights. She's also wearing an impressively sized hearing aid which obviously isn't functioning perfectly, given the volume with which her friend has to speak to make herself understood.

I order a plate of mixed crostini, *pappa al pomodoro* (a rather thick bread and tomato soup), a salad, and one of the steaks that had persuaded me to enter in the first place. I decide to wash down my meal with a Chianti Classico Dievole Novecento. I also ask the friendly Albanian waiter for a pen and paper to take down some notes, then slide the chair a few inches away from the table and extend my legs, and with my head lolling back admire the splendid chestnut beams that cross the ceiling of the old tavern. In this relaxed attitude, my thoughts returned to the project I've just undertaken.

In the meantime the waiter serves the woman who resembles the Queen Mother a plate of grilled *radicchio*. She takes one look at its rich, crimson color and claps her hands excitedly. "Ah, Tuscan *prosciutto!*" she exclaims.

The waiter corrects her, raising the volume of his voice slightly (he's obviously already encountered the hearing aid): "No, madam, not *prosciutto Toscano, radicchio trevigiano.*"

Now she's even more excited. "*Prosciutto* and *Parmigiano,* wonderful, my favorite!"

Without losing his professional aplomb, the waiter explains in passable English that the dish is in fact a variety of red salad, a speciality from Treviso, a town located close to Venice.

The Queen Mother nods at him with a smile on her face, then when he's finished, says, "How lovely —Venetian *prosciutto!*"

Fortunately her companion, who reminds me of Jessica Lange and who is probably used to these scenes, now intervenes and politely thanks the waiter in decent Italian, explaining that she'll make her friend understand.

I pour myself a glass from the bottle the waiter has opened

for me, in accordance with the local saying, *un bicchiere di vino prima della minestra e saluti il medico dalla finestra* ("A glass of wine before your soup and you can greet your doctor from the window"). I then think of how often it happens — as in the case with these two ladies, the Queen Mother and Jessica Lange — that I tag people by their resemblance to someone famous; is this a side effect wine has on me?

Returning to the subject of the new book, I realize that having to write an entire volume means I will have to conduct some extremely thorough research, consult the local archives, and interview a number of people whose expertise will enhance the narrative. I begin jotting down their names. I also make a note to include local proverbs and sayings, of the kind I just used a moment ago. Also, I do have some interesting material I'd written earlier, on the history of the Chianti wine and the intimate relationship the locals have with the nectar of Bacchus. All I need to do is find the file and polish it up. The project is beginning to come together in my mind.

In the meantime the tavern has started to fill up. Apart from the ladies and myself, there is now a young couple seated in the corner and exchanging loving effusions, provoking in me a sense of tenderness as well as a bit of envy. My relationships with women always seem to end disastrously, and I've convinced myself that, at this point in my life, I'm too compromised ever to endure another one. Which brings to mind another proverb: *Quando il capello tira al bianchino, lascia la donna e tieni il buon vino* ("When your hair starts to whiten, leave the women and keep the wine"). Perfect for my present circumstances.

Proud of having pulled that nearly lost local saying from thin air, I raise my glass and unashamedly toast myself.

Moments later, who should arrive but the Countess, accompanied by three distinctive gentlemen whom I guess to be in their seventies — still far younger than the lady they escort; the Countess is on the far side of ninety. I get to my feet, feeling obliged to go and greet her at her table. She is an extraordinary woman who is credited with convincing the Nazis to spare the village at the end of World War II, after they had decided to blow it up as they retreated. As such she is a local hero. She's also blessed by a kind of agelessness; I would defy anyone to guess how old she is, given the scarcity of wrinkles on her fine face, and the tall, proud way she carries herself. She doesn't even need reading glasses. And her wits are still razor-sharp. Even now, she drives her car daily into town.

In the village, it's said that as a young girl she would ride her horse topless through the forests, like a latter-day Lady Godiva, because she believed her breasts would benefit from the pure Chianti air. Whether this is so I will never (and wouldn't want to) know for sure; but if her mammaries are as handsomely preserved as the rest of her, I would certainly advise all the young girls to follow her example. Just think how tourism would benefit!

After having wished the Countess *"Buon appetito"* I return to my table and find the antipasto course waiting for me. I eagerly devour it while continuing to admire the tavern's interior, appreciating it all the more for knowing that until a few years ago, it was a dusty, disused stable. The restaurant is composed of two dining rooms divided by an ample stone arch. The larger room, where I'm seated, has a wooden beamed ceiling, while the other is surmounted by a typical Siennese red brick vault. The stone walls have been ably restored by a talented stonemason, the floor is tiled with rustic but elegant terracotta, and at the entrance, as I noted earlier, one is greeted by the welcoming fireplace where meats are roasted and vegetables grilled.

Now a group of three young girls has entered; I recognize them as members of the Dragon *contrada* in Siena. They are apparently inseparable; I can't recall ever having seen any one of them on her own, or even in different company. They sit down at the table next to mine and politely salute me with a chorus of *"Ciao."* Like most girls from Siena they are dressed very elegantly and are quite attractive in their sleek, modish dresses, unlike myself in my ripped jeans, my worn, collarless white shirt, and my army boots. I didn't even shave this morning, and judging by my scruffy hairstyle one would think I'm waging a personal strike against the entire hairdressing profession. With the girls now settled at the table next to me, I certainly look out of place.

When you dine alone, eavesdropping is simply unavoidable. I listen as unobtrusively as possible to the conversations now bubbling around me: to the Countess explaining why she believes the war in Iraq has turned out so disastrously; to the Queen Mother happily mistaking each new dish for something it's not, despite the efforts of the waiter and Jessica Lange to correct her; to the billing and cooing of the young couple, still holding hands and gazing at each other over a flickering candle. And overriding all this is the girlish cacophony at the table next to mine, as they continually and sometimes simultaneously start a number of different conversations — all of which strangely seem to wind their way back to an earnest analysis of the chronic colitis problem that afflicts one of them. For instance, they begin reminiscing about their recent trip to Thailand and the how hard it was adapting to the torpid climate and the spicy food — but oh, poor Lisa had to spend most of the trip affixed to the toilet. While I'm enjoying my *pappa* the girls recall the time they participated in a cross-country run, and how well they all did — except Lisa, who came in last because she'd had to pay the bushes several visits, and wasn't it smart that she thought to stuff a supply of toilet paper into her socks. Then, as I'm picking up the bone of my beefsteak with my fingers and gnawing away at the last bits of meat, one of the girls reports that she's going to be working for a few months on a project based in London — to which Lisa responds with a story of how, on a London holiday with her parents when she was a child, she didn't want to interrupt the sightseeing by insisting on a lavatory visit, and so tried to wait till they got back to their hotel — but miscalculated her intestinal fortitude and ended up evacuating in her seat on the London Underground at Golders Green. Finally, when I ask for the bill and am ready to go, they all — perhaps inevitably — relive the last time the Dragon won the Palio, which must of course include the memory of how, when the members of the *contrada* were swarming towards the terrace to collect the banner, Lisa was forced to push in the opposite direction, against all her fellow Dragons, with her hand on her stomach and an urgent look on her face.

At this point I can no longer contain myself and let a laugh slip past my lips. The girls suddenly realize I've been hearing all of Lisa's intestinal misadventures, and turn bright red and to try play things down. Lisa herself wittily says, "I've really made a shitty showing, haven't I ?" I am about to add the local farmers' expression, *Bevi bene e caca forte e non aver paura della morte* ("Drink healthily and evacuate vigorously and don't be afraid of death"), but at the last moment think it best to keep it to myself.

I leave the waiter a tip, say goodbye to the owner, and realize that I'm slightly sloshed again. I stagger on beneath a bright waning moon, which means that soon the weather will change.

The fresh air helps me recover slightly from my addled state. I decide the best thing to do is have a final nightcap at the *polisportiva*.

I tuck my pad of paper under my arm. Somehow, during all the conversations that distracted me during dinner, I've managed to take several pages of notes — and to draft a reply to Mia Lane.

From: Dario Castagno
To: Mia Lane
Subject: Re: A proposal for you

Dear Ms. Lane:

Greetings from Chianti/Tuscany! I wish to thank you for your e-mail, which I read with interest; I admit to being flattered that you've thought to contact me. I am intrigued by the project you propose on behalf of the publisher you represent, and have given it due consideration before agreeing to undertake it.

I have spent the day immersed in my beloved landscapes, reflecting on the proposal and my ability to meet your expectations. I've concluded that if what you require is a brief history of Chianti wine, and maybe some its folklore and legend, I can certainly give it a try. I'll send you this weekend a brief essay I wrote recently on this very subject, to give you an idea of how I would approach the book.

If however you seek more technical information on the subject, I doubt I'm your man but will be happy to introduce you to oenologists and sommeliers who will, I'm sure, be keen to meet the challenge.

Hoping that this initiates a mutually enjoyable collaboration, I send you my warmest regards.

A presto!
Dario Castagno

7

DOCTOR'S ORDERS

The headquarters of the *polisportiva* is in a building that for many years was the village school — no longer required for that purpose, given first the postwar depopulation of the area, then more recently the declining birthrate. It is now transformed into a kind of social club where the village elders meet for a drink and to play cards, and where the townspeople hold assemblies to organize the grape harvest feast held the last week of September. The members take turns at doing bar service, selling few cheap products under an annoying neon light. I could have avoided entering but for my desire for a nightcap and maybe a few words with someone that wasn't Orazio.

Among the customers was, again, Giulio, still leaning on his walking stick and busily emptying another large glass. If it's true that the more he drinks, the more he shrinks, he ought to dwindle on down to nothing before the end of the night. I can't help recalling the stories I've heard about him, how this tiny, cramped little fellow was once a tall, robust young man with the body of a Hercules, filled with boundless energy. Then his wife died and he started drinking — some say as much as six litres a day — and slowly, inexorably, he started to diminish. When I first moved to the village I tried to exchange a few words with him, but quickly realized he preferred to remain in his own silent world; so now when I encounter him, I offer him a polite smile and leave him to his solitude.

Now I spot Dino, another village character, certainly the heaviest weight in town, who has dozed off and is snoring like a chainsaw, his forehead pressed against the surface of a secluded table in the darkest corner of the place. It's just a matter of time before his tiny wife will appear, as she does every night, swearing and shouting a whole series of shrill imprecations, and ordering him to move his massive bulk out the door home where he belongs, and isn't he ashamed of falling asleep in public anyway.

Naturally the entire team of old men have gathered around the gaming tables, their glasses resting on the green velvet surface, playing the classic Tuscan card games *briscola* and *tresette*. They'll curse the Madonna if they receive a bad hand, and the spectators wait for one of them to play badly, after which they'll tease and mock him and loudly tell him what they consider were the right cards to have put down.

Observing them, I think of how years pass by remorselessly. I recall those players I've seen seated at these very tables who appear here no longer, their places taken by those who were once called middle-aged but are now unquestionably old, and who are next in line to go. One of these is Guido, who has been parked here on his wheelchair for a few hours by his sons, his expression, as it has been for some time now, inexpressive and vacant. Just a few years ago he was so vibrant, so full of life; he loved to boast of the African campaign that had made him a war hero. Observing him now, immobile with his aura slowly *glissando*, makes my heart sink; I'm convinced he can't wait to leave this world that no longer belongs to him, where he no longer even recognizes himself. And I wonder, perhaps inevitably, when it will be my turn to be among the ancients seated here.

At the counter I'm happy to run into the middle-aged village *dottore* with the improbable surname Becchini (undertakers), as he gulps down a *gotto*. He invites me to sit next to him.

"You drink?" he asks. That immediately reminds me that he ran some routine blood tests for me a few days ago; I feel a flurry of panic that he's going to tell me he's had the results, and that I've been drinking too much.

"Only twice a day during meals and in-between," I reply, and this makes him laugh. It turns out he hasn't yet received my test results; he's simply inviting me to join him for a glass.

"Remember what Ambrose Bierce wrote," he tells me "The teetotaller: a weakling who succumbs to the temptation to deny himself a pleasure."

Dottor Becchini is an exuberant fellow, and the kind of company I've been looking for all evening. For the most part, he's the medic we all would like to have, because of his capacity to play down even the most grievous situations and to act as a good friend as well as a physician. In other, rare circumstances it's best not to have anything to do with him — like the time he was called urgently by a local whose mother was having chest pains, late on the night before Becchini planned to go on vacation. He couldn't ignore his professional obligations and so against his will went to see the old lady. As he had no intention of missing his flight to Cuba he decided to solve her problem very rapidly. Without touching her or even asking the unfortunate woman any questions, he diagnosed an extremely rare and lethal disease and announced that in just a matter of hours she would be no more. Having said this, he immediately filled out a death certificate for her, telling the incredulous relatives simply to add the date and time she expired. Fortunately for her, at least fifteen years have passed and they have yet to fill in that blank space.

Dottor Becchini is very cultured, very refined, and there's no doubt that the palm of village intellectual goes to him. When I confess that maybe I *am* drinking too much and that I'm thinking of quitting, he lights a cigarette, then tosses back a *gotto*, pats me lovingly on the shoulder and lets out a hearty laugh, revealing his nicotine-stained teeth. *"Balle,"* is his reply. "As Gotthard Ephraim Lessing" - this is someone I've never heard of – "would say, 'One can drink a lot, but one can never drink enough.' And remember also Hemingway, 'Wine is proof of the civilization of mankind,' he said."

He then buys a round of *gottini* for the entire bar and lowers his voice, confiding that in fifty years of medical practice he has yet to see anyone die from an overdose of *vino*. "Remember the old saying," he says, *"Se berrai vino rosso rinnoverai il tuo sangue"* ("If you drink red wine, you will renew your blood"). "You're not going to become a teetotaller, now, are you?" he continues, using the Italian word, *astemio*, and making a sour face as he pronounces it. "It doesn't even sound right, does it? Like some kind of fatal disease. Very sinister. And really, how can you renounce the most precious fruit of our land?"

He raises his forefinger and quotes again, this time, I believe, the German philosopher Schopenhauer: *"Chi non ama il vino, il bel canto, e le donne rimane uno stolto per tutta la vita."* ("He who does not appreciate wine, women and song is a fool for life").

After this impressive series of quotes and proverbs, I don't dare contradict him; and so I find myself with a goblet full of rich red wine in my hand, sharing a toast with my friend.

Dottor Becchini, I learn, never really wanted to become a physician, and would have preferred to devote his career to his chief passion: languages. His widowed mother, who came from very modest roots, forced him to study medicine mainly because she believed that the *mamma* of a doctor can always walk with pride through the town, the envy of all the other women. But he hadn't completely abandoned his first love, and in his spare time had taught himself to speak and read fluently a multitude of foreign tongues, including Russian, Chinese and Arabic.

Despite my head now being in a wine-induced whirl, I try to follow his narrative — an arduous task because he is extremely talkative tonight. He maintains that the Italian language is a marvellous idiom, and as with most Latin languages one can perceive the significance of its words by their sounds alone. As he expounds on this, he fills up his glass and then mine, utterly ignoring my *"No, grazie."*

He chooses *il mare* (the sea) as a perfect example. "Just speaking the word, you get the idea of gentle, undulating movements, a sense of great vastness" — and he demonstrates by waving his hands before my eyes, mimicking the roll of the waves and making me feel suddenly seasick. He then continues with *terremoto* (earthquake), rolling the r's as he pronounces it. "Doesn't it give you the idea of something disastrous? Of the very ground itself lurching beneath your feet?" And here he sets his cigarette in the ashtray, gets up, and starts to sway his hips as though thrown out of balance by a tremor, though to me he looks more like he's making a bad go of boogie woogie dancing.

He then returns to his original subject, opining that English is a cold language without much sense, a perfect example being "teetotaller" — so neutral and harmless, unlike its baleful, lethal Italian counterpart. These language lessons continue until we finish the bottle of Chianti Classico Riecine. He then orders another glass for himself and one for me to keep him company *(Chi non beve in compagnia è un ladro o una spia* — "He who does not drink in company is a thief or a spy") but this time, fortunately, he heeds my *"No grazie,"* and I am able to go. While I'm heading for the door, the *dottore* shouts behind me, "Hey, Dario! . . . If you really believe wine is a man's enemy, you should remember what the Bible says: "He who flees in the face of an enemy is a coward'."

Then once again I am out in the silent streets. Curiously,

despite all the wine I've downed, I'm not feeling drunk — if anything just a bit tipsy. My head is a little weary and my walk a touch zigzagy, but on the whole I'm feeling fine; in fact, I'm suffused with an enormous sense of well-being — which is the great gift of our country's wine to us.

I lift my gaze and observe the spatter of the Milky Way across the sky, and at the same time think about Becchini and how many people in Italy bear curious surnames. Some are pertinent to the jobs they take, as if predicting them; and others, like in Becchini's case, decisively the contrary (or so we hope). When I moved to Italy as a child, for example, the government was composed of men named Piccoli (small), Storti (crooked) and Malfatti (ill-done). The Minister of Transport was named Formica (ant), the Minister of the Post and Communications was named Colombo (pigeon), and the Minister of the Interior was named Rognoni (kidney). Then there was the grocer named Pomodoro (tomato); the fishmonger named Fresco (fresh); a decorator named Raffaello (like the painter Raphael); a pair of bricklayers, Leonardo and Michelangelo; an orthopedic called Maniscalco (horseshoer); an anaesthetist unfortunately named La Morte, a Vatican liaison named Amen, and a terrorist ironically christened Pace (peace).

These memories accompany me right up to my threshold. I empty the mailbox and at the fourth attempt manage to insert the key into the lock. Inside, I flip through the various deliveries and find the usual bills, as well as three envelopes from the U.S. containing personal checks from people who have ordered and received the DVD documentaries I sell on-line. I enjoy receiving these letters, not only for their content but because I'm amused by the colorful, often picturesque checks that circulate in America. They differ so much from ours, which are stark and severe, with the bank name stamped on a gray or white background. Checks from Americans seem, on the other hand, to reflect the sender's personality. I eagerly open the envelopes and I'm not disappointed; one check features Wile E. Coyote chasing the Roadrunner, another is adorned with dozens of tiny hot chili peppers; and the last is all pink, with a background sketch of a pair of horses running freely across the plain.

The house is dull, dark and not very cozy; for the first time I feel strangely uneasy here. It seems too large for a solitary man like me. Is something missing? . . . Maybe a female presence? .

. .. To exorcize the unconfortable consideration I actually recite out loud a famous WC Fields quote that I recalled sounding something like "A woman drove me to drink and I never had the courtesy to thank her" and this makes me chuckle and helps disregard the uneasy growing sensation...... I thought I'd settled that....

I manage to avoid pouring one last glass of wine and I haul myself to my bedroom on the third floor. I select a volume from my library, one that I think may contain some interesting material for my Chianti wine research. Minutes later I'm under the blankets and my head starts to spin like a turbine; suddenly the wine I have again partaken too freely of, starts to manifest its disabling effects. I feel suddenly, overwhelmingly tired so I leave the book unopened, dim the light, and in no time fall into a deep slumber.

THE RISE OF THE VINE

The next day I manage to locate the essay I'd written earlier, and which I promised to send to Mia Lane:

∾

The tradition of viticulture in Chianti has prehistoric roots. We know the grapevine significantly preceded man, thanks to the discovery of fossil remains of the *Vitis Ausanie,* the ancestor of the wild vine, from as far back as the Pliocene age. So it's no surprise that the first human beings to settle here eventually stumbled onto the means of making wine. What's more surprising is that over time, they turned it into an art.

In the 9th century B.C. the people most prevalent in these lands — the mysterious, joyous Etruscans, who probably came here from the Middle East — gave official status to the succulent juice of the vine. Thanks to numerous colorful paintings they left on the walls of their tombs, as well as to the carved objects they buried in them, we have ample testament to the ways they used wine in civic and religious rituals. They seem to have venerated a god of wine, and both began and concluded each banquet by spilling their cups on the ground as a sacrifice to him, or by pouring them into a brazier placed on an altar.

Were these Etruscans, then, the people who passed down to the Romans the art of winemaking? The answer is almost certainly yes. Yet the Romans didn't appreciate the wines from Chianti as much as their predecessors did. They favored the full-bodied vintages of more distant, southern climes like Sicily, or even Greece. This partly explains the subsequent abandonment of Chianti in late Roman times. Production did manage to persist on a small scale, as witness Tito Livio's text *The Vino Nobile of Montepulciano*; and recently on the south-eastern border of Tuscany, an ancient cellar has been discovered, with amphorae dating back to Roman times — a few of which still contain wine!

We must give credit to the monks of the Middle Ages for having brought back the cultivation of vines after the barbaric invasions that overran these lands. In fact, a wine that they referred to as Vermiglio, which "had the characteristic bouquet of violets and irises," seems to be a precursor of our modern Chiantis.

From that point on, evidence of wine in daily life grows profuse. A document from A.D. 793 records the transfer of a plot of land destined for viticulture, in the vicinity of Montepulciano. A contract exists from 827, between the parish of San Salvatore and one Giovanni Aggiperga, in which the church agrees to give him land on which to build a house for him and his new bride, in exchange for a donation of five *congi* of wine (one *congio* being the exact equivalent of 3.283 litres) to a local feast.

Permits to plant vineyards in Tuscany began to multiply around the year 1000, and many of these refer to farms located in Chianti — such as a document from 1024 which mentions the purchase of property of San Petri in Avenano of *terra laboratorea et una de vinea* (lands to plough and one also for vineyards). Documents referring to properties within Chianti, dating from1022, 1035 and 1039, refer to Grignano, La Torraccia and Corte Vecchia respectively; others from 1151 pertain to the castles of Terrazzano and Montegrossoli. Of these, remarkably, only the latter has not survived, having been destroyed in 1550 by Charles V and never rebuilt, mainly because of its vicin-ity to an unattractive quarry that fortunately is no longer worked. I find it amusing that despite these ancient per-mits being a thousand years old, many of the localities they mention not only are still in existence and producing wine, but some are still owned by the same families.

It's interesting also to notice that wine was by no means sold cheap. On the contrary, in 1265 a *congio* was purchased for eight *denari*, a sum sufficient for at least twenty days' easy liv-ing in an expensive *pension* of the time.

Wine was a necessary component of daily life because of its nutritive value (which I have written on at length in my pre-vious books) — a value so universally recognized that wine was often used to complete business deals or even cement peace between warring powers. In the civil war that erupted between the Uberti and other prominent families in

Florence, endless negotiations finally gave way to a truce; and, as a historian of those times wrote, "instead of blood, wine flowed." He concluded, "It was common to fight among fellow townsmen; one day they would wage a war, the next you would see them eating and drinking wine together, boasting about who had been the most courageous."

We now come to an age in which viticulture exploded. Vineyards spread over the entire countryside. Looking at historical prints of Siena and Florence, we can also see that it wasn't uncommon for vines to be grown inside the city walls. This explains why we see so many thoroughfares with names like Vine Street, Old Vine Street, and New Vine Street — not to mention the San Jacopo Among the Vines. Obviously this boom created many new jobs, and the art of winemaking was catalogued among the *arti maggiori*. In 1282 the local producers formed the first consortium, with its own emblem and all.

The notaries employed by the consortium fixed the prices and recorded quality and color, as well as the dates the wines were put on the market in a "clear and comprehensible manner." Merchants had to subscribe to a register, and were obliged to purchase a certain number of containers, measuring glasses and other kinds of equipment. It was also declared illegal to construct *osterie* close to churches, or to sell wines to "criminals, robbers and bootlickers," the penalty for which was the closure of your shop — or, worse, seeing it burned to the ground.

In the 12th and 13th centuries we find an amazing amount of oenological documentation. The prestige of wine was so high that Pope Boniface VIII named it the fifth element, after water, earth, air and fire. By now osterias had become the meeting point not only for exuberant youngsters, but also for the literati and other influential personages. Passionate associations of wine lovers were formed; they would taste not only the local vintages but wines imported from Corsica, Sardinia, and Crete. Still, it was forbidden to sell wine on Holy Friday, and even on ordinary Fridays it was proscribed until the end of the reading of the sacred scriptures.

Meat dominated the menus of those times, often served with legumes and enhanced with spices or sweetened with honey. Obviously bread was the major source of nutrition, and curiously the famous Tuscan beans were as yet unknown — as were potatoes, tomatoes, coffee, tea and tobacco. Wine was by far the most consumed beverage, since the well water in the cities was of such dreadful quality. Even the gentle sex were avid consumers; a document from 1268 describes a group of women who, while waiting for the arrival of Corradino of Svevia, "to kill time emptied half a *staio*." Half a *staio* was about three gallons. A rise in wine consumption of course meant a rise in drunkenness, and new codes of behavior were formed to discourage excessive drinking. In 1289, a certain Bono Giamboni wrote, "Inebriety according to the teaching of Saint Augustine is a vile burying of reason . . . a rage to the mind . . . it is gratification for the demon . . . sweet poison . . . deprivation of dreams . . . it slows down one's ingenuity . . . makes one ill, betrays secrets and induces foul language." By contrast, we turn to Gregorio from Montecatini (maybe an ancestor of *Dottor* Becchini), a physician who maintained that "of all beverages wine is the best; it generates good blood because it contains similar substances. It clarifies infected blood, stabilizes body temperature, renders the mind happy, and betters the conversation because the latter becomes more colorful."

Also of interest is a treatise by a Sienese medic, who in 1256 proclaims himself a wine connoisseur and in fact warns of the negative effects of water. Another unusual document, dated April 1299, discusses the sabotage suffered by a vintner named Giovanni Boscoli, in Lucolena in Chianti. The judge ordered the *piviere* (sheriff) of Gaville to pay the sum of 18 *lire* to all the inhabitants of Lucolena because "during the night that separated the 26th and 27th March, someone had broken into the cellar and spilled the vat's contents to the ground." For lack of a culprit, the *piviere* was fined; after all, he was responsible for the town's security. And when wine is tampered with, *someone* must pay!

Lamberto Paronetto, a scholar who dedicated his entire life to the study of wine and who is considered one of the major oenological experts of last century, calculated that in one year in Florence consumption reached 6 million gallons (!). I can't imagine the banquets that were held that year (or maybe I can). Allow me to conclude by asking, given the evidence presented here, whether we can still in good conscience call these years the "Dark Ages"?

9

ADDIO UMBERTO

As I finish rereading my essay, my stomach begins to grumble; and no wonder, the sun has snuck below the horizon and the world's gone dark. It's time for supper. I descend the stairs to the living room, musing on how quickly time flies when I'm working. It's a good feeling.

The temperature has dropped dramatically, so I pile up the hearth with firewood from the stack Checco delivered a few weeks ago. While I'm busy getting the flames going, it occurs to me how lucky I am that I undertook to write that history of Tuscan viticulture, for no other reason than my own edification. The hours I spent leafing through old books and documents in the archives and public libraries, are now paying off in a way I never expected.

When the flames are crackling and no longer need my assistance, I go to the kitchen and fill a terracotta pot with water, rice and barley; after it's boiled I flavor it with a drop of extra-virgin olive oil, a sprinkle of red hot chili pepper, and grated parmesan cheese. I open a Chianti Classico Castello d'Albola, abiding by the wise old saying *Il riso nasce nell'acqua e muore nel vino* ("Rice is born in water and dies in wine"). After I've emptied my bowl I crack open some chestnuts I picked up in the forest a few days ago and left to soften them in a container of water, and place them directly on the glowing embers. As they roast I put on some music — a CD by Nick Drake entitled *Pink Moon* — and as it plays I dine, shelling each chestnut, one at a time, and devour it with a sip of wine. When the plate is clean and the bottle is emptied I decide it's time for bed. There are still chestnuts left, but I'm full.

Under the covers, as my eyelids droop shut, it occurs to me I haven't spoken to anyone all day — not even by phone. I'm turning into some kind of hermit. My only contact with other human beings has been by e-mail, but does that even count? — Wait, I did get a call earlier, from Orazio; but I didn't understand a word he said, and anyway he scarcely counts as human contact. I chuckle at this nasty thought, and as sleep overwhelms me I tell myself that in spite of the solitude I wouldn't exchange my way of life for anyone else's . . .

My slumber doesn't last long. I'm awakened by a succession of sharp knocks on my front door. Alarmed, I slip out of bed and peer out the window, and even in the dark I recognize the lanky figure of Michele lurking below. When I open the window he lifts his head towards me, but remains silent for a few moments; and when my eyes adjust to the dim light I see that his long, coal-black hair isn't tied in a ponytail as usual, but is waving loosely in the wind. He then raises a straw flask of wine for me to see, and in his gravelly voice calls out a single word:

"*Open.*"

I swiftly don a shirt and pull on a pair of jeans and descend to the ground floor. When I open the door he steps inside without a word. Immediately I realize something is bothering him. Before I can inquire he turns his sad, scared eyes on me and with a quaver in his voice says:

"Umberto is dead."

Umberto is his father — a man he respected but whom, because of a difficult (though not hostile) relationship, I have never heard him refer to as *papà* or *babbo,* two endearments Tuscans typically use for their fathers.

"He just suddenly fell to the ground this morning, with a glass of wine in his hand," he continues as I open the flask and fetch two glasses from the walnut sideboard.

"I'm sorry," I tell him. It's a banal phrase, but it's all I can manage to come up with. His eyes are swollen, rimmed in crimson, and as we spontaneously embrace I feel my own eyes moisten and the first tears roll down my cheeks.

I motion him to have a seat on the sofa, then toss a chunk of olive wood into the fireplace to get the dimming embers going again. We sit together and drink, finishing the chestnuts and the two-liter flask, and talk deep into the night about the virtues of poor Umberto. In spite of my sadness, I'm honored that Michele chose me to help him commemorate his father tonight.

৯

Monday morning arrives. That east wind carries scatterings of oak leaves from the branches and piles them in drifts across the landscape. Against this chill, desolate backdrop, church bells ring to announce Umberto's funeral. All the shutters in the village have been pulled down as a sign of respect.

I have altered my usual dress accordingly, formalizing my customary jeans and white shirt with a somber black jacket. When the funeral procession passes my house I come out and join it, adjusting my collar as I fall into step with the other mourners. We march in silence all the way up the steep hill that leads to the cemetery. The whole village has come to pay the respects to Umberto's family, a testament to how well loved he had been. For many years he'd made his living selling wine, and as Michele had said, he died with a glass in his hand. I feel certain this is the very way he'd have chosen to depart this life.

Some black clouds trawl overhead; despite this the village elders continue climbing the steep hill, determined to defy both the threatening weather and their own frail bodies to make this one last gesture of friendship to Umberto. I offer my arm to Clara, who's having difficulty with her walking stick; she is clad all in black, her head covered by a silk shawl. She looks timeless in her grief; she might have come hobbling right out of the 15th Century.

We reach the tiny cemetery, following Michele and his brothers, who carry the coffin with proud, mournful faces. As we pass through the gates a timid sun peers out from behind the dark clouds, and suddenly the hills erupt into dazzling autumnal color — vibrant reds, luxurious golds. It's like a heavenly salute for the departed.

As we watch, the coffin is lowered into the ground by the local council workers, while Michele steps aside to put a comforting arm around his mother, whose faint sobbing breaks the silence. At the end of the ceremony many people queue up to shake hands with Michele and his brothers, and to embrace his mother. By the sound of muted laughter, I imagine many of them have paused to relate some oft-related story or anecdote about Umberto to leaven their condolences.

From the corner of my eye I see Orazio drawing dangerously near, and to avoid being drawn into one of his interminable disquisitions I vanish by way of a path through the fields and head for home. Along the way I notice that the lizards are sunning on the rocks, taking advantage of the resplendent November sun that has now taken full possession of the skies.

I arrive home still in a funerary state of mind. I pour myself a glass of Mecacci and make a final toast to Umberto. After all, this is how he himself passed his life in these lands that he loved: each milestone marked with a similar raising of his glass. I feel in some strange way that he has set down a baton, and that I am obliged to pick it up; perhaps it's a function of beginning work on my new book. As I empty the glass I recall another local saying, *Il vino e le persone buone durano poco* ("Wine and good people never last long").

FROM THE RENAISSANCE
TO MODERN TIMES

Ironically, the very first mention of a wine denominated Chianti — all the way back in 1398 — refers it as a white wine. The document is a receipt for the purchase of six barrels for three florins, twenty-six coins and eight denari paid by a certain Francesco di Marcho to Tino Riccio. It was a second-quality white produced in Valdarno that was valued about half the price of the more prestigious wines produced in other areas of Tuscany, and far inferior to the red named Vermiglio, produced within the borders of Chianti.

In the 15th and 16th centuries the red wines of Chianti are still referred to as Vermiglio, and only in the following century do both the territory and the wine become universally known as Chianti. In this period, to protect the quality of Chianti wines, a league was formed that included the boroughs of Radda, Castellina and Gaiole; this League of Chianti still exists today.

The league's 1384 charter was updated several times — in 1413, 1418, 1429 and 1439. The last reform dates to 1444 and forbids any grape-picking before September 29 (San Michele's name day).

The regulations are extremely precise. The League states that its image would be highly damaged by anticipated harvests (set in advance to avoid picking fruits before they are ripe) because "wines could not be good and thus would be unmarketable." The application of their rules resulted in a dramatic rise in the quality and prestige of Chianti wines. As early as 1458 one Cristoforo Landino writes of "the valley of Chianti that produces such exceptional wines." I also like to quote the governor of Milan, Ludovico il Moro, who declares "comforting to his stomach" the wines from these lands and who ordered an abundant supply.

The ascent of the Medici in Florence seems to have contributed immensely to the popularity of Chianti wine. Take for example the 1459 visit of the Sienese Pope Pius II to the

Florentine court, during his trip to Mantova. He was greeted by Cosimo de Medici, who organized a sumptuous reception with sixty thousand citizens celebrating in the square. Sixty boys and eighty girls danced a series of ballets, while a hundred stewards carrying straw flasks poured Chianti for the festive crowd.

A few years later, for the wedding of Lorenzo the Magnificent, the guests were plied with more than one hundred barrels of Vermiglio. Lorenzo declared that the wine "makes your feet move faster and everybody hurries to drink it." Documents also cite a friend of Lorenzo, a certain Bertoldo, who "loves to drink, and dances when he hears the clinking of the goblets." Referring to his drinking companions, Lorenzo said, "If there are foes of wine, wine is their main enemy, and they will be stung by divine fury." Though he goes on to admit that "wine disturbs the mind and impedes the use of reason." Lorenzo was a passionate lover of the nectar of Bacchus, and would bestow on his friends enormous quantities of wine he personally selected for them. He also composed these immortal verses:

Viva Bacco e Viva L'amore
Chi vuol esser lieto sia
Di domani non c'è certezza
Quant'è bella giovinezza
Che ci sfugge tuttavia

Long live Bacchus, long live Love
He who wants to be happy
Be so, as there is
No certainty about the future
Youth is wonderful but nevertheless flees.

The painters of the Renaissance, such as Paolo Uccello, Benozzo Bozzoli and Domenico Ghirlandaio, depicted still lives in which wine was heroically at the forefront. Poets, literate men who attended the court of *Il Magnifico,* paid tribute to wine, proclaiming its virtues and dedicating poems and songs to Bacchus. I won't cite them all, but will allow this fragment to represent all: " . . . and it is mainly in good wine that I have faith, and I believe that whoever thus believes shall be spared."

An amusing and controversial figure of this era was Pievano

Arlotto, who, so the story has it, paid a visit to his doctor one day. When the latter was informed that his patient was drinking a bottle of wine a day he immediately ordered him to give it up. Arlotto abruptly put on his hat and headed for the door; the doctor followed, waving the bill at him, but Arlotto refused to pay, because "what you prescribe is not a remedy."

To the Cardinal of Pavia, Arlotto uttered a phrase that became a classic Tuscan popular saying: "In each grape there are three stones: one for sanity, one for mirthfulness, and one for drunkenness."

Another anecdote finds Arlotto dining at a tavern with some friends. When they finished the wine they drew straws to see who was to go and refill the demijohn in the cellar. Arlotto lost, and when he resurfaced with the wine he said, "Now we need a lottery to see who goes to the cellar and closes the taps I left running."

Arlotto died after ninety-two — presumably happy — years.

After the death of Lorenzo the Magnificent, his son Piero proved an ineffectual ruler and the Medici were soon banished from Florence, which also suffered invasion by Charles VIII of France. The French appreciated the Vermiglio very much; at this point in history it was considered by far the area's most prestigious wine. With the return of the Medici in 1512 the people went wild with ecstasy and wine flowed in abundance. In 1515, on the occasion of a visit from the Pope, drinks were offered free (though some malicious gossips reported that everything else was made more expensive to make up for it).

In short, the people got used to drinking well and made sure that wine was preserved and served in proper receptacles. A document dated 1517 finds Francesco degli Albizi reminding Filippo Ricasoli that wine must be taken from "refilled and fresh barrels." In 1523, when a member of the Medici family was elected Pope Clemente VII, a fountain was erected outside the Palazzo Medici, on which "two showers were installed that sprinkled wine into barrels, and the people would fill flasks and other containers." Alas, a period of bitter conflicts followed; the Chianti area was sacked, and many castles and villages were destroyed by the Lansquenets.

But wine remains the area's greatest conqueror, and many are the names of those it recruited to its ranks. Two great navigators, Amerigo Vespucci and Giovanni Verrazzano, lived and produced wine in Chianti, as did Leonardo da Vinci who practiced viticulture as a hobby and apparently painted his Mona Lisa in a villa close to Greve in Chianti. "The discovery of a new wine is increasingly better for mankind than the discovery of a new star", Da Vinci stated

This was of course a golden age for the visual arts, and painters of the caliber of Antonio Bazzi (better known as *Il Sodoma*) frequently depicted scenarios celebrating wine; the great Albertinelli even opened two *osterie*, one of which he named *Il Pennello* (The Paintbrush). He wrote, "I used to paint flesh and wine; now I serve them, and everyone praises my good wine." Michelangelo was a regular there; he was a wine buff who always had at least two different vintages on his own table, one of which he ordered directly from a certain Lionardo di Buonarroto. In a letter to some relatives he wrote, "I prefer two flasks to eight shirts." In another letter he complains to his supplier Lionardo of the quality of a recent delivery: "If the wine was good when you sent it, then the deliveryman ruined it during transport."

In 1556 Battista de Tadda sculpted the columns of the Palazzo Vecchio with bunches of grapes. Caccini erected the statue of Autumn with a satire that transports the precious fruit. Vasari painted a vision of Chianti in the *Sala del Cinquecento* as well as a young Bacchus, and Cellini invoked a scene of farmers picking grapes. The great astronomer Galileo Galilei wrote, *Altro il vino non è se non la luce del sole mescolata con l'umido della vite* ("Wine is nothing but the light of the sun mixed with the moisture of the vine"), which he later rendered more succinctly, *Il vino è un composto di umore e di luce* ("Wine is a synthesis of mood and light").

At this point, wine was a centerpiece of Tuscan culture and an indispensable element of everyday life for citizens from all social and cultural strata. Over the following centuries the product improved considerably, and began its triumphal conquest of lands beyond the Tuscan borders.

჻

I read this chapter out loud to myself a few times; it sounds good. But maybe it's wise to wait for the literary agent's verdict before writing anything else. Though if she likes it, I think I will dedicate it to Umberto, whose inspiration is in nearly every line. I pop open a bottle of Chianti Classico Castelvecchi and I offer him a *brindisi* before the usual ritual routine of lighting the fireplace and downloading the e-mails.

Having completed both tasks, I have dinner to prepare. I slice an onion and chop some celery, and sautée them in a pan with olive oil. I then cover the vegetables with tomato sauce and a couple of sweet red peppers, add a pinch of salt and pepper, and let it simmer for about twenty minutes. Then I pour the entire contents into a steel casserole containing salted boiling water, toast several slices of stale bread, and place them at the bottom of a terracotta pot. When the brew has a decent texture and flavor, I pour it into the terracotta container and put it on the embers in the fireplace. I crack two eggs over it, taking care not to break the yolks, and sprinkle the surface with grated parmesan cheese. Ten minutes later I am enjoying my *acqua cotta* accompanied by the excellent Chianti Classico Castelvecchi in front of a crackling fireplace, listening to a collection of Mia Martini's very best. With my stomach full and my soul full of grace, I slip off my boots and recline on the couch; minutes later I'm asleep, tightly embracing a willing cushion.

11

THE FINAL TRUSS (Part One)

It's late morning and I'm just returning home from my usual run through the woods. I quicken my steps because I hear the phone ringing in the living room.

I lunge inside and grab the receiver, and through my gasping I recognize Andrea's joyful singsong at the other end.

"*Ehilà.*" he says. "What're you up to, old boy ?"

I swipe my sleeve across my brow, blotting away the sweat. "Just returned — from a jog — in the woods," I manage to pant.

"I hope you ran an extra couple miles for me," he says. "I just passed the quintal the other day." I can almost see him patting his stomach in punctuation.

Andrea has always had the capacity to make me smile. His quick wit and easy familiarity are irresistible, and he has a pun ready for any eventuality. Lately I've intuited that he's worried about me; he can't seem to accept my increasing isolation and the rarity with which I call on any of the old gang. He sees this as a negative turn and is constantly trying to rope me in dinners or parties, so much so that I'm running out of credible excuses for declining. I do appreciate his attempts, in that they are evidence of his affection for me, and I'm always appropriately grateful; but it's also a little irritating because I really do feel whole and self-contained, and very much at peace with myself. There's no cause for anyone to worry.

"So, Andrea," I say, returning to the subject at hand, "you've been putting on bit of weight, eh?"

"Depends on how you look at it. See, I *intended* to put on six kilos but only managed four, so it's like I'm actually down two. Am I right?" He roars with laughter, then turns serious. "Listen, old boy, I've organized a Truss for Tuesday evening, and you've been assigned course number one."

"What?" I exclaim. I have to sit down; this news has made my weary knees go weak. "No way, Andrea! Not a Truss! It's been five years since the last one, and with good reason. We're all too old now."

"I knew you'd be enthusiastic," he says, pretending to have misheard me. "Leo's joining us too, as usual."

"But . . . Tuesday, you said?" I shake my head in disbelief. "*Today* is Tuesday."

"Why, so it is," he says, as if he hasn't known it all along. "Sorry for the short notice, old boy. Well, then, see you tonight at the usual place." And before I can utter another word, he's hung up, leaving me with my jaw on my chest.

I make a move to dial him back, but stop myself; I know he'll only ignore my call.

So. There it is. I'm stuck with another Truss.

"Truss." Just hearing the word makes me shudder. It doesn't actually mean anything; it's one of many nonsense terms Andrea has invented over the years. But he applied this particular one to a silly game we played in our youth, along with Leo. Each of us would enter the old walled city of Siena through a different gate, and had to make our way to the center while drinking a glass of red wine in nine previously designated bars located on a predetermined course. Then we'd meet in the middle, completely sloshed, at a bar on the Piazza del Campo, for a tenth and final glass; after which we'd go and celebrate by stuffing ourselves with a mammoth dinner at Enoteca I Terzi.

Before each Truss, Andrea would walk my route, stopping at the bars I was to visit and paying for each of my drinks in advance. I would do the same for Leo; and Leo, for Andrea. It had been fun, when I was younger; but I am young no longer, and have absolutely no desire to get rip-roaring drunk tonight. Still, it would be deeply difficult and very unpleasant to get out of it now; and so in honor of our ancient friendship I give myself up to fate and prepare to participate.

I take a shower, chug down a bottle of mineral water whose label boasts of its ability to "purify the liver," then don a pair of worn jeans, military boots, and my customary white shirt. It's still a bit early so I pass the time by leafing through an erotic comic book. Finally, at six o'clock I go out, start up the engine of my filthy old Fiat, and head in the direction of Siena — all the while cursing Andrea, Leo and the Truss, under my breath.

Following the rules of the game, I park outside the gate known as Porta Pispini and walk Leo's route, visiting the nine bars he will be entering shortly, and paying for his upcoming drink at each of them. Despite several years having passed since the last Truss, I'm surprised that some of the bartenders recall both me and our game. A few of them even snicker as I fork over the cash and make cracks about us "never growing up."

Having completed Phase One I head over to my own starting point, which commences at Porta Ovile. Moments after I cross beneath the splendid medieval gate, I duck into the first bar, where the host, Claudio, greets me with a volley of his contagious laughter, his head lolling from side to side in disbelief. Despite the intervening years he remembers exactly what to do: he takes a glass from the rack and fills it to the brim with a deep red Mecacci and slams it down on the wooden countertop without saying a word. I take it up, like the challenge it is, and empty it all in one go. Might as well begin with a bit of bravado! I wipe my lips on my sleeve, nod to Claudio, and pivot on my heels, and in the space of an amen I am back out in the street. As I start the steep ascent Claudio calls after me in his resonant baritone, "Good Luck!" Which I appreciate. I'll certainly need it.

At the top of Via Vallerozzi, on the border of the She-Wolf and Porcupine *contradas*, I enter Fabrizio's enoteca, which as usual is full of tourists. The barman is of course awaiting my arrival and has filled an elegant crystal goblet with an important Chianti Classico Badia, a Coltibuono. I avoided making a show of any kind — no swirling or sniffing — which would otherwise be appropriate considering both the prestige of the wine and the fine goblet it's being served in, and instead swallow the contents in one greedy gulp. Fabrizio, who is busy explaining the mechanics of storing and serving wine appropriately to a party of Canadians as they sample a Vino Nobile Vigna Asinone, pauses long enough to give me a friendly farewell wink. As I head towards the door I feel the eyes of all the Canadians burn into my back, as Fabrizio reveals that I am the author of the books he has displayed on a nearby shelf. I wonder if some of them will buy the book, then read it and think me a hypocrite for my long dissertations on the value and importance of wine — remembering that they'd seen me polish off a glass of Vino Nobile like it was Coca-Cola!

Now I'm on Siena's main street, still feeling fairly sober, and surrounded by a throng of people of all ages — many of whom, at the sight of a familiar face, stop to have a chat, creating an annoyingly complex traffic jam. It's also sales season, and I notice that many shops are choked with crazed-looking women brandishing shopping bags emblazoned with the names of famous Italian designers. It takes me a while to wend my way through this human flotsam and reach the third bar on my route, which is actually not a bar at all but a small café owned by the beautiful Clarissa, who beams a smile at me as I enter. Her intense, navy-blue eyes light up as she leans far over the counter to kiss me.

"You know why I'm here," I say with a little sigh in my voice.

She laughs and pours me a Chianti Classico Meleto from an open bottle, then goes back to the espresso machine to finish filling orders for her other customers — most of whom are employees of the bank next door. Envy them, for they are able to take their coffee breaks here at Clarissa's, which is renowned for serving the best brew in town.

Before I leave, Clarissa grabs my wrist and makes me promise to give her best regards to my two crazy colleagues, Andrea and Leo. I'm not sure I want to do that, but I agree for her sake. Seconds later I am again treading the ancient granite slabs of Siena, breathing in the fresh air — which by now is helping me to stay upright. I'm feeling the first twinges of drunkenness, and I'm just a third of the way home; I'm not at all confident I'll be able to finish this Truss under my own power.

But I can't worry about that now. Summoning the path from my memory, I depart the main street and its crowds and duck onto a much more peaceful thoroughfare passing beneath a stone archway. Here is where things will start to get difficult, because I have to tackle three bars in quick succession. The first is called Planet Basket, and as the name suggests it's sort of meeting point for fans of the local basketball team. It's a nice, cozy spot, its walls covered with photos of players from all over the world who have at some point in their careers worn the glorious jersey of Siena. When the team wins a game they wave its green and white banner on a mast bolted to the wall at the entrance.

Inside I meet a couple of regulars, and when I explain that I'm here on a Truss with Andrea and Leo their eyes grow wide, as if to say, "You *still* do that?" . . . The embarrassment of which helps me find the strength of will to chug down glass number four, presented to me by a young bartender who has no idea what to make of me.

As I sit a bit unsteadily on my stool, my friends laughingly propose to stand me another drink, to toast my fortitude; I politely decline. Mainly because my fortitude might not survive it.

By now I'm definitely feeling the cumulative effects and I am slightly euphoric. I realize this as I enter bar number five and commence chatting casually to a couple of seniors I know very well. I'm in the territory of the Caterpillar *contrada* and so it's not unusual that many of the faces here are familiar to me, and I find myself lingering a few extra minutes (breaking the rules) to discuss the upcoming elections for a new *Rettore* and *contrada Capitano*. After I leave, I realize I am halfway through.

Not bad, I think.

Then I ask myself, *Who was I just talking to?*, and cannot quite remember.

One block on I enter Fabio's little wine bar, which I find empty; by contrast, my glass, poured generously from a straw flask, is now full. I realize from the severe look of the old bartender — whose shiny, raven hair is slicked back with what appears to be an abundant application of Brylcreme — that something isn't right. Is he upset because I'm his only customer tonight, and I'm only staying for one, prepaid drink? . . . Whatever the problem is, it's not the evening to inquire, and I take advantage of his silence to leave immediately and head for the next bar on the list.

I enter Via delle Vergini in the Giraffe *contrada* and mount the stone steps to Piazza Provenzano, dominated by the Church of Provenzano to whose Madonna the July Palio is dedicated each year, and where the members of the victorious *contrada* rush as soon as the race is over, singing loudly, in Latin, the Te Deum, with tears of high emotion streaming down their cheeks. Maybe it's the effects of the wine, but suddenly I feel a shiver race down my spine as I recall that recently I myself have lived that scenario, when my own *contrada*, the Noble Caterpillar, triumphed one July afternoon after having gone without a victory for fifty seemingly endless years.

I stop to observe the church's façade and as if by magic the silence is broken by the echoes of drumbeats coming from the Owl district. I instinctively set off in this direction, and catch teenagers practicing the art of flag tossing to the military rhythms of an accompanying drummer. *This is why I love Siena*, I think; *where else on the planet can you find teenagers so keen to learn the ancient medieval arts?*

Suddenly my head is in a whirl; the wine has gotten to me, my gait is unsteady, I'm having trouble walking a straight line.

I lean against a wall, take a deep breath, and convince myself that everything will be fine if I just pause a few moments and regain my equilibrium. All I have to do is get through the last few bars and then this will all be over.

I summon up all my stamina and, with the beating of the drum still pounding in my ears, return to my route and enter a filthy *osteria* for my next serving. This is where the local alcoholics meet, and there are many here tonight, bending over the crooked wooden tables, their red noses and bloodshot eyes downcast; some play at cards, others merely mutter curses at the universe. I shivered at the thought that I might not be quite so out of place here — that if I continue living this kind of life, I might even end up a regular. I rapidly drink down the third-rate wine, served up in a lurid red glass, and beat a hasty retreat from this dump. Despite some sudden and rather severe problems with basic ambulation, I manage to find the main street again, but I feel completely out of place in this surging crowd of people. I have trouble distinguishing faces — they appear deformed, out of focus — and the monuments surrounding me seem moments away from collapsing onto my head.

Forging ahead, I enter the eighth bar, where the *figli di papà* (the rich youngsters) gather for their aperitifs. There are many of them here tonight, wolfing down tiny slices of bread topped with caviar or truffle sauce, crowing about the latest Porsche model, and sporting expensive suits and the most up-to-the-moment haircuts, their wrists weighed down by their bulky Rolex watches. The bar is packed to the brim, and I have difficulty making my way through all these smug, spoiled children to the counter. When I finally arrive, the barman — whose face is as responsive as that of a grouper grilled in aluminum foil and ringed by potatoes — has no idea what I'm talking about. "You want a glass of wine without paying?" he says, glaring at me with his dull, seafood eyes. I'm having some trouble stringing together a coherent phrase, so our exchange is going nowhere fast. I have a growing feeling my personal Truss might end right here; but a second bartender suddenly comes to my aid, explaining to the grouper that I have a drink prepaid by the bald fat guy who came in earlier — "You remember," he says, "the one who knocked over an entire tray of mayonnaise tarts."

The grouper goes off to get my glass of wine; but perhaps it would have been better if we'd been left at a stalemate. My head is spinning like a gyroscope, and I can no longer walk like a normal human being. After I down the wine — in three short swallows, as though making it disappear quickly will diminish its power! — I need to draw on all my thirty-odd years of experience as a drinker to keep myself upright as I head towards the toilet. It's like riding a surfboard, except the waves that threaten to knock me over are actually inside me. Despite all my best efforts, I stagger a bit and knock into a pair of well-dressed brats who recoil at my touch, and shout "Piss off!" and "People like you aren't welcome here!" I limit my response to a mumbled apology, carefully avoiding any discussion of my right to be in this place — I'm scarcely capable of rational argument, and anyway, nature is calling . . .

After voiding my bowels, I go to wash my hands, and catch my reflection in the mirror; now it's my turn to recoil, and in sheer horror. My skin is a pallid yellow, with greenish tints. My eyes are red and swollen. I unbutton the top of my shirt, pull up my sleeves, and stick my entire head under the running tap, being careful not to swallow a drop of water (against the rules of the Truss). Then I look at myself once again — matted and dripping, like a half-drowned dog — and solemnly swear to myself, "Never again, old boy!" I even consider abandoning the Truss and just going straight home . . . but my pride prevails, and I steel myself for my visit to ninth bar, which is just off the main entrance of the Piazza del Campo.

Once again I stumble out onto the streets and proceed slowly — almost glacially — with the palm of my hand pressed against the ancient city walls to keep me from collapsing on myself up like a folding chair. I bypass Il Casin de Nobili that in times gone by was an exclusive club; it is surmounted by a number of statues of local saints whose heads are turned towards the eternal rival city Florence, as if threatening the rapacious natives of that place to *Keep away*. As I look up at them, I have the impression that they aren't so much looking out at Florence, but looking *away* from *me* — averting their holy eyes from the pathetic spectacle I've made of myself. San Ansano in particular seems particularly rigid with disgust at my condition. I lower my head in shame and creep into Danilo's bar, which is actually a tiny take-away pizzeria. The wonderful aroma of the pies hits me like a blow; I would dearly love a slice, but alas, eating, too, is against the rules.

Danilo seems very concerned by my appearance, and asks if I'm okay. I give him a thumbs-up. He doesn't look wildly convinced but says no more — merely hands me an envelope. Suddenly I feel the hairs on my neck prickle with alarm. An envelope? . . . Why would anyone leave an envelope for me here? This can only be bad news . . .

I grope for my eyeglass case in my back pocket, and after several furtive attempts that threaten to bring me crashing to the ground, manage to retrieve it and to fumble the glasses onto my face. I then tear open the letter, and I can see that it's written in Andrea's big black capital letters . . . but I can't actually make any more sense of it. I shyly hand it back to Danilo and ask him if he'll read it out to me.

He gives me another worried look, then begins: "Dario! Leo and I have decided to make the route slightly more challenging, and so Danilo will pour you a grappa that you will have to consume in a single swallow. Having done this, you'll find us at the usual bar for the grand finale! Congratulations old boy, you've made it. Andrea."

Just the thought of drinking grappa makes me want to throw up all over these delicious pizzas. Even at the best of times, I loathe the acrid smell of this liqueur, its harshness on the tongue, the aftertaste that clings permanently to the palate, resisting even the most determined assault by toothpaste or mouthwash. And then there are its aftereffects, too terrible to contemplate . . .

But I'm stuck now. Danilo has pushed a shot glass full of the clear, lethal liquid across the bar at me, and now stands ready to witness my consumption of it. I make the sign of the cross (backwards) and toss it directly down my throat.

Immediately I can feel it flow though my veins and shoot directly to my brain. In spite of myself, I feel a little thrill of relief. True, I am completely cooked, but somehow I've made it. I've endured another Truss.

As I leave the pizzeria, Danilo opens the door for me and again tells me he's very worried about me; I try to give him another thumbs-up, but I'm no longer quite certain where my thumb is, and my index finger goes up instead. This has exactly the opposite of the reassuring effect I'd intended. But in truth, the thought of reaching the Campo has somewhat revitalized me. I have no problem finding the main entrance to the square, and boldly make my way towards it — only to realize, seconds later, that I'm not within the magnificent Piazza del Campo, but in a shop that sells women's lingerie. It's at this moment I realize that I am completely gone. To make things even worse, a very elegant saleswoman, trailing an irresistible scent of peach, approaches me and asks if I need help.

I'm appalled at the idea of admitting my condition to this radiant beauty, so to avoid embarrassment I grab the first thing within reach and hand it over to her, managing to blurt out, "I, I, I'll take this." Several minutes and several dozen euros later, I'm back outside with a jungle-pattern G-string tucked in my back pocket, and a growing sense of nausea gnawing at my innards. The entrance to the Campo, I now see, is right next door to the lingerie shop; my aim had been just a *little* bit off.

I stumble down the steps — which I'm sure have been some-how made steeper overnight —and as I slowly descend them I'm buffeted by the overlapping voices of the swarm of people around me, to the point at which I'm convinced they're all say-ing "Ciao Dario! Ciao Dario!" The square itself seems to throb like a human heart, expanding and contracting with each beat. My stomach is in a turmoil, and my breath could be registered as a chemical weapon. Then I spot Andrea and Leo at the bar Il Palio, miraculously as fresh as roses, helping themselves to handfuls of chips and nuts offered by the house. As soon as they see me on the threshold, pale as a ghost and unsteady as a flick-ering candle, they both point at me and collapse with laughter. Andrea roars, his jaws wide, revealing the paste of nuts and chips he's been mincing in between his jaws. Leo, on the other hand, doubles over, and starts beating his palm on his right leg.

When they've collected themselves, they come to my aid, each hooking under one of my arms and dragging me to the counter.

"Why so late?" says Leo. "We were getting worried." His tone is sprightly — arch — the tone of someone who is enjoying tak-ing the piss out of someone else.

"You stink like you fell into a wine barrel," Andrea adds.

Meglio puzzar di vino che d'acqua santa ("Better to smell of wine than of holy water"), I managed to stutter feeling proud of remembering such an appropriate old saying despite the con-dition I'm in. But my pride is diminished by my shame at need-ing their help; how is it that I'm so much worse off than they are? Aren't we all the same age . . . ?

"Ready for the final drink, old boy?" Andrea asks with a grin, as he signals the waiter.

In accordance with tradition, the last wine is a flute of sparkling Brut Cà del Bosco. We raised our glasses in the air and clink them together.

"To the final Truss?" Leo proposes, and he swallows down the lovely vintage as though he's actually thirsty for it.

Seeing this, a horrible suspicion claws through the thick layers of alcoholic fog that shroud my brain. Still hampered by my slurred speech and close-to-comatose state, I blurt out:

"Hey, hau ish eet that yu ish sho shoba?"

"Now, now," Andrea says, as if putting off a whining child. Then he turns to Leo and says, "Actually, what we *should* have toasted was *Dario's* final Truss. Can you believe that at forty years of age, he still has time for foolishness like this?"

"You're right," says Leo impishly.

The full horror of what has happened is beginning to dawn on me, and the realization must show on my face.

"Come on, Dario," Leo says in a lofty upper-class accent, "we're both married with kids. Surely you never really believed we have time for this puerile, silly game." He shakes his head and adds a *tsk tsk tsk,* and fussily rearranges his ponytail.

At this point, taken by a sudden rage, I cry out *"Shon of a bishh,"* and launch myself towards my so-called friends, missing them both rather widely, with the result that I land face-first on the terracotta tiles.

Both Andrea and Leo reach down and grab me under the arms again, and lift me back up on my feet. Unfortunately we're not alone in the bar, and a small crowd has gathered to observe the pathetic scene. Now it's Andrea's turn to intervene. "How sad, a renowned local author performing these lurid spectacles in public."

Having heard this remark, an attractive middle-aged American woman, whose hairdo is a sort of a new-age version of Doris Day's pageboy, steps up to the scene and asks if she has heard correctly. "Is this Dario Castagno? Who wrote the books about his life in Chianti?"

Andrea confirms this in his colorful English: "Si, Madam, the too-much drunken writer."

The woman is visibly impressed. She quickly adjusts her cottony hairdo, and faster than The Flash manages to extract a lipstick from her Prada handbag and deepen the red of her lips.

Then she is approaching me with her arms wide, and I start to panic. I don't know what she wants from me, all I know is I don't want it from her. My only gambit is to breathe at her — emitting a toxic gush of wine, grappa and *prosecco* laced with gastric juices; more than enough to flatten her expensive hairdo. But this doesn't stop her; she grabs my shoulder, boldly hands Andrea her camera, and asks if she can have her photo taken with me. I embrace her and whisper in her ear:

"Sha love ju."

To prevent further humiliation, Leo and Andrea now drag me back outside, and out of reach of the postmillennial Doris Day. The crowd, seeing my condition, parts to make way for us, either out of pity or disgust. I wish I had a bag over my head.

As they lug me to the enoteca Leo says, "So, you enjoyed the innocent joke we played on you?"

"Bashtadsh" I snarled.

"C'mon, old boy," Andrea urges me. "The dinner is on us"

As always, the Enoteca I Terzi is packed with clients of the so-called *Siena bene;* bank directors, local administrators, professionals, and rich tourists. On Tuesdays the menu is set. There are fish, oysters, lobsters and all kind of exquisite Mediterranean crustaceans. My companions literally deposit me at the table, then Andrea orders me a triple espresso, and for himself a plate of mayonnaise to drown his fish in.

As the espresso begins somewhat to restore me to my senses, Leo and Andrea confide that originally they'd planned to take part in the Truss, but at the last moment decided to play a joke on me. "Because, old boy, you'd gone and forgotten about your closest friends," Leo explains. "So we had to have a little revenge."

I actually smile when I hear this; because, after all, it *is* a pretty funny prank, and they really have succeeded in making me feel guilty. I can no longer manage to be angry, despite having been their victim. As we sit, and eat, and laugh, it slowly comes back to me: the importance of real friendship; how I've missed my best friends without even realizing it; and how much it must have hurt them. I deserved this, I even asked for it. Now I have to watch them down bottle after bottle of *prosecco*, while I endure the punishment of limiting myself to San Pellegrino mineral water.

Nodding at my bottle, Leo says, "Isn't it you, Dario, who's always saying that water makes rust, and that the fish pee in it?"

Trying to ignore his taunts, I take a fresh gulp; but Andrea chimes in, "Remember my *nonno*? He would always say, 'Those who refuse to drink wine, may God deprive them of water.' Also, 'Water gives you nothing, wine makes you sing' — remember?"

"I remember," I admit. "And if I'm not mistaken, your late *nonno* Lottieri also remarked one day that *L'acqua rovina I ponti il vino la testa* ('Water may ruin bridges but wine ruins your head.')

Leo snickers. "Remember, Andrea when your *nonno* caught me as a teenager, mixing wine with water? He was appalled. He told me, *Quello che mescola l'acqua con il vino merita bere il mare a capo chino* ('He who mixes water with wine deserves to drink seawater upside down,' is what he told me.")

We continue in this vein, trading memories and proverbs and roaring with laughter, until the owner, Incarnato, slightly irritated by the commotion we're making and obviously having followed part of our conversation, hands us the check and offers us another famous maxim, *Dove puo' il vino non puo' il silenzio* ("Where wine can , silence can't,") which of course makes us laugh even more, but also gets his message across.

It's time to leave. I convince my friends that I'm feeling sort of fine, after the meal and the coffee. I tell them not to worry, I'll take the anti-breathalyzer route home, but *without* stopping to visit Alberto.

And with that we go our separate ways. I head towards my rusty Fiat, with the sensation that someone has driven a railroad spike directly into my skull. Fighting against this agony, I put my hands in my pockets and pull out my keys. My eyes suddenly catch sight of a purple one I'd almost forgotten about. Suddenly I recall that it belongs to my dear friend Viviana; it's the key to her apartment, which she gave to me years ago, with the instruction that if I were ever in trouble while in town I should use it. I'd taken her up on the offer several times, but not in a very long while.

Still, why not use it now, I think. It beats driving with this head.

I'm again on the main street, which is packed with rendezvousing teenagers, exchanging longing looks and sweet phrases. I have to re-cross the Piazza del Campo, which is now backed up with a parade of the *Selva* (Forest) *contrada*, still celebrating their August Palio victory; and after snaking my way through the throng I find myself on the stoop of Viviana's medieval apartment building. I wonder what she's up to, I think. I can't possibly imagine, but I'm sure she will be happy to see me after all these years.

I enter the building, climb the three imposing flight of stairs, and delicately place the key in the lock, trying not to make any noise lest Viviana is asleep. I seem to recall that her bedroom is the first on the right. I open the door delicately, find my way to the bed, then slip off my boots and slide myself under the blankets. I can immediately feel the warmth of a female body, and impulsively I embrace her just as I've done so many times in past years.

As soon as I touch her soft skin a scream pierces the night, which starts my head banging in anguish. Then the light on the side table explodes into brilliance, and before I can understand what's going on I'm kayoed by a tremendous blow to my right eye.

12

THE FINAL TRUSS (Part Two)

I finally arrive home at five in the morning, after a precarious journey in which I several times narrowly avoid plunging into a ditch, due to being blind in one eye and thus having no depth perception. I feel an idiot and want to break down and cry, but I don't have enough energy for that kind of emotion; all I can do is gasp a few curses at Andrea, Leo and myself, and collapse onto the bed, exhausted.

I spend the rest of the night — or rather, morning — twisting and turning beneath the sheets, three words beating relentlessly in my ears: *"Dario you're screwed . . . Dario you're screwed . . . Dario you're screwed . . . "*

I ignore the phone, which rings intermittently in the living room — timing its intervals so as to jar me awake each time I'm on the verge of slipping into deep slumber. I could get up and take the receiver off the hook, but I'm too tired to move, so I have to endure the torment of the insistent ringing.

Finally, when the phone has again jolted me out of incipient slumber, I notice that the clock reads 12:18. I decide it really is time to get up and respond. Rising from the bed, however, is a titanic task; I can feel my face twist in pain, even as my limbs, three times heavier than I remember, resist obeying the commands my addled brain is making an effort to dispatch.

I stagger down the stairs and lurch over to the phone, lifting the receiver off the cradle a moment too late; there's only a dial tone. I look longingly back upstairs — it's so tempting to head back up to bed and the protective custody of my covers — but I force myself into the bathroom. My vision is fuzzy and my mouth is dry as Death Valley, and it's really no surprise that I don't recognize the parched, gray, hunched figure who gapes back at me from the mirror.

That can't really be me, I think, as I pull at my cheeks and check my gums, as though looking for evidence that I might be somebody else.

My right eye is black — actually mauve — and is closed up tight. I make no attempt to open it; it would be hopeless. My upper lip has swollen so that it looks like an inner tube, with a crust of dried blood dangling from it like a bush rope in the jungle. To put it simply, I look seriously frightful.

I open the shower and place my head under some cold running water until my hair is drenched. The sensation makes me gasp; I feel immediately more awake, though no more glad to be alive. Then, while delicately dabbing my injuries with a towel, I try to reorder the events I went through last night. Gradually the pieces fall into place, like a jigsaw puzzle coming together before my eyes

First the Truss comes trickling back, wincingly, pub by pub . . . then my meeting with Andrea and Leo, and the realization that they'd made a fool of me . . . the cringe-making performance I gave at the rendezvous point . . . the attempt to sober up at dinner . . . and finally the oh-so wise decision to spend the night at Viviana's, which resulted in confusion, screams and a blow to the head.

And then? . . . I try to summon the recollection from the dank recesses of my warped memory.

I seem to recall being awakened by a series of sharp slaps to my face. When I opened my single functioning eye, I could make out, swimming in the air before me, a face I recognized — that of old *Maresciallo* of the *Carabinieri*, Iuzzolino. I tried to greet him, but he kept striking me even when it was apparent I was now conscious; in fact he actually amped up the force of his blows, hitting me with even more vehemence. Then he grabbed my shirt front and started shaking me, snarling over and over again, "Dario, you're screwed," and at the same time boring into me with eyes both bloodshot and brimming with hatred. A large vein in his forehead was protruding, as if engorged with pure rage.

He was accompanied, I now remember, by two younger officers; one was busy talking into a phone, while the other scribbled on a notepad the words of a young, sobbing girl who had her back turned to me. From what I could see of her, she was extremely athletic; she had a crew cut, and was dressed in camouflaged print military shorts and a sleeveless T-shirt that showed off a body of impressive musculature. I noticed that the back of her neck was tattooed with some kind of winged green dragon.

When the first officer finished his call he came over and mumbled something which caused Iuzzolino to release my collar. I dropped back onto the mattress, my heart beating as though I'd just run a double marathon.

I was allowed to leave. My head was still spinning, but I managed to pull my boots back on and stumble to the door, where I noticed that for the second time in only a few hours I had drawn a crowd. The stairwell was packed with people from the other apartments, who had come out in their pajamas and robes at the sound of a woman's screams and the *carabinieri's* sirens. They took a step back when I appeared, and regarded me with a mixture of hatred, fear and disgust, which was really the least I could expect, considering my split lip, black eye, and shirt doused in blood. I felt like as if I were in a western movie — and not as the guy in the white hat, either. No, I felt like the outlaw who was being run out of town by the sheriff.

As I groped my way down the steps, Iuzzolino's voice thundered down the stairwell after me: "Listen up, Dario! Next week I'm retiring after thirty years of service, and in all that time you've given me nothing but grief! Let this be the last time you break my balls, or when I go out I'll take your head along with me!"

And that, blessedly, was the end of the night.

Now that I've got the whole, awful chronology straight in my head, I decide it's probably best to lie low today — stay in the house and recuperate, and avoid any new trouble. I make myself a cup of *orzo* and stretch out on the couch — but I have to get up again in a moment to fetch some cold milk to add to the brew; I can't stand the hot liquid against my injured lip.

I've just achieved a tolerable temperature and taken my first sip, when the phone interrupts me.

"Pronto," I say into the receiver, in a low, hoarse voice.

And suddenly I am being pummeled by a volley of furious words from Viviana. "Dario! I just had to call and thank you for a really memorable night. The *carabinieri* woke me out of a deep sleep to tell me someone had broken into my apartment and got into my bed, which my cousin happened to be using at the time, and that her shrieking had woken up the whole building and brought the entire police force out with their lights flashing. Then they told me the stranger was *you*. What the hell were you thinking? Are you out of your mind?"

"Viviana," I say, trying to interrupt, "listen to me! I can explain!"

Eventually she calms down and said, "Fine, then. Explain. And this better be good."

"It's simple," I say, trying to make the story as brief and innocuous as possible. "First of all, I didn't *break in* to your apartment. I'd somehow survived a Truss with Andrea and Leo, but I didn't think I could drive home, so I decided to take advantage of the offer you once made and use the key you gave me in case I ever needed — "

"What?" It's her turn to interrupt. "Dario, it's been *eight years* since you last crashed at my place. I haven't even *seen* you in the past two years. What the hell makes you think you can just waltz right through my door like I made that offer yesterday? What goes through your mind — presuming you still *have* a mind, which I'm beginning to doubt?"

I try to offer more explanations, but I can't get a word in edgewise. "My God," she continues, "if I'd been home in bed last night you'd have given me a fatal heart attack. But I wish I had been, rather than subjecting my cousin to that awful shock. Poor kid, she's in Siena for a kickboxing tournament and had nowhere to stay, so I offered her my place while I'm on assignment in Rome. I thought I was being nice. I didn't realize I was putting the poor, sweet girl in *your* drunken path. She's only seventeen!"

I make a few attempts to add some word of explanation, but she continues to barrel right over me; and in the end I decide it's best to let her get all her anger out of her system.

"If you're going to ask for forgiveness, forget about it. The poor girl thought she was going to be raped by a *sex maniac!*" She pronounces the last two words with the same elongated syllables she'd used for *"eight years"* — she's nailing me to the wall with her diction.

"And the fact that you'd just completed a Truss is no excuse at all," she adds, with no sign of slowing down. "My God, aren't you all a little old for that kind of juvenile behavior? At least you're single, I can't imagine what Leo and Andrea's wives have to put up with on a daily basis. There's really no hope for any of you, at this point. You're terminally adolescent."

I realize I have an opening here; she's shifted the full brunt of her fury off of me, and turned it, however glancingly, on Leo and Andrea. I can use this brief respite to my advantage; so I seize control of the conversation.

"Listen, Viviana," I say, "maybe you're right about Leo and Andrea and me. But you're making too much out of this incident. I mean, I'm sorry I frightened your cousin, but she's hardly the defenseless little girl you make her out to be. I saw her, she's built like Mike Tyson. And as for helpless, she gave me a swollen lip the size of a bowling ball, not to mention a black eye the size of Pamela Anderson's breasts."

I'm cut off by the dial tone; Viviana has hung up on me.

I stare at the receiver for a few moments, like an idiot, unable to believe she'd really cut me off that way. Then I gently lower the phone onto its cradle and sit down and consider the whole situation. Maybe Iuzzolino and Viviana are right, maybe I never *will* grow up. I've tried, certainly, but there seems always to be something to pull me back to the old behaviors. I'm a victim of fate. I may as well just give in to it.

And so I descend into a sulk and spend the remainder of the day lying low, feeling sorry for myself. But the recent spate of surprises hasn't quite abated. As I'm slouched on the couch, dipping some whole wheat cookies in my orzo, I hear a feeble knock on my front door. I open it only to find Andrea before me, looking very trim in his expensive gray Armani suit and carrying his elegant leather briefcase at his side. In contrast to his dashing apparel, however, he wears a demented look on his face; he appears sick — his skin pale green. He says nothing but brushes me aside, drops his briefcase as he sweeps past me into the house, and bolts towards my kitchen. I follow, and find him hunched over the sink, where he extracts a handkerchief from his pocket and wets it under the tap. Then he slipped off his Cesare Paciotti shoes, doffs his jacket and tie, and lowers himself onto the couch, placing the damp handkerchief gingerly on his forehead.

"Good afternoon, Andrea," I say. "Do come in."

He doesn't even look at me, but lies there gasping for several minutes; I sit down across from him, determined to wait however long it takes to hear his story.

Finally, he's ready. "Old boy" he said, his voice so feeble I can barely hear him, "before you tell me what the hell happened to your face, let me just fill you in on what I did after I left you and Leo last night. I was on my way to my car, when I started thinking, what a shame it was that all those prepaid drinks were going to waste. So I decided, why not have a few? They were meant for me, after all."

I nodded. "It's nice to know Leo didn't waste all his money."

"He didn't waste any of it," he says with a groan. "I don't know what came over me, but I ended up having every last one." My one uninjured eye opens wide with shock, and he says, "That's right, I did a Truss all by myself."

I stifle a laugh and let him continue. "As you can imagine, I went to work this morning with a mammoth headache and a stomach in turmoil. Unfortunately, my boss called me into his office and insisted I taste some terrible walnut liqueur of his own production; he's so proud of the stuff I couldn't possibly decline without offending him. Well, I had a single shot, and no sooner had he asked what I thought of it than I puked all over his brand-new cherrywood table."

I let out a single laugh, so big it almost reopens my split lip.

"Oh, yes, I imagine it's sweet revenge for you," he says bitterly. "Anyway, he gave me the afternoon off — less out of sympathy, I imagine, than to get me out of his sight. So if you don't mind I'm going to take a nap right here and try to recover a bit before I go back home." He shifts the handkerchief on his brow and said, "But first, tell me how you got so mauled."

So I recount my own misadventure, including my beating by a seventeen year-old girl and my subsequent encounter with Iuzzolino. When I finish, we gaze at each other in silence for a moment, then dissolve into helpless laughter; which exhausts us both. I leave Andrea to fall asleep, closing the shutters for him as I depart the room; then I go to my office to check my email.

Among the multitude in my in-box, is the one I've been hoping to receive.

From:	Mia Lane
To:	Dario Castagno
Subject:	Re: A proposal for you

Dear Signor Castagno,
Thank you for your prompt reply. I was pleasantly surprised to receive so swiftly the material that you sent over the weekend, and found it extremely well written and informative. It was interesting to learn about the

history and traditions of Chianti wine over the centuries and you must have done a great deal of research to gather all those dates and anecdotes. Unfortunately I must inform you that this isn't exactly the kind of narrative the publisher is looking for. I've read your previous books and very much like how you capture the intimate character of the country, its people, and its wine; we're looking for something similar — along the lines of more direct personal experiences. We are particularly interested in light, amusing stories, perhaps about those times that you overindulged your love of these wines, and some diverting situations you found yourself involved in.

I apologize for the misunderstanding and for making you lose precious time; obviously I should have been more specific, but am hopeful we can count on you for future collaboration.

Best Regards
Mia Lane

I gaze incredulously at the monitor with my only functional eye, my mouth agape. Far from a scholarly treatise on Chianti viniculture, it appears as if they're asking — never mind how delicately they phrase it — for a litany of my booze-ups and hangovers.

"Piece of cake," I say aloud, suddenly alive with enthusiasm. I have plenty of material; in fact, am I not actually living the epilogue of a chapter right at this moment? With a supporting character one floor below me, emitting snores loud enough to rattle the windows in their frames?

I smile, thinking that at the time Mia Lane was writing this message I was already completely sloshed, facing down Iuzzolino in Viviana's apartment. I wish I'd known; I could have said to the old bastard, "Listen: this is *research* for a *book.*"

In fact, a lot of my life has been research for this book. All I have to do is to dig in my memory for the most entertaining stories. Of course, my memories of these incidents can be a little wobbly, given the circumstances. But I'll worry about that when I have to.

In the meantime, I decide to write up a full report on what I've just experienced while it's reasonably fresh in my memory.

I feel a sudden impulse to toast this new beginning with a glass of red; an impulse I easily manage to suppress. Instead, I pop a CD into the stereo — one of Lucio Battisti's best, *Una Donna per Amico* (which I've chosen in honor of Viviana) — and begin to set down this account of my last, disastrous Truss.

13

THE FINAL TRUSS (Conclusion)

By the time I finish writing the sun has set, and Andrea is now awake. He's seated on the couch sipping a hot cup of mallow tea and munching on a piece of moldy toast he found in some forgotten corner of my pantry. He's also smeared it with the last squeeze from an expired tube of mayonnaise. Never mind, it's clear after last night's Truss that nothing he puts into his body can ever kill him.

We spend the next hour or so talking about how we've both changed over the years; unlike me, however, most of Andrea's changes seem to have come not from within, but from his wife. She keeps him on a very short leash, putting him on a strict diet and rationing his calories. "She even forbids me mayonnaise," he moans, as he tries to squeeze a few last drops from the ancient tube. Considering the hour and his apparent longing for real food, I invite him to stay for dinner, but he declines with a sigh; "My mother-in-law is coming over," he says, "and frankly, it's easier for me to just go home now, and not have to argue with my wife about it later." Suddenly my solitary life doesn't seem quite so bad.

I walk Andrea to the door, where he retrieves his leather briefcase, dons his jacket, and reknots his tie. He's just about to bid me goodbye when his phone rings. He takes it from his pocket and looks at the Caller I.D.

"It's Leo," he tells me, and there's relief in his voice; clearly he'd expected it to be his wife. He flips open the phone and says, "*Ehila* Leo! What's up? . . . No, I'm not home, I'm at Dario's. Why?" His brow furrows as he listens, and he looks up at me in some concern. "You say you're in trouble?"

Suddenly he puts down his briefcase and goes back to my couch, and sits down. He listens a bit more, and suddenly he starts to laugh. He says, "Well, that makes three of us, then."

And suddenly I realize what has happened: Leo, too, decided not to let the opportunity for a Truss go to waste. I sit down opposite Andrea and wait to hear what happened to him. Andrea, by now, is beating his forehead in amazement.

"You say you passed out cold on the bench outside Porta Romana? . . . I can't believe it! You were actually woken up by Iuzzolino in person at five in the morning? . . . Oh, he asked if you'd taken part in a Truss, did he? No, he's not psychic, it's just he'd already had a run-in with Dario." I can hear Leo's laughter from the other end of the phone. "He'll tell you all about it later," Andrea says. "For now, finish telling *your* story." He listens some more, nodding, then puts his head back and laughs, and says, "Sure, sure, no problem, we'll see you soon." Then he flips his phone shut and looks at me with a grin.

"Well?" I ask, impatient with curiosity.

"His wife ran him out of the house with a baseball bat, and now she's changed the locks and won't let him back in."

I shake my head. Maybe Viviana is right: none of us will ever grow up.

"Anyway, he's on his way over here." He flips his phone back open and begins dialing. "I think I will remain for dinner, after all . . . Hello, sweetheart? It's me. I have some unfortunate news . . . "

After giving his wife the most banal of excuses (he has to work late because of a difficult client), he goes off to buy some steaks, sausages and ribs, while I stay behind to light the fire. Seated by the hearth, feeling the heat of the crackling flames, I begin to medicate my injured eye and lip with the best remedy available: a five-liter pitcher of Mecacci.

Here we go again, I think as I pour my second glass; and then a more appropriate local saying occurs to me: *Per fare un amico basta un bicchiere, per mantenerlo non basta una botte* ("To make a friend all you need is a glass, to maintain one takes more than a barrel").

Andrea returns with a bag full of meats (and a king-size tube of mayonnaise), and minutes later we hear the roar of Leo's scooter approaching (he has never owned a car). We head to the window in time to see him take off his crash helmet and shake out his ponytail; he looks a little bit the worse for wear, but a couple of glasses of red are all he needs to put him right.

We end up devouring the grilled meats directly with our hands, seated on the floor before the fireplace and emitting loud, appreciative belches, chewing with our mouths open and drying our greasy lips on our forearms. It's satisfyingly primitive. The main topic of conversation is of course the Truss and all its myriad complications — Iuzzolino, my black eye, Viviana's kickboxing cousin — and this inevitably inspires us to recall other pranks we've played in the past. Our hoots of laughter are eventually interrupted by Andrea's phone ringing — it's Leo's wife, now worried about him and trying to track him down. Andrea assures her that Leo is safe and sound, that he's sorry about the previous goliardic night, and will return to her soon.

When we empty the jug there is a moment of temptation — but after looking each other in the eye for a few moments, we decide that no, it's not a good idea to refill it; in fact it's best to just call it a night and get some sleep.

As we say goodbye we clutch each other in a collective bear hug, and when I close the door behind them it occurs to me that this has been an unexpectedly felicitous ending for our disastrous final Truss. I myself am so contented that I feel like cashing out right on the couch, with the sweet notes of Tim Buckley playing behind me as a sleep-time soundtrack. And so I do.

OUT AND ABOUT

The following morning I feel decisively better; a good night's sleep has dampened the nauseous effects of the Truss. Alas, it can't soothe the psychic bruises that will remain raw and vivid for many days to come. Still, I'm in a better mood than I deserve to be, the nine o'clock sky is limpid, and the temperature is fresh and delightful. I'm in the perfect frame of mind to sit down and write, but decide it's wise to wait for Mia Lane's reply; I don't want to bolt ahead before getting her okay to continue.

I find no messages from her in my in-box, but I wasn't really expecting any; it's just twenty-four hours since I had last emailed her. As long as I'm here, seated before the screen, I take care of some other correspondence; then around eleven I turn off the computer and sit comfortably on the terrace, immersing myself in the warm sunlight and amusing myself with a book by a talented young Bolognese author named Gianluca Morozzi

Suddenly a single ray falls across my Bianchi racing bike, which I parked here a few days ago with the intention of tucking it away for the coming winter months. I gaze at my faithful companion, with whom I've covered tens of thousands of miles over the years and even competed, with negligible results, in some local amateur races. Its yellow hue suddenly brightens with reflected sunlight, and it seems almost as though the bike has come alive and is pleading for one last ride before the long winter hiatus.

"Why not?" I say aloud. The weather is unseasonably mild, and a brisk ride will help clear away the last, wretched vestiges of the Truss.

I tear off my jeans and shirt, don my cycling gear, oil the chain and put air in the tires; during which preliminary activities I also decide on my route. I'll make for the top of Monte Luco, right where the RAI-TV antenna booster is placed — a landmark visible in the far distance from my house, since it's one of the highest peaks in Chianti.

Cycling through these sloping hills is not a simple task. A minimum of training is necessary to be able to handle the near total absence of level ground and the continual appearance of vertiginous inclines, which can make even a short ride an extremely demanding one. As my village is located at the top of one of these steep hills, for the first several miles it isn't necessary to touch the pedals; gravity does all the work for me. I take particular care not to brake when my wheels pass over the slippery leaves shed by the oak and chestnut trees, and which contribute considerably to the risk of wiping out — a risk that is amplified today because I've got no depth perception, what with my left eye still swollen shut.

I bypass an ancient monastery, immersed in a vast olive grove, now property of the local university. Some farmers are preparing for the coming harvest, setting up ladders and surrounding the trees with ample nets to collect the fruit. A light breeze flaps at the branches, churning up the leaves and stirring their various colors, from green to gray and almost silver on the back. Soon I will be picking my own fruit, the preamble to transforming it into the precious extra-virgin olive oil that I supply mostly to overseas clients and friends.

Despite the fact that I'm fully suited and the sun is quite warm, I feel a slight chill when I reach the bottom of the valley and slip into the filmy fog that envelops it. Minutes later I'm on the main drag of Chianti; here the road starts to climb, and at last I am compelled to start pedaling, the exertion of which always warms me up. I switch to a more demanding gear, lift my backside from the seat and start to push my weight into the pedals; soon I achieve a regular rhythm. After about ten miles the road again dips into a descent, and I reach the lowest point of the entire route; then after having crossed a new bridge over the Arbia river, erected in place of the one that collapsed in the 1993 flood, I turn in the direction of Montaperti (which, as my longtime readers will know, is where the Sienese army annihilated the Florentines on the 4th of September, 1260). For the second time the road arcs upward, and again it becomes necessary to extend my torso over the handlebars. My heartbeat soon roars in my ears and pearls of sweat dampen my forehead, which I've swaddled in a bandana, Red Hot Chili Peppers-style.

I pass an impressive 17th century mansion, and through its wrought-iron gates I catch sight of an arbutus bush bearing an incredible bounty of ripe fruits, as well as an impressively laden persimmon tree; I've always been fascinated by the way this tree sheds its leaves but not its mushy orange fruit, giving it a bizarre appearance — like a modern art installation with plastic balls in place of fruit.

After a few miles I leave the boundaries of Chianti and find myself crossing a much more barren landscape. Here I come across several ranches where Arabian horses are bred for racing. Today some of these magnificent creatures are galloping about in their corral, happy-go-lucky, instilling in me a similar sense of giddy freedom.

Now the hill becomes even steeper, and I approach my favorite series of hairpin turns and corkscrew bends; then the road swoops up and down in succession, giving the sensation of being on a roller coaster, and to avoid losing speed I have to change up and downshift the gears both rapidly and continually. In the midst of all this maneuvering I manage to take in the beautiful countryside, with its ancient farmhouses scattered untidily among the hills; most of them are now rented out as holiday homes and their shutters will remain closed until next season. Those still inhabited by locals, on the other hand, are readily apparent by the thin brown smoke that seeps from the chimneys before dispersing into the wide blue sky.

In a clip, I enter and exit Castelnuovo Berardenga, a town I adore and which for some odd reason hasn't yet been discovered by tourists; then I head towards San Gusmè, a tiny hamlet at whose entrance one is greeted by the curious statue dedicated to Luca Cava. It portrays a man crouched down and evacuating his bowels, and it's this unprepossessing figure to whom the annual village feast at the start of September is laughingly dedicated. (The reason? If you pronounce Luca Cava very rapidly it sounds like *Lui cacava* — "He shat.")

Now that I'm back in Chianti the vineyards are again an omnipresent feature of the landscape, but in this season they are not at all attractive. As soon as the harvest is over they assume beautiful amber and crimson hues; but after only a few weeks they shed their leaves and stand utterly denuded, their rows of barren branches resembling a sad military cemetery.

I head towards Monteluco and the road rears up before me once again, this time reaching its maximum slope. The only sound is the tinkling of the bells around the necks of the sheep grazing lazily in a nearby field, who are guarded by a magnificent example of a Tuscan herding dog, a *pastore maremmano*. Each time I reach this stage of the ride and pass the sign that announces the upcoming twenty percent ascent, I invariably consider giving up, and ask myself why I put my body through such an arduous task. At the halfway mark, panting and gasping, I always vow to give up drinking and smoking. Soon my pulse is pounding beyond normal human limits, and the lack of oxygen distorts reality — in fact only recently, when I made this ride in sweltering midsummer heat, I had mystical visions due to the strain: I was positive I could see Saint Peter and Saint Paul spurring me on. Only when I got closer did I realize that the two figures I had mistaken for biblical stalwarts were really two friendly shepherds waving their staffs at me in encouragement.

I keep climbing, very slowly, trying to dose my strength. I feel my legs fill with lactic acid; my calves are stretched to their maximum and I risk pulling a muscle if I'm not careful. If I stop here, starting up again would be impossible.

It takes another forty minutes to reach the peak, swaying rhythmically all the way, my head bent over the handlebar. Sweat trickles down my face, right through the drenched bandana, irritating my eyes and even sliding into my open mouth. Inevitably I end up swallowing some of it, and I have the impression that it tastes faintly of Chianti wine, which shouldn't surprise me considering the quantities I've downed in the last few days.

I'm so focused on tackling the mountain that I ignore the splendor of the landscape surrounding me; an infinite vista that embraces three of the major Tuscan provinces. Finally I obtain the summit, and as I cruise past the big TV antenna I can raise my head, catch my breath, and compose myself for the long downhill leg that takes me to the hamlet of Castagnoli, Castle Meleto and through Radda in Chianti then Castellina in Chianti before confronting me with the final hill that leads me back to my village.

I feel utterly spent, but gratified. I check the little milometer; I've covered 87 miles at an average speed of 16 mph, and considering my age and physical condition I feel proud of my performance. After a long shower I reward myself for having pedaled so productively by opening a Chianti Classico Aiola 2003. I propose a *self-brindisi* and down the first ruby mouthful: even better, because I've earned it!

15

SUDDENLY, ELIO

Eventually I notice that during my absence I've received an e-mail from Mia Lane.

From: Mia Lane
To: Dario Castagno
Subject: Re: The Truss

Dear Mr Castagno,
I received, read, and very much appreciated your chapters on the Truss. The entire situation is hilarious, and I laughed out loud while seated at my computer, unfortunately disturbing my tabby cat who's in the habit of coiling up on my lap while I work. I find it incredible that this misadventure occurred only yesterday; maybe destiny took a hand, because this is exactly the kind of story we're looking for.
I admit that after having read your previous books I suspected that characters like Andrea and Leo had been slightly exaggerated, if not entirely fictionalized, but you've convinced me that they're genuine. I'm certain you must have a bounty of other such crazy episodes you can relate, and I can't wait to "meet" the other people that live in your world. For instance, the *carabinieri* officer Iuzzolino must be someone you crossed paths with many times, judging by the tone of your relationship as presented here. I really look forward receiving more material from you.
In the meantime, best regards and I hope you're recovering from your injuries.
                                                        Mia Lane

From: Dario Castagno
To: Mia Lane
Subject: Re: The Truss
Attachment: The Truss part three

Dear Mia

Ciao! Pardon me if I use a less formal tone this time, but as I'm certain our exchanges are bound to be more frequent, it seems more convenient for us both. So please put aside the Signore Castagno and simply call me Dario. I'm delighted you enjoyed my tragicomic Truss experience. At least I now know my blood wasn't spilled in vain! I must admit, it was far more satisfying writing it down than living it. If we do include it in a book, do you think we'll inspire a Truss craze in the States? . . . Possibly we'd have to pay a royalty to Andrea, who invented both the game and the name. A bottle of wine ought to cover it.

I'm attaching an additional chapter to round out the adventure, because an epilogue of sorts occurred only last night. I hope you enjoy it; I think it makes for a perfect ending.

Meanwhile, my eye is slowly recovering and I can open it a bit now, though my sight is still blurry. The swelling in my lip no longer looks quite so alarming, too. Now it just looks like I've had silicone injections.

Tomorrow I will begin work on some new chapters that feature Andrea, Leo, and why not, good old Iuzzi in person. Regarding some of the interesting local characters you refer to from my previous book, you'll be interested to know that just today, while cycling through my hills, I encountered an old friend of mine.

I was about halfway through my usual route and stopped for a drink from a freshwater spring close to Castle Brolio. I wasn't alone for long; an elderly man pulled up in his Jeep and took some plastic jugs from his trunk to fill with the cool, clear water. I recognized him from his ample lope and his reversed-pear shape body. I had first met Elio when I was a fireman in Siena many years ago; in fact he was my chief, and soon became a role model — a *maestro* of life.

Despite that more than twenty years had passed since I'd

last seen him, and that I was wearing cycling gear, a bandana and sporting a disfiguring black eye, he recognized me immediately. He squeezed me with all his might, actually raising me off the ground, he then gave me a big kiss, grazing my cheek with his bristly beard and leaving it rashed as though a carpenter had scraped it energetically with sandpaper.

Old Elio is a bizarre character, much like the surname he bears: Strambi (Italian for *odd*). He's ridiculously vital; he has the strength of ten plough-horses. Whenever I think of an old Tuscan farmer, Elio's is the face I see. And he was virtually unchanged after all these years — except for his thin fuzzy hair, which was no longer pitch black but now a dull gray. All the rest was as I remembered: his friendly smile, tiny black-pea eyes, and jutting jaw. His massive head seemed to be resting directly on his collarbones, as though his neck hadn't been able to support the weight of it and had sunk right into his trunk. His wide shoulders resembled those of an Olympian swimmer, and his hefty biceps are like iron, which in fact is characteristic of the Strambi family.

From the pelvis down, however, he is strangely unprepossessing; his legs are long and spindly, and seem better suited to a ballet dancer than a Chianti farmer. Sometimes, observing him, I have the impression Mother Nature overlooked a slipup on her assembly line, and somewhere else on the planet there is someone boasting a long neck, willowy arms, and a lean torso walking around with legs like redwood trees.

Even Elio's voice is distinctive. His voice box emits a sound both feeble and shrill, giving the impression that he's speaking in falsetto. My colleagues at the fire station and I often laughed when he barked orders at us, joking that he could easily join the Bee Gees.

He never feels the seasons; he's always been completely meteorologically apathetic. In frigid winter he wears the same sleeveless shirts he does the rest of the year, and in summer can work the rocky fields for hours beneath the scorching sun without swooning. He performs with enviable mastery any type of job, from the merely physical to the dauntingly skillful. If he needs to chop wood or tote huge boulders, he'll do it without flinching; he can forge metal, and yet his blocky fingers are also capable of weaving delicate baskets from straw and painting astonishing watercolors. He cures his own salamis and hams, which I recall as being exquisite, and makes homemade red wine and sweet *vin santo*, both as genuine as he is. He drinks them in very large quantities at any time of day, in accompaniment to his frequent snacks.

Courage is another of his virtues. I remember very vividly a time during my term of duty when he ran into a burning kitchen, picked up the heavy butane gas bottle that had caught fire as if it was a mere bundle of branches, carried it on his shoulders down three flights of stairs, then dashed outside and threw it into a ditch where it exploded seconds later.

He married a minuscule woman whom he adores, and a friend of mine who lived in the apartment below them swore that every night Elio and his lady made love so that his chandelier would rock back and forth and the ceiling would creak and groan. This only ceased when Elio called out at the climactic moment, in his very marked Tuscan accent, *"Che toro tu hai trovato!"* ("What a bull you found!")

I heard a story about him having to knock down a wall that separated a room from a wine cellar. Every blow of his club brought him closer to his goal, and when the sweet odor of must at last began to waft through from the adjacent room he seemed to go crazy, like a shark when it detects the presence of blood. When finally the wall collapsed before him, he vaulted over the rubble and dashed towards the barrel, then placed his mouth to the tap and rewarded himself for his effort, as though he were drinking water from the font where I now encountered him.

He insisted that I join him for a bite before continuing my ride. He produced some bread from his straw basket (one of those he'd made himself), sliced it, then applied two slices of ham (again of his own production) and handed them to me. He offered me some wine (once more, his own) which I politely declined since I was in the midst of my ride, so he got up to return the bottle to his jeep (Japanese production but give him the equipment. . .) At the last moment he turned his eye on me and said, *"Chi beve per mangiare, mangia per vivere"* ("He who drinks to eat, eats to live"). So of course I changed my mind, and he sat down again and poured me a glass. When I wanted to dilute it with some spring water he reminded me that *il primo bicchiere deve essere pretto, il secondo non annaquato, il terzo senz'acqua, il quarto come il primo ed il quinto solo vino* ("The first glass must be pure, the second not watered down, the third without water, the fourth just as the first, and the fifth only wine").

I remained with him a good half-hour, chatting over old times, before saying goodbye with a final *brindisi*. When I had emptied my glass (the fifth, as a matter of fact), he added: *"L'amico è come il vino fatto ora che il tempo inacidisce o migliora"* ("A friend is like a newly made wine that time will either better or turn sour"). We promised to meet again, and until then he embraced me and placed in my bike's bottle holder a parting gift of his own wine.

You see Mia, Chianti is also beautiful for this reason: one can spend an entire day without meeting anyone at all, and then suddenly out of the blue you can encounter a character like Elio, a creature shaped by these hills, a simple, genuine man sprung up from this soil and brimming with stories to share. He belongs to that category of big hearts always there when needed, one of the last of a long line of Chiantigiani, a race sadly in the throes of extinction, a romantic survivor of a remote time.

As promised, I will send you a chapter tomorrow. I've just this moment finished a bottle of red wine so, for now, I guess its time to go to bed.

Goodnight Mia
Dario

16

THE BIRTH OF ANDREA

I rise early the following morning, and after my usual cup of *orzo* I pack my laptop into my duffle bag and walk up the hill to my outdoor office. The last thing I did before going to bed was to promise Mia Lane a chapter, and I have every intention of keeping my word. I sit down at the table under the large oak tree and reflect on the many times I've been involved with Andrea and Leo in, shall we say, "awkward" situations. It seems as if our proximity to each other sparks an unusual chemical reaction that results, more often than not, in chaos.

Judging from her last email, Mia seems to be particularly intrigued by Andrea. He certainly is a unique character, a generous man with a peculiar wit and a devilish sense of fun; in brief, a true friend and companion, of the kind I wish everyone could have. I've already written in a previous book how I came to know him; but given that this book is to be about my more extreme experiences with wine, Andrea is sure to be an even larger presence — since more often than not he was directly involved. So why not take the opportunity now to pull back the veil, and reveal his true identity?

જી

We all call him Andrea Giubbolini, but for many years I knew him as Luca Resti. To explain this paradox, I must go back some fifteen years.

It was the beginning of the 1990s, and Luca was going through an extremely difficult time. He was depressed by his job in the insurance department of the local bank, and the future seemed bleak to him. So he decided to give everything up and move to Costa Rica. Why Costa Rica? He couldn't really say, and it seemed odd to us that he was suddenly so obsessed with it, especially since he'd never even been outside Italy before. But he was determined to live there, and to open a bar on the beach.

He was the only child of a well-off family with whom he still lived at age 26 – which isn't uncommon for a single man in Italy. His parents had always spoiled and coddled him, and from the time he was a teenager he was allowed a tremendous amount of freedom. But recently they had curtailed his privileges and even imposed a rigid curfew on him, all in an attempt to make him take his job more seriously; he was failing at it, and this alarmed them. They wanted him to have a steady career and a solid retirement fund, and in fact it was his father who had got him this job, by working his connections with all the major bank directors until one of them finally bit.

But Luca didn't appreciate his father's efforts on his behalf and dreaded turning into an average, boring Italian with a pre-programmed life, spending the rest of his days dressing in suit and tie and adhering to rigid timetables.

Costa Rica, he decided, would be his salvation. Every night he descended on the local bars and talked his friends' ears off about this major change in his life while downing a positively immoral quantity of wine, until closing time forced him to get up and go home. Inevitably the following morning he would arrive late at work with "sailor's eyes," unshaven and disheveled and smelling like a distillery, and pass the day as productively as the potted plant outside his office.

Curiously, despite Luca's habit of consuming oceans of alcohol, he managed to hide this proclivity from his parents. He never took a glass of wine in their presence, not even during weekends or on holidays or festive occasions. But as his Costa Rican plans grew more rooted, he became increasingly careless. He would return home stooping and swaying, and rise the next morning sullen and gray-faced and swallow headache-relief tablets by the handful. His parents weren't stupid.

They were fond of me, and I returned their affection and esteem; Luca had many times confided that they admired the way, at twenty, I was already living on my own, having created my own career and forged my own independence — as if this were something very much out of the ordinary.

Now I found myself in the awkward position of being sought out for advice on their son: Had I noticed, they wanted to know, anything weird about Luca's recent behavior? I answered that I hadn't, because in truth Luca was acting no weirder than usual.

One day I answered the phone to find his father on the other end, his voice shrill with alarm; he told me that at three in the morning he'd been awakened by noises on the landing — and when he'd gone to investigate had been struck dumb by the sight of his son trying to insert his keys into the door of a neighboring apartment, muttering angrily and cursing his failure. When his father called out his name, Luca turned and gave him an idiotic smile, mumbled an incomprehensible apology, then quickly shuffled past him. He was now seriously worried.

I wasn't sure how to respond, so I reassured him that Luca was going through a difficult period, what with having to become more independent, and would soon get through it and be fine; but in all honesty his behavior was beginning to worry me as well.

Luca and I had a friend in common, Massimiliano, who had been called on duty for military service. He organized a midweek farewell party at a disco he rented for the occasion, and invited both Luca and me to the festivities. But Luca, after accepting, made the mistake of finally telling his parents about his plans to relocate to Costa Rica, so upsetting them that they forbade him to go to the party.

I decided to intervene by using my influence with them. I knew that they were reasonable, open-minded people and were only worried about their son's recent bizarre behavior. I had no problem convincing them he would be safe with me; I promised to pick him up, keep an eye on him, and then bring him back at midnight, sober and in shape for work the next day. I also told them, confidentially, that I didn't believe Luca would ever really go to Costa Rica; talking about it was just his way of letting off steam.

And so the night of the party I arrived to pick up my friend. Each time I visited his house I felt as though I was entering a wax museum, because everyone who lived there looked like someone from the movies. His father, a big man who reminded me of the actor Ernest Borgnine, greeted me at the door with a wide, friendly grin; he shook my hand firmly as if to seal our verbal agreement. He then brought me in to the kitchen to greet the remainder of the Resti family. The grandmother was the spitting image of a postwar Italian actress named Tina Pica; but alas, she was not only deaf but suffered from both Alzheimer's and acute flatulence. She sat next to the stove, emitting almost imperceptible hisses from her beneath either flank, which fortunately were nearly odorless. As usual she mistook me for someone from her youth and asked whether I'd finished reaping the grain, and if so was I willing to take out her older sister to dance *liscio* at the village feast. Luca's mother, who looked very much like Jane Fonda (though a tad plumper), was busy cooking dinner; she greeted me with a wink and a kiss on the cheek. She and her husband were extremely cordial and welcoming; Luca's father passed me a glass of *vin santo* and poured one for himself; it was a vintage he and his relatives produced themselves on a small vineyard close to Montepulciano. "We're relying on you, Dario," he said as he sipped his wine; "keep an eye on Luca, and get him home at a decent hour, and *sober* so he can work tomorrow." Once again I gave him my word.

Luca appeared moments later; as usual he had kept me waiting while he meticulously arranged his ridiculous forelock over his balding head with far too much Brylcreme. By 7:30 we were seated in my run down Citroen CX I possessed all those years ago, the Rolling Stones blasting from the speakers, and when I took the exit onto the highway Luca grabbed my arm and said, "Stop!" I slammed on the brakes, thinking something was wrong — but in fact, Luca had merely spotted one of the itinerant vans that sell delicious tripe sandwiches.

"Lampredotto?" he proposed, and I approved. This had always been a shared passion of ours, a delicacy that has since become something or a rarity. It's composed of tripe (the lining of a cow's stomach boiled in a vegetable broth) served with salt and pepper inside a *rosetta* roll of bread.

The only drink that goes with it is red wine, and Luca characteristically added to each bite a slosh of mayonnaise from an aluminum tube he kept in his inner pocket for just such an emergency. One sandwich only whetted our appetite for a second, and the second for a third, and of course all had to be washed down with as many glasses of wine. We ate and drank standing close to the van's counter, not bothering to talk much because of the deafening roar of the cars and trucks barreling by us on the highway, not to mention the hideous groan of the generator the vendor was using to power his kiosk.

At nine o'clock I parked my Citroen in the dusty lot outside the squalid, gray, prefabricated edifice that had been transformed for the occasion into a discotheque. Judging by the number of cars already there, the place would be pretty full.

Luca seemed relaxed and happy and everything appeared to be under control. At the entrance our invitations were examined by the bouncer, who was dressed in the uniform of bouncers everywhere: military camouflage sleeveless T-shirt and pants, dark sunglasses, a crew-cut, and the unmistakable plug inserted in his ear. He wore a profoundly intelligent expression, of the kind you might find on a boiled octopus. His muscles were unnaturally large, very likely the fruit of years of illegal testosterone pills, and so bulky that he could barely move in any natural way; he couldn't even turn his massive neck — he had to swivel at the hips to look behind him. Even when he was inert, he looked likely to burst at any moment.

Our invitations approved, we entered the club and were immediately swallowed up by a horde of gyrating youngsters on the dance floor, jumping up and down perilously close to the stage. Everyone seemed to be having a good time pogo-dancing and jostling each other aside with friendly thrusts and shoves, while at same time exchanging meaningful looks with the girls — as though all the hijinks were for their approval.

Massimiliano came to greet us and thanked us for coming. He had already shorn off the long, blond, curly locks which used to tumble down around his shoulders; I almost didn't recognize him with his new military look. He was electric with joy despite the fact that the next day he'd be settling in for a long stay in some drab barracks in Lebanon. Clearly he wanted to make as much as possible of his last night of freedom.

We decided to toast his departure with a *brindisi* at the bar, and squeezed our way through the mass of sweating youths, gyrating wildly to the music. The band was The Rumble Fish, a ramshackle local group who responded to the enthusiasm of the audience by playing with unbridled passion, not even pausing between songs.

When the crowd ejected us on the other side of the room, we pulled ourselves together and started drinking. As usual I limited myself to red wine, while Luca insinuated himself into a group of youngsters who were challenging each other to sessions of tequila bum-bums. Immediately I remembered the promise I'd made to his father. I excused myself, leaving Massimiliano to the care of some newly arrived well-wishers, and grabbed Luca by the arm. I gave him a shake, and then, as if I were his big brother, said: "C'mon old boy, quit drinking, you

109

know where that will lead. Just set your glass on the counter and let's go dance." I reminded him that I wouldn't put up with any "fucking about." He looked me straight in the eye and reassured me that all was well, and that he'd join me as soon as he'd finished talking business to an insurance colleague he had by chance just encountered.

I danced a good twenty minutes alone before I realized Luca was still at large, and more angered than worried I returned to the bar — where I found him gulping down one tequila after another, as though it were mineral water gushing from a mountain spring.

This time I had to be more brusque: I took the glass from his hand and threatened to drag him back home. Then it happened: he snatched the glass back and with a foggy gaze told me that I had no right to bother him. He stared at me with as grave an expression as I'd ever seen him wear, and announced:

"You've obviously mistaken me for someone else. I have no idea who you are, my friend!"

"What the hell are you saying, Luca?" I protested. "Have you gone completely off the rocker?"

He shook his head slowly and said, "I don't know who this 'Luca' is. My name is Andrea, Andrea Giubbolini." Here he chugged down another shot of tequila and turned to the people at the opposite side of the bar and said, "I'm a grown man and I'm off to Costa Rica! Everybody raise your glass to the sunny paradise of Costa Rica!" And then he picked up someone else's wine glass and tossed its contents down his throat before its owner could realize what was happening. Now I was worried, extremely worried.

I lost my patience and forced him out onto the dance floor, where the band was performing an Italian version of Duran Duran's "Planet Earth."

The strobe lights hit me full in the face, and I was momentarily blinded; when I blinked myself back into sight, Luca was gone — he'd melted into the mob. I immediately commenced searching for him, but knew it wouldn't be an easy task, finding one man in all that crowd and din. Of course, I reflected with a grim chuckle, I was looking for Luca *or* Andrea, so maybe that would double my chances.

I ran into Leo among the crowd and asked whether by any chance he'd run into our mutual friend. "I did," he said, looking perplexed, "but it was a little odd. I called out, 'Ciao, Luca,' and slapped him on the back, and he just turned to me and said, 'Sorry, old boy, you've got me mixed up with somebody else,' and then he left me standing there with no idea of how to respond."

Now I was seriously alarmed. I explained to Leo the entire situation, the promise I'd made and the way Luca had turned the tables on me, and begged him to help me find him. He agreed, but our search was derailed by friends who'd just arrived and who invited us to join them in a *brindisi* for Massimiliano, which of course we couldn't turn down.

When we managed to be break free again we were so eager to resume our search that we collided with two stoned teenagers who were just waiting for an excuse to start a brawl. Somehow we managed to talk our way out of that situation and continued our search, looking everywhere, in the toilets, in the dark corners of the disco, making our way through throngs of sweat-slicked youngsters. Everyone we spoke to seemed to have seen Luca somewhere and then lost track of him. I started to panic as I realized it was past one o'clock. But what could I do? My charge was nowhere to be found.

Mired in defeat, I parted from Leo and headed out to the car park with a Skiantos song serving as the soundtrack for my failure. I was just feeling the enormous burden of responsibility on my back, when — with a shock that nearly killed me — I spotted Luca, a magnum of *prosecco* in his hand, arguing with his father!

My blood froze, my saliva dried up. Luca was in an unforgivable state, drunkenly spewing at his father and shaking the bottle at him, and trying to convince him that he had "got the wrong guy" because he was Andrea Giubbolini, not Luca Resti, and he was off to Costa Rica. His father wasn't having it; he pushed him against the hood of his car, grabbed the magnum from him and threw it into a bush, then raised his fist. With less than a moment's thought I leapt between them and tried to block the blow; and for my efforts was rewarded with a sock in the eye that sent me flying. Luca's father's mouth foamed with rage; he ordered me to stay away from his son, then grabbed Luca's ear, opened the car door, and gave Luca a kick in the backside that sent him right into the rear seat. Even as he slammed the door on him, Luca was still protesting that he wasn't his son, he'd got the wrong person. I heard the roar of the engine, and while I was yet struggling to get to my feet I saw the tail lights disappear in the night.

To make matters worse, the boiled-octopus bouncer now arrived on the scene; he had already summoned the police, and they appeared moments after he did, while I was still wiping the dust of the car park off my face. A young *Maresciallo* Iuzzolino appeared before me, took of his beaked cap, scratched his head, and said, "Dario, this time I'm going to ruin your miserable existence."

I don't recall how I prevented him from doing this . . . but I do remember that Luca's insistence that he wasn't Luca, which began in earnest that night, continued with such dogged insistence that even his poor, beleaguered parents gave up with a shrug, and allowed him to be Andrea Giubbolini . . . and so he is to this day.

I certainly didn't do a good job of managing him that night, and felt extremely guilty about it; however, his obsession with Costa Rica did fade soon after, and in a few days' time his father called to apologize and to invite me to a family dinner. We remain on good terms to this day and still occasionally recall that crazy evening with laughter.

By the way, Tina Pica is still alive; she's 104 and as gassy as ever. And Andrea has yet to cross the Italian border.

§

After concluding my account of Andrea's "birth" and sending it to Mia, I turn off the computer and feel a sudden longing for *lampredotto* — served with green sauce, salt, and pepper — but having no possible means to satisfy my craving, I open instead a much less exciting can of *canellini* beans. I pour the contents into a pan in which I've briefly sautéed a sage leaf from my front garden in some golden olive oil.

Minutes later I've devoured the last of the legumes and sopped up each drop of oil with a slice of stale bread. I open the window and sit rather perilously on the sill, my legs dangling beneath me, and sipping some Chianti Classico San Felice. I pass the time by observing the flickering lights of the village of San Marcellino across the valley until I've finished the bottle. Then I move back inside, take up a collection of short stories by Niccolò Ammaniti and insert a CD of the best of the late Rino Gaetano, and settle down to read, and to dream.

17

THE TENNIS EXPERIMENT

I open my eyes but remain immobile for a time, gazing out the window at the sky — in particular, at the slow dissolution of the milky white trail left in the wake a plane that took off minutes ago from Firenze Peretola. The plane itself is still visible, though rapidly ascending. I idly wonder what sensations the passengers are feeling, as they look down at the rolling Chianti hills from such a majestic height. I smile as I realize that while they are looking down over Chianti, I'm looking up at them — we might be said to be exchanging gazes.

When the plane finally recedes from view I get up and begin my usual routine— first checking my email to see if any orders for my olive oil or requests for my tours have come in. And indeed several have. I reply to them, one by one, and am about to sign off when I receive in real time a brief message from Mia. It is almost eight o'clock over here — making it eleven o'clock the previous night in L.A.

From: Mia Lane
To: Dario Castagno
Subject: Andrea/Luca

Ciao Dario,
 I've just finished reading the true story of Andrea/Luca and think it's ideal for the book. It made me laugh fit to bursting. But what, may I ask, is wrong with you? You seem very gentlemanly and well-mannered yet obviously you have a capacity for getting into trouble that is well beyond the accidental. In the past two days you've send me a pair of stories, both of which are thematically similar despite the events being separated by twenty years. Same friends, same police officer — even another black eye for you! Is this a pattern in your life? . . . I find myself hoping it is. In fact, I challenge you to come up with

another episode in which the four of you appear once again. Behaving your worst, of course.

Fondly
Mia

I notice with pleasure the continuing evolution of our e-mail exchanges. They've become diverting; fun. I'm now rather intrigued by this woman about whom I know nothing — except that she has a name suitable for an American comic-strip character. I think about my manager, and how she most likely wouldn't approve of me sending any material to an unknown woman without having previously come to an agreement of any kind. She would have every right to be furious and to consider me a greenhorn sucker. On the other hand, this kind of forging-ahead behavior has always been part of my character; I'm very instinctive, and in general I tend to trust people — and in fact have paid the price for gullibility more than once. I shrug off this thought during the walk to my office under the oak tree; but it's become too cold to sit down and write — November has at last decided to be November — so I turn back, deciding to reply to Mia from my "home branch."

To:	Mia Lane
From:	Dario Castagno
Subject:	The Challenge

Cara Mia
Buongiorno! You're forcing me to realize not only how full of incident my life is, but how similar that incident is — like the leitmotif of Ravel's "Bolero," which I adore and which in fact I'm listening to right now. All the same, I will take you up on your challenge, and in fact here's my response — an account of an episode that occurred many years ago:
It had been a few months since Andrea and I had descended into a terrible new habit. We would meet every evening at a tumbledown dive, a lurid *osteria* located in a dark, humid alleyway. Here we would waste all our spare time downing wines of the worst quality in the company of shabby, disreputable alcoholics who stank of cold, stale sweat, and whose rotten breath would have

made the sewers of Calcutta seem a field of lavender by comparison. A dense layer of smoke, released by the worst brand of dark national cigarettes, clung to the low ceiling, through which seeped a garish fluorescent light whose filthy tube hosted the remains of dozens of flies who had died there, trapped and roasted. I'm certain the oldest carcasses were residues from the Sixties, or even earlier. The fetid stench of excrement wafted from the windowless men's room, where the toilet bowl was an island stranded in an ocean of urine.

Surely the degree of masochism we displayed by patronizing such a place would have made us excellent subjects for a psychological monograph; because we were truly despised by each and every one of the old farts who surrounded us, and who had nothing to spare or share with us. They hurled murderous looks at us each time we dared to cross their threshold. The only person who made any kind of effort to be civil to us was the bartender, but only because we were among the very few customers who paid their tab without begging for a discount — or, worse, ending up on his black book that he kept furtively under the cash desk.

To balance the immoral quantities of wine and grappa that flowed down our throats, we nourished ourselves on the most appalling salamis containing the highest possible cholesterol content. We stuffed ourselves with *soppressata*, *buristo*, and draining fat sausages — and of course Andrea would make it even worse by adding shots of mayonnaise squeezed directly into his mouth from the tube he always kept in his breast pocket. We consumed these heart-crippling meals on the greasy formica countertop, eavesdropping on discussions of past Palios that often degenerated into blasphemous imprecations and even threats of violence among the regulars, who in their long lives had managed only to drink very much and work very little (if ever). At closing time the bartender would lower the shutters, then commence the difficult task of getting the drunken mob to depart. Often he had to literally shove them out into the street, and more than once he was forced to summon the police because so many refused to leave unless he offered them one last round of last drinks (though of course it was never the last) while beating their fists men-acingly on the lopsided wooden tables.

After a few months of assiduous visits to this depressing *osteria*, Andrea looked up at me while ordering a *gottino*, and smoothed his ridiculous forelock as he always did when about to announce something important. With a firm tone — but with less admirable diction, since his mouth was filled with a mash of minced *soppressata*, mayonnaise and wine — he made the point that maybe we had gone slightly over the top and that we should per-haps seriously consider changing our habits. Then he adjusted his distended belly so that it hung less obtru-sively over his belt buckle, and proposed that the next day, instead of rendezvousing at this dreadful joint, we meet instead for a tennis match.

Surprised by the suggestion, I replied that it wasn't a bad idea to mend our wastrel ways, but as to tennis, I had never played and had never wanted to; it seemed to me boring, and far too upper class for my tastes. But Andrea was surprisingly insistent, and barraged me with a series of relentless arguments — which I'm sure he had rehearsed beforehand — including the fact that I was born in Wimbledon (as if that alone were enough to make me a player), so that in the end I decided to give it a try.

We left earlier than usual, offering a farewell round of drinks to all the infamous old ruins, and Andrea explained the gesture by grandly announcing that we were about to change our lives and that, as a result, this would be our last visit to the bar. As soon as he said this, applause broke out from darkest corner of the joint, and one of the real stinkers stood up, raised his glass and with a triumphant sneer said, *"Finally* you two are hauling your sorry asses out of here" — and grinned in satisfaction, revealing a ragged set of crooked, nicotine-stained teeth numbering no more than four. And with that, we left that place for good.

Andrea made an appointment for us at the Virtus Tennis Club for 7 p.m. sharp the following day, and generously offered me the loan of a racket. I was still grumbling a bit about the whole plan, so he handed me an envelope that contained the result of a recent blood test. When I read to my astonishment his alarming cholesterol and transaminase levels, his sudden enthusiasm for a change of life started making sense to me.

The following day after work we met as we'd arranged at the tennis club, where we would baptize our new life. I found Andrea in the changing room sporting a ridiculously worn-out Seventies Lacoste outfit that was several sizes too small and made his belly seem as if he were in the ninth month of carrying twins. He'd also fastened his forelock beneath an elastic headband, which made it look something like a mouse caught in a trap. But at least he was wearing a tennis outfit. I, however, had donned the first things I found in the armoire: a black, torn t-shirt with the red-tongue Rolling Stones logo blaring from its front, soccer shorts, and a pair of All Star training shoes full of holes. My outfit provoked whispers of hilarity from the club members in the locker room, all of whom, I noticed were wearing extremely expensive Sergio Tacchini ensembles, so that they seemed hired for the filming of a commercial for that detergent whose slogan is "Washes so white that even whiter is impossible." Andrea handed me a very heavy ancient wooden racket; I suggested that after our match he donate it to the local archaeological museum. Then we tried exchanging a few volleys. Andrea had played in his past and it showed, as he had no difficulty sending the ball over the net, while I was a complete, spastic neophyte. The few times I didn't miss the ball entirely I was actually very good at sending it careering into the adjacent court, disconcerting the ivory-clad snobs whose game was thus interrupted and who rewarded me with icy, patrician glares.

But Andrea's past experience couldn't get him past his present physical limitations, so that his fat took the same toll as my flailings. After just half an hour we were both gaping and gasping and damp with sweat, and we decided to call it a day.

From under the shower Andrea proposed a green salad and a mineral water at the clubhouse. I agreed; but while we dressed he changed his mind and proposed a pizza and orange crush at Bianca's pizzeria. Again, I agreed. Then, while he was busy at the mirror massaging Brylcreme into his forelock, he proposed a bean soup at the tavern.

Yet again, I agreed. But all this talk of food had gotten me hungry; so as we headed for the car, I suggested we go and pay good old Fosco a visit.

Andrea looked at me with an expression of instant accord. "Fosco really knows how to grill a steak," he said, almost reverently. "And maybe . . . just one glass of red wine? What harm can a glass of red do?"

I could think of no harm at all; and so minutes later I was seated inside Andrea's Volkswagen, zipping across the deserted Chianti hills towards La Pinetina di Fosco. We basked in pride at our new athletic lifestyle, and made plans to have an early night and meet again the following day at the tennis club.

Andrea pulled up under a well cured pine grove that Fosco maintained with maniacal care, and in which he ran a small diner — only in the warm months, as a pastime; he didn't need to make a living from it, as he was wealthy and had an honorable pension. The place contained four wooden tables, a barbecue pit, and a small kitchen camp. We were happy to be the only clients that evening and when he saw us arrive he greeted us with open arms and a beaming smile. Our good old friend Fosco was looking hale and hearty as usual; he kissed our cheeks and invited us to sit, then returned with a two-liter flask of wine.

"Hey, buddies, taste this," he exclaimed proudly as he filled our glasses. "A friend of mine produces it just for me from a small vineyard close to San Marcellino, it's *fantastico!*"

Andrea placed the cup to his lips, took a sip, and swirled it momentarily in his mouth before swallowing. "Sublime," he announced with a smack of his lips and raising his glass in sign of appreciation — a slightly exaggerated verdict, to please Fosco.

We then updated Fosco on how we had quit our old degenerate life and had begun a new, healthy enthusiasm for tennis, and that for this reason we were going to have just a steak and a green salad, and would be limiting our drinking to one glass of red and plenty of water.

Fosco lowered his head and stared at us as though we had announced we were each going to have a sex change; then he turned his gaze skyward, as if talking to the Almighty, and said, *"Dio mi guardi da chi non beve vino!"* ("God save me from those who don't drink wine!"). Then he shrugged and reminded us of the farmer's saying: *"Il vino di casa non imbriaca"* ("The house wine doesn't make you drunk") and filled our glasses to the brim, ignoring our pointed *"No grazie!"*

He then proposed a dish of anchovies while waiting for the steaks. Andrea gave it only a moment's thought, then nodded in approval — after all, what harm could anchovies cause? — and Fosco added that he also had a very freshly made *soppressata* and would we like some of that as well? Andrea shot me a furtive look, as though seeking my permission to say yes.

I was only too glad to be his accomplice. "Two slices of *soppressata*, as far as I'm concerned, have never done anyone any harm," I replied to his visible satisfaction.

With a crafty smile, Fosco left us to prepare the dishes, during which time he entertained us by singing in eighth rhyme, a traditional form of poetic improvisation; we would give him a theme and he would come up with a verse on the spot, even as he prepared our meal. The more outlandish the theme, the more dazzling his rhymes.

Later, after having devoured a tray full of *crostini* and *bruschette*, we wolfed down a plate of *tagliatelle* in hare sauce, a *ribollita* ("To replace the carbohydrates we'd used playing tennis," was Andrea's justification), a mixed grill of steaks, pork chops and sausages ("Proteins are essential to prevent muscular strain"), all washed down with abundant red wine ("For the circulation and better efficiency of the blood vessels").

Fosco then recited from memory some canti from Dante's *Inferno;* as we listened we finished off the third bottle of wine produced by Fosco's friend in the small vineyard close to San Marcellino, a wine which now seemed to us quite *fantastico* indeed, so much so that after applauding Fosco's recitation we cracked open a fourth. (We had to have something with which to toast him!) By now the stars were glittering in the sky, adding an appropriate atmosphere to what was turning out to be a lovely, light-hearted night. Fosco disappeared for a moment, then reappeared bearing a tray of *dolci* his wife had made ("Sugars are essential for energy, are they not?") and a series of sweet *vin santo* wines ("As a reward for having been so athletic this evening").

Just when we decided it was time to go I heard the sound of a Vespa from around the bend; it drew nearer and then ceased. A silhouette emerged from the dark, and the closer it got the more familiar it seemed — yes, it was Leo! I interrupted Andrea, who had his back to the front door and was seriously expounding on top spins, drop shots and backhands, all of which we had to work on improving the following day. Andrea turned, saw Leo, and let out an exclamation of welcome.

It had been a while since we'd caught up with Leo, as he had been on a long trip to India. Andrea immediately called for Fosco and ordered a fifth of the *fantastico* produced by his friend in the small vineyard close to San Marcellino. We exchanged friendly backslaps and for the next hour or so listened raptly to Leo's detailed adventures in Asia, until Fosco, who had kept silent vigil from a certain distance, politely interrupted us, pointing out that he had no intention of sending us home against our will, but it was three in the morning and his wife was probably getting worried.

We settled for a final toast and then, tired, happy, and filled to the brim with food and wine, we said goodnight (though maybe good morning would have been more appropriate). Fosco closed up shop behind us, and Leo hopped his Vespa and went off in the opposite direction to ours.

We returned home on a gravel road, talking about Leo and envying his experiences in India. Andrea chose to insert an AC/DC cassette — if only to keep our eyelids from drooping shut — and then it happened. An enormous wild boar suddenly leapt in front of us. Andrea screamed and slammed on the brakes; the wheels locked and we skidded across the dusty road, and the impact was inevitable. When it happened, we were hurled forward; I smashed my nose on the dashboard and Andrea banged his forehead on the steering wheel.

A moment's eerie quiet followed. Instinctively I brought my hand to my nose; it came away covered in blood. But from my brief examination the nose didn't seem to be broken. Andrea pushed aside his forelock and massaged an enormous bump that was growing in the middle of his forehead. The engine was no longer running and we remained in silence a few seemingly endless seconds, until Andrea in a feeble voice said, *"Mamma mia*, what a disaster! . . . It just suddenly appeared from nowhere, did you see? . . . There — there was no way I could avoid it!" He then lapsed into a series of very typical Tuscan imprecations. I found a pack of tissues and daubed my poor nose, then opened the car door and stepped out to check the damage. The bumper had come off and a wheel was crooked. As for the boar, it was lying on the road in a cloud of dust whose motes were slowly settling to the ground. Andrea joined me, and despite the slushy state we were in we had to decide what to do now.

There was no use calling out for help on that desolate, pitch-black road; even if we did eventually get someone's attention, they would have had to summon the *cara-binieri* — which meant Andrea being subjected to a breathalyzer test and almost certainly having his license confiscated. We concluded that the wisest plan would be to sleep in the wrecked car and at sunrise, having shed our alcoholic handicap, go and seek help.

Andrea, though, proposed to haul the dead boar back home in his car. At least by selling the meat to a local tavern he would make back some of the money required to fix the Volkswagen. And so, tired, drunk, and bruised, we got hold of the animal's feet and with extreme difficulty piled its bristly cadaver into the back seat. We covered the poor beast with a blanket Andrea produced from the trunk, and without making any further comment we climbed into the front sea and tried to get some sleep.

I managed to doze a bit despite Andrea's shatteringly loud snore; it sounded like a wheezing groan, punctuated by a lament from the pit of hell. In fact, when his snoring finally stopped, the silence that followed was so profound that I was jolted out of my restless half slumber, and when I opened my eyes I found Andrea piteously massaging his lump, which had turned an unattractive shade of green.

"Finalmente!" he said, clearly annoyed. "I couldn't sleep, the way you've been snoring like a sawmill."

I was a bit confused by his remark and drowsily replied,

"What are you talking about? I've never snored in my life. *You're* the one who was going at it like a lawnmower."

"Don't be ridiculous," he said. "I sleep like a lamb."

We were just beginning to argue the matter further when a heart-shredding snort from the back seat made it clear who the real culprit was.

"Madonna!" Andrea shrieked as we both clambered our way out of the car, in a state of drunken panic.

We slammed shut the car doors behind us and once again found ourselves standing on the dusty road, our hearts thumping.

"This is a ridiculous dilemma to be in," I snarled.

"Hey, don't blame me!" Andrea cried. "I can't help it if the beast is too stupid to know we killed it!"

We stood shivering in the cold while the car gently rocked as the boar resettled its weight. We now had to figure out a new plan, as not only did we have a wrecked car and were still addled by the wine, we had the additional problem of a fierce wild animal nesting comfortably in the back seat. The first thing to be done, obviously, was to release the boar. We decided to open the rear doors and, now that the sun was just peering above the horizon, hope that the boar would be inspired to step out and seek some breakfast. In the meantime, Andrea and I could go off in search of help. We carefully opened the car doors, then quickly trotted away lest the boar by some chance felt like jumping out and giving chase. But it seemed content in the back seat for the moment, so we were able to slow down our pace. Then, each nursing a massive headache — due both to our hangovers and the blows we'd taken in the accident — off we went.

It suddenly occurred to us that anyone we encountered in our present state — bruised, battered, our shirts drenched in blood, gripping onto each other as we hobbled along the road — might justifiably be afraid to stop.

"We look like the cat and the fox in Pinocchio," said Andrea, referring to the famous Tuscan children's tale.

I laughed. "You're being optimistic," I said. "I'm sure we look more like a pair of zombies who haven't quite returned from the dead."

About half an hour later, during which Andrea had been

uncharacteristically silent, we finally heard the engine of a car approach. We felt a rush of relief; we had been saved! Our joy died instantly when we saw that the vehicle was a *carabinieri* jeep on patrol, and were mortified when we realized the driver was old Iuzzi in person. Our paths had continually crossed since we were teenagers, and despite the countless times he had promised to ruin us, he had never actually done so; we figured he was actually a good guy and that he was in some bizarre way even fond of us. But still we would have preferred someone else; he might not take us into custody, but depending on his mood he could make our next few hours very uncomfortable ones. When he saw us he rolled down the window, removed his beaked cap, ran his right hand through in his hair and then stroked his thick moustache and said, *"Gesù Cristo."* He invited us to get in the jeep and we related to him the entire incident exactly as it happened — minus a few small details, like the five bottles of the *fantastico*. And the exact time of the impact. Which left him the impression that we'd been playing tennis, had a green salad and mineral water at Fosco's afterwards, and then while returning home at dusk had run into a wild boar. Possibly he might have questioned the idea of Andrea or me managing to depart Fosco's in so pure a condition, but he was too distracted by the detail of the dead bore miraculously resuscitating in Andrea's backseat.

He drove us back to the wreck. The doors were still hanging open and the boar had taken advantage of them and departed, never knowing how close he had come to being served stewed in local restaurants.

Iuzzolino kept us the entire morning filling out paperwork. When he finally let us go, he shook his head in dismay and with a long sigh said, "Will you ever grow up, either of you?"

And then we were free. We had the entire evening ahead of us, as we couldn't play tennis because of our injuries and so we chose instead to go for a bite at our usual *osteria* — the one to which we had grandly announced we would never return.

The usual mob of sad sacks were all still there and needless to say were surprised to see us. The bartender, while pouring us our usual reds, nodded his head towards our bruises and asked what had happened to reduce our faces to a pair of four-seasons pizzas.

"We played tennis!" we told him in unison.

He looked at us with an extremely dubious expression, then lowered his head and said gravely, "You *do* know that the rules of the game are to hit the ball into the opposite court — not into your opponent's face?"

"I've always said that sport ain't good for you," added an old man we had nicknamed Ciotolino (Little Bowl), who had been eavesdropping. Andrea and I gave each other a look and then dissolved into laughter, until the tears were rolling down our cheeks. Ciotolino stared at us, completely confounded; and after that the least we could do was to offer the old fart a glass of wine.

He didn't like us; but he accepted.

೩

I carefully reread the chapter before sending it to Mia, pointing out that I have clearly won the challenge — even though I have slyly substituted a broken nose for a blackened eye.

I decide to have dinner at Paolo's, a local enoteca. I order a *tagliata* with arugula and a bottle of Chianti Classico Corsignano. When I return home I feel a sudden impulse to dance, so I move the sofa against the wall and insert a collection of Eighties hits — and immediately start dancing like a raving mad lunatic until I literally knock myself out.

In the morning I feel another strong impulse: to write. But first I want to nourish my soul by taking in some of the beautiful vistas autumn affords, and what better way that to take a jog? The weather is colder than it was for my last run, but that doesn't prevent me.

When I return home I find a text message on my phone, sent by the estate manager of the farm I normally use to pick olives:

Dottor Castagno,
Please be informed that we have decided to commence the olive harvest and if the weather permits we should finish in a few weeks. May we expect your presence at 8 a.m. tomorrow?

I reply with a very succinct:
Yes.

18

WELL OILED

I think it only polite to inform Mia that I will be out of touch for a few days due to the demands of oil making, and that until I've finished the harvest, pressing, and shipments I will unfortunately have no time for correspondence.

After signing off, I make lunch — plain spaghetti with a tomato sauce loaded with garlic (another advantage of not having a fiancée) and two entire hot chilli peppers. From the wine rack I select one of my favorite Chianti Classicos, Antico Podere Casanuova, and propose a *brindisi* to myself as good auspices for the upcoming harvest.

I eat the spaghetti reclining in front of the TV — sipping my wine and switching back and forth between a dated Brazilian *telenovela* and a ludicrously staged wrestling match. The soap opera, broadcast on a local station, is so poorly filmed that the protagonists appear to be jaundiced; at first glance they might be The Simpsons. I wondered whether they are all meant to be suffering from chronic hepatitis. The antagonists in the wrestling match are two massive, hairless giants pumped up with hormones who bellow at each other and throw themselves with ridiculous phoniness around the ring, to the ecstasy of their cheering audience. I watch for a while, trying to figure out what is supposed to be so entertaining about these swaggering, masked, pot-bellied stuntmen cavorting like circus elephants.

Suddenly it occurs to me how many of the commercials (which seemed to interrupt the shows at increasingly short intervals) are devoted to female hygiene; over the course of just a few minutes I see smiling young girls playing volleyball to publicize a tampon; then middle-aged women discussing a recommended solution for vaginal discharges; then a mother who halfway up a mountain realizes that her daughter (who is climbing with her) has annoying itches "down there" and pro-

duces from seemingly nowhere a tube of a miraculously soothing cream (I have no idea how the daughter manages to apply
it while suspended several hundred feet in the air); and finally
a woman wrapped in a bathrobe who has solved her intimate
problems with a new brand of deodorant.

At a certain point I give up and switch off. While heading for
the computer I consider how fortunate I am not to possess the
apparently very problematic female organ. Moments later I
find Mia's response to my e-mail.

From: Mia Lane
To: Dario Castagno
Subject: Re: The Challenge

My dear Dario,
The chapter you sent was hilarious and yes, I admit
defeat; you certainly won the challenge. I perfectly
understand that you'll be extremely busy for the next few
days; I only wish I could come and help you pick your
olives rather than sit all day in front of a computer. I'll
miss not hearing from you, certainly, as your stories have
been transporting me daily into a world so attractively
different from my own. I must be frank and confess that
the air of mystery that surrounds you has been intriguing me as well; I feel privileged to have assumed this
unusual role of "confessor" to a man I've never met, and
getting to learn so much about his private life.
It seems every day brings a surprise: I'm an avid consumer of olive oil, and today I learn that among your
many activities you also are a producer of the stuff. How
long have you been doing this? I would like to learn
more, if possible. But only when you can spare the time.

From: Dario Castagno
To: Mia Lane
Subject: Extra-virgin Olive Oil

Dear Mia,
I'll miss exchanging e-mails with you as well, as I seem
to have found a very precious "pen pal" in you. However
it's only for a few days.

I'm more than happy to read that I intrigue you, and that you envy the life I lead. I feel very fortunate that I can live the way I do; it is of course not without its drawbacks, but it allows me the kind of freedom I cherish.

Regarding your interest in how my small olive oil venture started: alas, you won't find any interesting material for the book there. It was simply a consequence of my job as a Chianti tour guide. You see, Mia, I've always had a particular attraction for the newly pressed oil — or the *olio novo* as we refer to it in Tuscany - its intense aroma of freshly mowed grass, its dense consistency and strong flavor, and the pleasant tickle it leaves behind in the throat. These characteristics, added to its irresistibly opaque, almost phosphorescent green hue, make it by far the prince of products in these parts. Often during tours with my clients, I devoted much more than a few simple words in describing the virtues of the freshly made oil, and I'm sure sometimes I bored them with my enthusiasm.

The harvest takes place in late November through the beginning of December. This is the off season for tourists, who won't return till Easter, when they come storming back by the thousands. Unfortunately the oil by then has already lost most of its original color and flavor and for this reason I was rarely able to get my guests to taste extra-virgin olive oil at its very best.

In 1998, together with a younger friend of mine named Stefano with whom I share this same passion, I took into serious consideration the idea of supplying *olio novo* to individuals living overseas. To be able to do this within a few days of its pressing and with door-to-door delivery, we had to go through a whole series of bureaucratic gyrations, including permits, certificates, and all other kinds of annoying of red tape. We were also well aware that due to the scarce quantity produced from the local trees, making a consistent profit would be improbable; but our goal was only to break even, and to provide an annual supply for our own families.

Having settled this, we had to give the venture a name. We decided to dedicate the product to the people who had probably initiated olive growing in Tuscany: the race we call the Etruscans. Their own name for themselves, we've now discovered, was Rasna, and so over a stewed rabbit and a bottle of Brunello Siro Pacenti, the Rasna Extra-Virgin Olive Oil snc project was born.

The original habitat for the olive tree was decisively vast, the basin of production being practically any coast that faces the Mediterranean sea: Southern Europe, the Maghreb zone of North Africa, and a good part of the Middle East. It's evident that for the plants to grow and to survive (which they do, even for thousands of years) requires decisively mild climates. Chianti isn't quite the ideal habitat, located as it is in the inner lands of Tuscany with peaks of elevation that can reach almost a thousand meters. Also, winters here can be extremely frigid and in exceptional cases can reach almost Siberian temperatures, as testified by the freezes of 1929, 1956 and 1985, each of which devastated the oil industry. Consequently, the vast majority of trees here are just over twenty years old and produce a tenth of what a tree can produce on the coast; thus the consumption of their oil is almost exclusively destined for its producers and for a privileged few who have the forethought to reserve it long before harvest. It seems odd to pass through the profusion of olive groves that cover the Chianti region, and then discover that the local markets carry only oils produced in other parts of Italy — or even in some cases imported from neighboring countries.

There are a number of large companies within Chianti that purchase cheaper oils in bulk from outside our boundaries; they bottle it and then place it on the market with a label that specifies "Bottled in Chianti," inducing the consumer to believe he is purchasing a local product.

So why even bother cultivating olives here, you might ask, given the near impossibility of making a living out of it? The answer is really very simple: its excellent quality.

We must credit the Romans for having recognized the mixture of elements here that contribute to making the Chianti oil a superior one, and for importing the tree from the coast and cultivating it inland. The elements I speak of are the altitude, which guarantees a more salubrious environment and thus less conducive to parasites; the distance from the salty sea breeze; the rocky soil; and indeed the young age of the trees. These are the factors that make the Chianti oil so prestigious and yet so rare. Gosh Mia, I hope I haven't ended up boring you as well. Tell you what, I'll spare you a discourse on the organoleptic qualities extra-virgin oil possesses; I think you already comprehend why I undertook this task as a kind of mission. Its greatest reward is the satisfaction I get when I receive enthusiastic feedback from my affectionate clientele. Sharing my love of this oil with the world — that's what makes the entire chore well worth the fatigue.

℘

I decide there is no harm to use up the rest of the day at home doing nothing. Minutes later I'm listening to the radio through speakers placed strategically around the living room, an intensely heartbreaking song by Luigi Tenco gently overwhelms me. As I follow the lyrics I recognize it as the number he performed at an Italian music contest some forty years ago, only a few hours before blowing his brains out in a hotel room, leaving the entire nation reeling in shock. I still recall the magnitude of the trauma — indeed I still feel it today, especially when hearing his voice.

My body is sunk deep into the couch cushions, my gaze captivated by the crackling flames in the hearth. The pile of logs I'd carefully stacked and set alight a mere hour ago is now a shimmering inferno; I can feel its heat against my face, and am reasonably certain, from its greedy vigor, that it's reached its zenith. From this point the flames will slowly diminish and the temperature wane by degrees, until in a few hours' time nothing but a heap of fluttering cinders and dull ash will remain.

Abruptly I snap my head towards the entrance; under the strains of the music I've heard something — a kind of muted blow; probably a feeble knock on the front door. As I rise, my first guess is that I'm about to be greeted by Orazio, who has a tendency to turn up unexpectedly. But I promptly change my mind, as he would never content himself with a single rapping of his knuckles; he'd stand there insistently hammering with the palm of his simian hand, setting the house aquiver and risking knocking the door right out of its frame.

But there is no such pounding; nor even a second knock, and as I approach the door I consider that the sound I heard may have been merely the wind — or maybe it was nothing at all, just my imagination at work, summoned to life by my profound reaction to the music.

But in fact I do have a caller: a tiny man with a rather gloomy appearance. His head is tucked into a Chicago Cubs cap, from beneath the rim of which he looks up at me with sad, doleful eyes — the pupils pale blue, the whites watery and dimly pink, like the bland stratum of watermelon that's closest to the rind.

His hollow cheeks are inadequately hidden by a scruffy white beard the consistency of cotton candy, which dangles right down to his abdomen. Beneath it is an overly large sweater whose hem droops about his knees, and a pair of a recently purchased stone-washed jeans and track shoes. As is ever my habit, I find myself seeking a celebrated look-alike for him, and am torn between Bashful, from the ranks of Snow White's seven dwarfs, and the eminent neurologist Oliver Sacks.

"Mr Kestanio?" he inquires in the trembling voice of one who is aware his presence might not be wholly welcome.

"Yes, that's me," I reply; then, taking pity on his evident insecurity I add, "Like to come in and share a glass of wine I've just opened? We have a local saying that a bottle of wine requires sharing. And think of it: have you ever met a wine lover who is also a miser?"

The little man is visibly startled; he obviously wasn't expecting such a reception. "That's is extremely kind of you," he says while accepting my handshake. "I'm Zachary, from Seattle." He removes his cap, revealing a head that is completely bald save for a few disorderly tufts sprouting at unattractive intervals. More than a scalp, it reminds me of what remains on a rugby pitch after a tough six nations' match.

I fill a goblet and hand it to him, inviting him to take a seat on the couch while I lower myself onto the terracotta ledge of the fireplace so I can face him. "Seattle is a nice city," I observe — not merely to break the ice, but because I indeed spent a very enjoyable few days there, so much so that it's one of my favorite cities in the U.S.

My guest smiles in agreement but offers no further conversation. He looks about him in seeming anxiety, as if uncertain how or why he's suddenly found himself here. "So what can I do for you, Zachary?" I ask, to give him a gentle nudge.

He explains that he's read and enjoyed my books, and while attending a university convention in Siena he's taken advantage of a day off to visit my village. He had lunch at the local tavern and asked the waiters question after question about me, until the staff suggested he just come and visit me in person. He was at first reluctant, but they assured him I wouldn't mind and would even happily sign his books, so he decided to give it a try.

He asks me now to forgive the intrusion, which of course I do, and he begins to relax, more than ever after having announced the Jewish saying that 'Over a bottle of wine many a friend is found.'

We chat a bit more, and when we've emptied our goblets I ask if he's up to a walk.

Minutes later I find myself climbing the hill behind my house with this increasingly amiable sixty-something American, enjoying myself by bringing to life for him the places he's read about in my books. We stroll by the villa owned by the famous female jockey who competed in the Palio some fifty years ago, whose experiences I reported in *A Day in Tuscany;* then on to the monument to the partisan fighter Bruno Bonci, another of that book's protagonists. We sit at my "office" table under the oak tree, where I point out to him the house in the valley below that I once shared with Cristina, and where I wrote *Too Much Tuscan Sun.* I then take him to the castle that belonged to my friend Matteo, and direct his gaze to the field in the distance where in 1260 the Sienese army defeated the Florentines in epic battle. I explain for him where exactly the Chianti hills commence, and describe the boundaries of the various Tuscan provinces. Zachary's facc lights up at each new place I point out; he seems blissful, even euphoric, and I'm sure he must be asking himself if I do this with every person who comes knocking on my door.

We continue walking and soon enter the village cemetery, as I think he will appreciate the opportunity to pay homage to Tonio, who was prominently featured in both of my books. Zachary stands in front in silence, his head bowed respectfully with what to me seems a mixture of both affection and esteem. Afterwards we greet a pair of elderly ladies putting fresh flowers on their husband's graves; their weathered faces look like prunes, as they long ago lost their youth due to years of working the fields.

We make our way back to the village through an olive grove in which the shadows of the trees chase each other without a pause; and then we find ourselves before the rusted sign that is now an integral part of the landscape, and which announces our arrival at our destination. Zachary looks up at me, his eyes still watery but no longer ringed with sadness, and asks me why I've chosen to live in a newly built townhouse rather than in an antique stone dwelling like those for which I express such passion in my books. I laugh because for me, too, it is a strange incongruity that I should live the way I do, but it's a matter of simple economics. It's still my dream one day to own and restore such a house, but at the moment it is beyond my means.

Ironically, I tell him, I actively opposed the construction of the very townhouses where I now live, and had even persuaded the residents to sign a petition to prevent them from being built. At that time I was living as a tenant in a beautiful old farmhouse; then one day the owner informed me that he was terminating my lease so he could make the place into a bed-and-breakfast.

I considered at that point getting a mortgage, and called a friend of mine who manages real estate to ask if there was anything available in the area. I soon discovered that there was — and by his descriptions I realized he was talking about was the very houses whose construction I had so vehemently opposed. I ended up buying one of them, causing general hilarity in the village.

Zachary roars with laughter at this story, and proposes we have a final glass at the local bar. The usual mob is all there: Giulio downing his umpteenth liter of the day, Michele idly leafing through the paper, Orazio trying very hard to explain something to Manola the bartender. Emanuele is, fortunately, on his way out, and when I pass him on the threshold he gives me a creepy smile, baring his nicotine-stained teeth. I notice with a shudder of revulsion that his shoulders are flaked with dandruff and that his skin is a mess of psoriasis.

He seems in fact to be openly decaying, and I wonder maliciously whether he'll make it back home or maybe just decompose entirely en route.

I share with Zachary the news that some of these characters will be featured in my next book, and he eagerly produces a camera and begins taking snapshots of me with them. He then asks Orazio if he'll take one of just the two of us together. Knowing it would take less time for a painter to render us in oil than for Orazio to figure out and operate the shutter of a camera, I snatch it from Zachary's hand and handed it to Michele instead; and it is he who graciously does the honors and takes our picture.

Finally I accompany Zachary to his car, after having signed his books and given him one of the last bottles of my 2005 olive oil, reminding me I have olives to pick the following day. He sits behind the wheel and turns on the ignition, then rolls down the window; I notice that his ivory beard is now splotched purple with wine stains. He asks while revving the motor if I've ever considered giving tours again, because in his opinion I've presented Chianti with so much zeal and ardor that it's a shame I no longer share my passion with others. I promise him I'll consider it, and see him off with a wave.

After he drives away I pivot on my heels and trek home to my life of sibylline silence. As I enter my door I pause to observe the moon suspended in the black hammock of sky, pocked by stars, I feel as free as the air and once again I try to comprehend the restless fascination these hills have on me

Inside, the logs on the fire have collapsed, lifting a cloud of lapillus. I do my best to reanimate the embers, then sit on the couch sipping at my Mecacci and thinking that I should really start reorganizing my life.

℘

After dinner I decide to make it an early night so as to be fit for the following day at the olive grove. Yet I don't fall asleep immediately; instead I find myself wondering about Mia — how old she is, what she might look like, what kind of clothes she wears, how she moves. Strange as it is, I have no clues from which I can infer the slightest thing about her. I don't even know if she's married, or indeed her age. Suddenly I wonder if it might be considered rude that I've never asked her anything about herself; all I've done is talk about me.

I shrug off this thought, as this isn't a dialogue in a singles' chat room; we're working on a book — a book, moreover, that concerns my experiences and my opinions. So my conduct thus far is fully justified.

Even so, I must admit . . . I'm growing extremely fond of her.

19

THE FRUIT OF OUR LABORS

It's still dark when the alarm goes off, obliging me to turn on the bedside lamp. I don a boiler suit and boots suitable for the role of an olive picker, which I am to assume in less than an hour. I open the window just as the sun starts to peep over the hills, and am jolted awake by the unexpected cold that gusts in at me. I add a thick wool sweater under my worn-out Belstaff jacket, a holdover from my motorcycle years — in fact, the only item I still possess from that period.

As soon as I get into the car my fingers seek out the heat vent switch, almost of their own volition. Then I shift into gear and pull onto the road, which at this early hour is barren of any other traffic.

The estate to which I'm heading produces mainly Chianti Classico wine but maintains as well a good number of olive trees. For centuries it belonged to a local family. Since Rasna was founded it has always supplied us the entire quantity of olives we require — which, due to our limited clientele, is the production of just a few hundred trees.

Now that the sun has risen entirely, I can see that the sky is completely cloudless thanks to the *tramontana,* a cold wind that blows from the northeast and sweeps the skies clear like a broom. I've never been a fan of cold weather but I feel no disappointment today; I know only too well to expect this kind of climatic condition when harvesting olives.

I dial Stefano's number on my cell phone to check that all is proceeding as planned. We have divided the chores of the business; while I pick the fruit, he and his wife Elisa prepare the certification and documentation required by customs. Later, after the pressing, the three of us will meet at our small warehouse where we will team up to bottle, label, pack, and finally deliver the shipments to the courier.

To reach the farm I must cross the entire Chianti area from

west to east, and because my mind is preoccupied with oil it comes naturally to observe the many olive groves which I otherwise would pass without notice. As I appraise the trees' silvery bark I reflect on how I've always been attracted to this particular plant; it is the symbol of victory and glory, which for thousands of years has supplied wood for carving, fruit for nutrition, and most of all oil — for use as fuel, to cure the sick, for the manufacture of cosmetics, and more. A biblical tree, it is also the symbol of peace and quietness; think of the olive branch the dove presented to Noah to indicate the end of the universal flood. It also represents strength, as when Athena won the challenge with Poseidon thanks to the gift of the olive donated by the mortals. And it betokens prestige: Homer describes Ulysses' bed, made from a centuries-old olive tree.

I stop for breakfast at a popular bar along the road. There are many cars parked outside, of which probably the majority are owned by my "colleagues" — other olive-pickers who are heading for the groves. As I'm about to face a long, hard, chilly day I wolf down a substantial meal: two slices of bread stuffed with a fresh *soppressata*. Indeed when my eyes fall on its moist, pink meat through the counter pane, I have the impression it's actually inviting me to eat it. I accompany it with a Mecacci wine, in defiance of the local saying that *il vino al mattino è pesante a mezzogiorno è buono la sera è ottimo* ("Wine in the morning is heavy, at midday is good, and in the evening is wonderful"). A quick look at the other customers reveals I'm far from the only one breaking this particular rule.

Among the diners I spot Marcello, a senior fellow I had the pleasure to work with in my winery days, some twenty years ago. He was old back then; now he seems positively ancient — and yet no less sharp for it, as he recognizes me immediately and waves his wrinkled hand in my direction. I approach him where he perches on a wooden stool and we exchange a few words, catching up. He offers me a glass of red that for politeness's sake I can't refuse; then he scolds me gently for not yet having a ring on my annular.

He also surprises me when he points out that I'm wearing the same old jacket and the overalls I used to wear in the cellar at the winery, and that I still have the piercing in my left ear. "You haven't changed a whit since you were a teenager," he says, summing up. I decide to take it as a compliment.

I leave Marcello, thanking him both for the wine and his parting invitation to the *porcellata*, the dinner Tuscan farmers traditionally give the day they slaughter their pigs, and at which nothing goes wasted. This highly anticipated event takes place in a couple weeks at his farmhouse close to Poggibonsi.

Back in the car I'm feeling a tad light-headed; but then, the dashboard clock reads just 07:55 and I've emptied two full glasses of wine already. All I need now is to run into Iuzzolino on patrol. He would never believe I'm on my way to work — he'd presume I'm just returning home from some all-night rave party (or worse, a Truss).

For the last part of the drive I think lovingly about Marcello's crevassed, warty face and how he resembles a venerable old olive tree, crooked, bulbous, and — let me just say it — ugly; but the plant itself has no aesthetic importance, all that matters is that it be fruitful and yield up its bounty, by all means Marcello does that too. "God bless him!" I think, and instinctively raise my hand from the steering wheel as though toasting him.

As usual, the farm's foreman greets me with a ridiculous *"Buongiorno, Dottor* Castagno," a wildly inappropriate honorific considering my status as a high-school dropout (and especially so if he knew the reason I got expelled). I get the impression that he has never quite understood why I insist on being there picking olives with a bunch of immigrants, old-age pensioners, and mental deficients.

I ask permission to form my usual team and he consents. So for the sixth year in a row, it's Pietro, Alessio and me.

Alessio is an old buddy with whom I went through primary and middle school. He's strong and a hard worker, but is afflicted with a serious mental dysfunction. This impediment is, alas, a family trait; when they hit their thirties something in their brains stops functioning, and they all become simply idiotic. Now, like all his relatives, Alessio habitually wears a ridiculously gawking expression; even worse, it is several years since he simply stopped speaking. The only time he opens his mouth is to release a sudden burst of laughter, inevitably for no apparent reason and at regular intervals of about ten minutes, no matter where he is or what he's doing. He lives with his father and six brothers, and considering how many they are, gaiety is an element that can't be missing within those walls. As they all behave in more or less the same manner, the subjects for conversation must number zero to nil, but someone's laughter is surely always rippling in the air. Not that there's much air to be had – not with all seven of them squeezed into a minuscule stone edifice that at first glance seems suitable for no more than a pair of slender newlyweds.

My other companion, Pietro, is a more complex character, and happens, as I discovered, to be the late Fosco's younger brother. Like Fosco he is a member of the Giraffe *contrada* in Siena and an eight rhyme champ; I've known him since the first year I picked olives at the farm. He possesses an enviable wealth of self-taught knowledge, and the small, silver-framed specs and the blue bask pulled over his snow white hair make him resemble a professor at some left-wing university. I guess him to be in his late seventies; he is literally devastated by Parkinson's disease, with which he manages to contend with heartbreaking dignity. He's very well aware of being at the end of his long life and is very fond of me for the esteem I clearly hold him in, and the inexhaustible pearls of wisdom he dispenses are his repayment for this debt of affection. As he himself would say, *Quando il vino è dentro l'uomo la saggezza è nella bocca* ("When wine enters you, wisdom enters your speech"). Spending long, wintry days picking fruits is tedious work, but in his company it can be a joy because we pass the time talking warmly about whatever subject I wish.

The foreman assigns me a white Lamborghini tractor whose trailer is stacked with cases of plastic containers which, as required by recent EEC dispositions, replace the sacks in which we used to deposit the olives. Also in the trailer are the ground nets to place at the foot of the trees.

I climb aboard the tractor and look out at the orchard awaiting me. The farm possesses all five varieties of local olives; personally I like my oil to be a blend of Leccino, Moraiolo and Correggiolo, and prefer not to add Frantoio or Pendolino. I turn the key in the ignition, the tractor rumbles to life, and off we go. Pietro sits next to me trembling like a leaf, while Alessio perches on the edge with his legs crossed, laughing to the winds.

I drive over a number of rocky fields covered by a gentle sprinkle of green grass that glows under the bright, cold sunshine. We spread the canvas cloth— which resembled a parachute — under the first healthy Moraiolo we encounter; then Alessio scampers up the trunk like a Macao monkey and starts detaching the fruits from the upper branches, while Pietro and I, less limber, commence work on the lower ones. We drop our pickings onto the canvas below us, and when we finish denuding the tree, we collect the olives and deposit them in the crates and load them onto the trailer, then set off in search of a Leccino and then a Correggiolo, and then start the process all over again with another Moraiolo — and so on, throughout the day. It becomes a cycle, a series of recurring tableaus, with Alessio always at the top of the tree laughing, and Pietro and me down below.

With a good dose of malignity I think that if Pietro only had more strength, he need simply press himself against the tree's trunk and the tremors of his terrible disease would be enough to shake the fruit right off the stems. But alas, there's no such escape from this wearying work.

While Alessio's joyful laugh continues unabated, Pietro and I discuss various topics until I ask him how many local proverbs he knows that relate to olive oil. He pauses a moment, removes his bask and runs his fingers through his snow-white hair, then adjusts his specs and recommences picking as he speaks.

"Have you ever thought, Dario, that oil is a synonym for calmness? Of a cool, quiet person we say, 'He is as silent as oil,' and when the sea is calm, it's an oil too. When something has been brought off with no mishaps we say it went 'as smooth as oil;' an evident reality is 'as clear as oil,' to 'throw oil on the waves' means to calm a stormy situation."

Knowing Pietro I'm not the least surprised by the breadth of his reply and encourage him to continue.

"Even the truth is like oil, is it not ? *Viene sempre a galla* — it always comes to surface. When a city expands we compare it to a *macchia d'olio* — an oil stain. If I were to say that you 'don't add oil and salt' it signifies not adding anything of your own or not wanting to mind anyone else's business."

Suddenly he turns and regards me, his trembling head giving added poignancy to the sad eyes that meet my own. "My own life," he says, "is like the guttering flame of an oil lamp that will soon be out." The full weight of this inevitable truth lodges between; then he breaks the awkward moment with a wink. Almost simultaneously the midday bells chime, signaling the lunch break. Alessio descends with a single agile leap, and we sit with our backs against the trunk to protect us from the dagger-like wind and also to allow our faces be caressed by the brilliant sun.

Pietro extracts a small wheel of pecorino cheese and asks me to slice him some bread, because with his shaky grip he might do himself an injury. Alessio has an abundant helping of lasagne left over from his previous night's dinner, which he eats out of a military mess tin. I, for my part, unwrap a deliciously fennel tasting *finocchiona* sandwich that I had the bartender prepare for me earlier this morning.

Pietro reaches into his rucksack and produces a flask of wine, then hands it over to me while noting, *"Mangiare senza bere vino è come murare a secco"* ("Eating without drinking wine is like building a dry stone wall"). I take a long gulp and hand it back to Pietro, who passes it on to Alessio. I feel light-hearted and happy to be in their company, performing those simple gestures of fellowship. After a few minutes Alessio goes off to relieve himself behind a bush, and when he returns with his silly grin, I feel, I don't know why, a momentary and peculiar twinge of envy for him.

With the lunch break behind us, we continue working until sunset. Pietro manages to extend his ruminations on oil for the remaining hours of the day. He recalls his grandmother's remedy for an annoying sty was to stare for three consecutive mornings at a phial containing olive oil. Children who suffered from metritis were customarily administered sage leaves fried in olive oil, and it was for many years normal to soothe any aching part of the body by rubbing oil on it.

From the medicinal Pietro segues into the spiritual, describing the uses of olive oil in religious ceremonies. Olive branches are still used today on Palm Sunday, and in the not so recent past were burned and the ashes scattered on window sills and in barnyards to ward off hail and thunderstorms. The blessed oil is used as an ointment for the newly confirmed and as viaticum for the moribund, and before electricity was used to fuel the church lamps whose light refers to eternal salvation. It is also used in occult rituals and to defeat jinxes and hoodoos, and one must be careful not to spill even a single drop outside of a container as the proverb warns, *A spander l'olio toccano disgrazie* ("To spread oil invites adversities"). "In this case," Pietro reminds us, "the remedy is to throw a pinch of salt over the shoulder."

Pietro lowers his voice and whispers, "There is another old saying, *Agli olivi un pazzo sopra ed un savio sotto*" — meaning, "The Olive trees requires a fool above and a wise man below". With a nod, he indicates the spot where Alessio hovers over us. "It doesn't refer to us, exactly. What it means, is that the branches must be pruned with relentless determination, almost as if you are assaulted by a sudden fit of madness, while the soil in which it grows requires fertilization, nurturing, and quiet care."

Inevitably we come to the principle use of oil: as a condiment. Pietro reminds me of the proverb *Quando condisci l'insalata con il sale vola, con l'olio canta e con l'aceto vai pianino* ("When you dress the salad with salt, fly; with oil, sing; and with vinegar, go slow") — or better still, use *il sale del sapiente, l'olio del sciupone e l'aceto dell'avaro ed invita un pazzo per girarla* ("the salt of the erudite, the oil of a profligate, and the vinegar of a miser, then invite a lunatic to mix it").

At dusk, with the trailer now full, we return to the farm cheerfully singing in eighth rhyme and happy for the prosperity of the day. I arrange to meet my companions again the following morning with hopes that it will be equally pleasant.

I return home tired and smelly, and with my hands impregnated with the oleos substance released by the fruits. I open a bottle of Chianti Classico Capaccia and listen to an old cassette of Francesco Guccini before taking a shower, and go to bed looking forward to the next day in Pietro's and Alessio's company.

In the end, it takes several days to gather enough olives to satisfy all my orders; these are then crushed at 3 a.m. on a chill, dark November day. The quality is excellent and the level of acidity far below the 1% that is the limit an oil may have and still be designated Extra-virgin. Together with Stefano and Elisa, I work night and day bottling, labeling and shipping the oil to our clients. And thus the 2006 Rasna crop enters the archives.

Returning to my regular routine, I require a few days to catch up with my work and to reply to the avalanche of emails that have accumulated during the week. I also send Mia a couple of bottles with instructions how to make the best use of the oil, and — as she seems to be interested in all aspects of my life — a detailed account of my days in the groves.

Just a few weeks later, Pietro will die, alone in his house, on Christmas Eve, and I will be shocked to learn that he was 94 years of age and not in his seventies as I had erroneously believed. He will be buried in a tiny cemetery in Chianti close to his wife, a son who sadly never reached his twenties, and his brother Fosco. He is an extraordinary figure to whom I owe a great debt, and I'm certain my Rasna clients will be pleased to know the oil in their dispenser is partly the result of Pietro's labors.

After his funeral I will uncork a Chianti Classico Querceto and raise a goblet to him, saying aloud, *"Pietro vorrei tanto ma non potrai tornare indietro"* — a ridiculous improvised epigraph that is yet perfect to commemorate poor, noble Pietro.

20

UNA GIORNATA PARTICOLARE

The sky is still amazingly immaculate, the air crisp, and while I have breakfast I decide that after days of catching up on my work I ought to give myself a little reward. I drop a line to Mia, telling her that I am putting off writing for one more day so as to relax and clear my head. My desire is to spend the entire day outdoors. The cycling season ended a few weeks ago and a run would occupy me for no more than an hour or two; thus the best activity would be a long stroll through the hills.

I have a companion who regularly accompanies me on my hikes and I have no doubt he'll be willing to join me. I pick up the receiver and dial Mauro's number; Loris, he confirms, will be thrilled to spend the day with me wandering in the woods.

I don my trekking gear and take a few moments to trim my goatee, trying to make the two sides match. I never manage to achieve perfect symmetry — one side is always a few millimeters thinner or thicker than the other — but I've learned to content myself with whatever results from the first attempt, because if I continue to go at it, correcting, reshaping, inevitably I end up shaving the whole thing off.

I quickly tidy up the house, stopping when it's clean enough to meet the standards of an average single male Mediterranean. Then I head out to the village store, where I purchased a ham sandwich that the gruff proprietor slices by hand while puffing on his cigarette — pointedly ignoring the severe laws against smoking in any public buildings. I select a bottle of Chianti Classico Isole e Olena and place it in my rucksack, and exchange a few words with Clara who as usual is sporting one of her colorful hats; she's just popped in for a copy of the daily newspaper.

I move on to the square, then duck down a tiny alley where Mauro's house is located, in the oldest part of the village. The key is in the lock so I feel free to open the door and enter; I make my way back to the living room where Mauro is seated, contentedly smoking his pipe before a crackling fireplace, and in the company of Loris. As soon as he sees me, the old Irish Setter starts wagging his tail energetically; he rises up on his hind legs and claps his paws on my chest, his tongue lolling to one side and trailing saliva onto the tiled floor.

Mauro is a pensioner who suffers from an annoying hip problem and is thus more than happy to hand over Loris for the day. Emilia, his wife, is busy plucking feathers from a fat thrush in the kitchen, and when she hears my voice she too comes into the living room, still holding the unfortunate volatile by its neck. She places the bird on the marble table, wipes her hands on her apron and gives me an affectionate hug. "Are you hungry?" she says, and before I can reply she takes a slice of toasted bread from the grill over the fire, sprinkles it with a pinch of salt and a drop of *olio novo,* and covers the surface with a leaf of black cabbage, then hands it to me with a lovingly smile. Mauro, not to be outdone, tops a glass of his newly fermented wine and shoves it into my free hand. What else can I ask for? I feel like I'm in heaven.

Mauro places Loris's collar around the dog's neck and hands me the leash. I tell him my plan, which is to hike all the way to Belvedere, and as a result I'm not likely to return till after sunset. Politely they insist that I stay for dinner, and knowing very well Emilia's talents in the kitchen I accept without hesitation.

I'll unhook Loris once we enter the woods, because he is very obedient, but for the first part of the walk, which is along the road, I keep him on the leash just to be safe. I am very fond of this dog, and of the perpetually weary expression he wears on his face, which somehow reminds me of Humphrey Bogart.

Minutes later, with Loris tugging excitedly on the leash so that I'm at risk of falling into the road, we pass by Mauro's perfectly tended vegetable garden, and finally, when I start treading on the narrow path, I'm able to free him. We enter an oak forest and I help myself to the last soggy arbutus fruits of the year while Loris, following his hunting instinct, starts ferreting out pheasant and jack-rabbits trails, his nose grazing the rocky surface covered by decomposing leaves.

Suddenly I'm overtaken by a sensation of serenity and ease. I adore being on my own in the woods, even if I'm aware that I'm only apparently alone — as the many eyes of the wild animals are doubtless fixed to my person from innumerable hidden places among the bushes and branches. In these moments I'm possessed of such wonderful calmness; walking relaxes me unlike any more physically challenging open-air activity. The woods in this season are still brimming with color, the trees still shedding and not yet completely bare. The leaves run riot across the spectrum, from amber and yellow to dazzling crimson, and provide a sharp contrast to the vines, which have already acquired a decisively winterish aspect, being completely naked and seemingly asleep.

The ubiquitous daisies still grow where the sun beats down, and in the woods it is possible to encounter a rare variety of broom that blossoms only at this time of the year. But the general feeling is of a falling off of summer's rich profusion of life. Even the birds have mostly migrated south, but if one is lucky it's possible to catch a glimpse of the timid golden oriole popping out of a shrub, showing off its splendid, bright Dijon-mustard colored plumage.

While descending deeply into the valley I keep in mind to summon Loris every now and then, lest he stray too far from me; he promptly appears instants later, breathing heavily and giving every appearance of being a thoroughly happy soul.

The vegetation in the lower part of the wood is thicker and I have to be careful not to rip my jeans on the prickly blackberry thorns and bramble bushes. At the bottom flows a small stream bordered by ferns; I ramble up the bank until I find the narrowest place to cross over, then take care not to wet my feet — unlike Loris, who plunges ecstatically into the water, completely immune to its frigid temperature. I wade across fairly easily, taking care not to slip on the soft, musk-covered rocks.

On the opposite side I start ascending again; here the wood is a mix of poplars in the lower part and pine trees further up, and suddenly I'm out of the forest and in a vineyard where a magpie lazily perches on one of the chestnut poles that hold up the vine hedges. At the far end of the vineyard I spot an old barn that has been transformed into a holiday home and whose shutters are closed until next Spring, when it will be once again rented out to some foreign family.

Here the path connects to an ancient road whose cobblestones were patiently set down centuries ago, and which leads to a massive villa — alas completely abandoned today — with an impressively wide open gateway and an elegant avenue boarded by ancient cypress trees leading to the front entrance.

The last time I was here I found the gate barred; so now I can't resist passing beneath its arches. Suddenly I find myself in an ample garden where nature has taken over, engulfing the marble tables and statues, choking them in tangled ivy and wild Canadian vines. Off to my right I notice a small chapel, its entrance vandalized; inside I find only a small portion of the altar still standing, surmounted by a chalk bas-relief that portrays a little *putto*.

My eyes fall on a gray marble gravestone with 18th century dates etched upon it; the names I presume belonged to people who had once inhabited the villa. Loris follows me, slightly intimidated by this desolate ambience, his tail tucked between his legs. Clearly he'd like to turn back. But now that I see the main door of the villa is also open, my curiosity wins over my reluctance and I decide to continue the exploration.

On the ground floor the halls are completely barren of furnishings, with the exception of the kitchen, which still has an oven — but only because it's built into the wall. There's also an enormous fireplace whose main beam has been removed. I climb up the travertine steps that compose the wide central staircase, gripping the wrought-iron balustrade, and reach the second floor, where I count over twenty bedrooms, some of which have a small balcony and others their own bathrooms — in one of which an iron tub yet remains, resting on four supports made to resemble lion's paws.

All the glass in the windows has been smashed and the shutters are rotten, ready to drop off their rusted hinges. Even on the third floor the desolation is total, except for an impressive terracotta stove in the corridor and an eerily abandoned wheelchair that in this rather spooky context causes a shiver to scamper up my spine.

Loris has now had enough; he turns and scoots back down to the ground floor, and this time I follow him. As I head back out to the garden I try to imagine what that villa looked like full of people, humming with life. I imagine scenes of servants busily performing their chores, adding cords of wood to the stoves and to the hearths; maids scrubbing the hallways and dusting the living rooms, making up the beds and beating carpets; cooks preparing meals in the kitchen, with steam and smoke and sounds of hissing and bubbling. Each of them would be making his or her small, ceaseless contribution to the smooth daily lives of the wealthy noble family that had been lords there.

I conjure up the halls as they must have looked decked out with expensive furniture, with precious crystal chandeliers dangling from the ceilings and enormous pictures adorning the walls, oil paintings of country scenes or portraits of ancestors in hand-carved gilt frames. I imagine shelves packed with books, leather-bound ancient texts; a grand piano seated on a floor covered by precious oriental rugs; sumptuous sofas and polished oak tables. And all around, the normal scenes of every-day life: hordes of happy children cavorting in the vast garden, carts pulled by oxen coming and going and loaded with the fruits of the farmer's endless endeavors, animated negotiations between visiting intermediaries and brokers, the parish priest coming to celebrate mass on Sundays, friends and relatives from nearby towns arriving in horse-bound calashes and traps to spend a leisurely weekend.

Now all that remains is the elegance of silence; there is no trace of past glory, no remnant of activity or posterity, just the slow but inexorable decline of a property forgotten by the modern world, one that nature is reclaiming, slowly swallowing it like a boa constrictor does its prey.

In the garden I sit atop one of the round marble tables that have been erected under a palm tree. From the rucksack I produce my sandwich and bottle of wine; it's time for lunch. Loris looks up at me expectantly till I open the sandwich and remove the fat from the ham and toss it to him. As he settles down to gobble it up, I open the bottle and give it a long, healthy swig.

Suddenly I feel ill at ease; uncomfortably out of place, despite the fact that I'm certainly not trespassing. But I feel *observed*. I rewrap the sandwich in its aluminum foil, pack it back in the rucksack, and make for the exit, followed dutifully by Loris who is clearly even more relieved than I to be outside the walls of this property.

I continue along the old country road and reach a stone farmhouse, where the family's estate manager must have lived with his family. Even here the abandonment seems total. The entrance is overgrown by a variety of wild rose that has covered the stone wall and then crept along the arch as if aware that this was the most logical pattern to follow. The buds are withering now, but some drooping petals have survived and glow at me in the intermittent sun, a pleasant, pale pink.

I'm surprised to discover that on the ground floor there is a granite olive mill, as well as more relatively recent equipment to extract the oil mechanically. It's all rusted and unusable, and gives the impression of never having been used much anyway. To one side I spot a pile of demijohns wrapped in their customary straw baskets, though infested by mice nests, and everywhere heaps of paper and note pads on which are scribbled the quantities of olives pressed in 1974 (probably the last year the mill had been active). Loris is busy sniffing out the rodents and climbing atop the heaps, digging furiously with his front paws, his body bent forward, his tail pointing straight up at the sky.

I go up a floor and the surprises aren't over, as to my amazement I find it is still completely furnished with simple, plain wooden furniture, the type so fashionable today that everybody snaps it up at the local markets. The terracotta floor is covered in bat and owl droppings, and there are piles of newspapers and magazines from the sixties. I find a staircase that leads back to the lower level through a sort of storage room where there is an old hopper and a dismantled *strettoio* – a grape hand-press - , and a couple of *bigonce* — round-bottomed wooden tubs for carrying grapes at harvest time.

I have no idea of the hour, as I have never owned a watch, but judging from the position of the sun I still have time to spare, and so I continue on my way. I slog along a very muddy path where the sun never shines, that takes me to yet another desolate-looking farmhouse. Suddenly Loris comes to a halt, curls his lip and bares his teeth (making him resemble Bogart even more cleary); his fur bristles and he erupts into barking. Seconds later I realize why. There's a scruffy looking mongrel tied to a chain that runs on a steel wire, allowing it a certain limited range of movement. This dog strains against his tether and answers Loris's ferocious barking with his own.

This din abruptly ceases when a tiny, stocky figure appears and orders the dog to be quiet. He's wearing a multicolored poncho and a sort of black bowler atop his head; his jet-black hair is tied in a ponytail that plummets the full length of his backside.

He then turns to us and with a menacing voice asked what we're doing here. "Just passing through," I tell him. "We'd no intention of disturbing you." Then, having noticed his accent, I asked if by any chance he is Peruvian.

"Venezuelan, actually," he replies, and his face changes expression when I begin showing off my Spanish, telling him I'm planning to spend my winter vacation in his country. He grins, revealing a set of gold-capped teeth, then turns and calls out to someone inside the house; a woman appears at the window, holding a ladle and a bowl. He says something to her in a low voice, and suddenly she's smiling at me too.

Minutes later I'm sipping a Mecacci before a welcoming fireplace, writing down places on my notebook that my new friend insists I must visit when in Venezuela. Consuelo and Santiago are very pleasant company. They're amazingly alike; indeed my first guess is that they're brother and sister, but in fact they're husband and wife. Both are wider than they are tall, and are dressed in traditional Andean costumes.

Santiago tells me that they have come to live in this remote corner of Tuscany in order to look after property that was purchased several years ago by a wealthy American artist who has yet to obtain the permits to restore it. The problem, Santiago explains, isn't so much the actual structure but the impossibility of improving the surface of the ancient road; it is protected by the superintendence, which considers it an architectural landmark, and won't allow any automobiles to drive over it — as it stands now, only all-wheel-drive or all-terrain vehicles could conceivably maneuver it anyway. As the main road is several miles away, this explains why the entire valley is in such a state of decay: no construction crews can get anywhere near it.

In brief, their job is basically to live on the site and prevent the building from collapsing — which they have been doing for two years now. Frankly, I find it bizarre that they crossed the Atlantic Ocean, presumably to find a more prosperous life in Europe, only to end up in a tumble-down ruin in Chianti that has no central heating, electricity or running water, and that is miles away from any form of civilization. Yet they seem happy with the situation and seem convinced that they're better off — that, amazingly, their quality of life is appreciably higher than in their previous life.

After thanking them for their hospitality I say goodbye and, still thinking about this strange encounter and how paradoxical life can be, I continue my hike with Loris. I pass an abandoned olive grove, another set of rundown farmhouses, and then turn onto a path hidden by thick bramble bushes. I know this route very well, because it leads to Belvedere. This is a territory I often covered in my youth on my cross-country motorbike — except that I would exit this bramble-cloaked passage rather than enter it. Which is how I discovered that it was here at all.

Minutes later, there it is before me: my beloved Belvedere. I open the rucksack and pry the cork from the bottle and have a little *self-brindisi* in recognition of my having walked all the way here. Loris releases a small woof as if approving the sentiment.

This is one of the favorite abandoned houses of my teenage years, and it is exactly as I left it the last time I was here, more than two decades ago: the yellow sandstone making up most of the structure, the stables at ground level, the small tower, the worn and crooked stone steps. I pass through the entrance that opens onto the ample salon of the first floor; the simple charcoal portraits of my friends and me, drawn on the stucco walls by Monica; our names all scribbled above the entrance, together with commemorative verses penned by Foffo. So many evocative traces of that memorable spell in the mid-Eighties are still here.

There are the benches we improvised out of wooden planks resting on oak stumps gathered in the nearby woods; the beds made out of jute sacks we stuffed with hay; the old well we managed to fix using a rudimentary hand pump; the empty flasks scattered before the fireplace. Suddenly memories and images from a lost time seem closer and more powerful than my present reality; I close my eyes and take a deep breath, filling my nostrils with the damp air, and the familiar odors revive long dormant sensations that I had evidently never entirely forgotten, but stored in some drawer deep in my subconscious. A tear trickles down my cheek and filters through my beard before resting on my upper lip, inviting the tip of my tongue to flick it up and reincorporate it.

The Belvedere was a place where we escaped from reality, the final boundary behind which we found sanctuary from an adult world we resisted joining but would soon inexorably be part of. For a brief, magical instant I relive the remote emotions of lost youth; and it occurs to me that most probably we were the final generation who spent their free time frolicking in these woods, passing the long evenings roasting sausages on a crackling fire, playing the guitar and singing before the glowing embers — plunging into the sensations of life rather than mimicking them on a chat line or shutting them out with the ceaseless noise of computer games.

I sit on the bench and finish off the wine, knowing that *il vino allontana la malinconia* ("Wine keeps the melancholy away"), while gazing at the names scribbled on the walls, many of which belonged to people whose whereabouts are a mystery to me now, others of whom I still occasionally meet, and a few of whom have, alas, prematurely departed this world. Loris licks my face, bringing me back to the moment; I am very far from home now, and it's time to turn back as the sun is setting, signaling dusk.

The returning trek takes four hours, and to kill time I sing the songs of Lucio Battisti aloud, keeping myself company. It's too dangerous to enter the woods in such darkness, so I must opt to skirt around it in favor of a main road — which means, once again, hooking the leash to Loris's collar.

Emilia has prepared an exquisite dinner, penne with cream and fresh porcini mushrooms for the first course, roasted sparrows and thrushes for second. We all sit in front of the fire, where a very tired Loris has curled up on the mat, and dip some biscotti in an uninviting gloomy colored cloudy homemade *vin santo*. It turned out to be delicious proving the local proverb *giudica il vino al sapore ed il pane al colore* ("Judge the wine by the flavor and the bread by its color"). I tell Mauro and Emilia all about my special day in Loris's company — about the villa, the olive mill, the quirky Andean couple, the surprising number of abandoned houses, and my return to Belvedere and all the sensations that I rediscovered there. The old couple then tell me that the entire valley was once the property of a wealthy family who occupied the villa, and that the farmhouses were home to the families of sharecroppers who worked the lands for them. It had once been considered a model farm, and anyone who had the good fortune to live and work there was considered both privileged and well remunerated. They had been the first farms in the postwar period to install electricity, and the farmers lived in enviable hygienic conditions by the standards of the day.

Then when the old *commendator* passed away the property

was inherited by his daughter, who married a man so full of vice that in no time he depleted the whole fortune at the card table. The entire estate went bankrupt and the farmers were obliged to move into the towns and find employment in the factories, and since then it has all become a shambles.

The most incredible thing, they conclude as we finished the last of the *vin santo*, is that the proprietress is still alive — though she must be now at least a hundred and ten years old.

As I walk home I feel both tired and happy, and can't seem to stop reflecting on the extraordinary day I've had. Tired as I am, I manage to find the strength to check out my email before going to bed.

21

IN VINO VERITAS

From: Mia Lane
To: Dario Castagno
Subject: Welcome Back

Dear Dario,
Welcome back! I'm so happy you have time to dedicate to me again, now that the harvest is over. I was pleasant-ly surprised to find on my doorstep a carton containing two bottles of olive oil and, as suggested in the enclosed note, I'm using it primarily as a bread dipper. I had never tasted *olio novo* before and yes it is really delicious, and now that you've spoiled me I can't imagine how I'll be able to cope without. My heart will sink once I finish yours and must go back to using the dull supermarket stuff I regularly buy. Thank you for a very special gift, Dario; it was very thoughtful of you and I will savor every single drop.
I also received another unexpected surprise: your e-mail detailing your wonderful day of picking olives. I found your description enchantingly romantic, even though I'm well aware that spending entire days in the groves must be grueling work. How I would love to have a venerable old friend like Pietro, so full of wisdom and stories; and in a different way I'm just as fascinated by poor Alessio. How nice it is of you to want him on your team.
I must admit I missed not receiving any news from you; every time I scrolled down my list of incoming messages I'd hope to find something from Dario Castagno, but alas I had to wait an entire week before your name finally popped up again. Despite your silence you were never far from my mind. In fact there's been something unsettling me, Dario. In your previous books it was obvious to per-ceive your love for Cristina, yet to me you haven't men-

tioned her. It seems clear that there's no female presence in your life and that you are deliberately trying to avoid any kind of relationship. You seem to be an extremely warm and loving person but there's an aura of melancholy about you. I'm getting very personal, I know, and I don't ask that you answer me; I'm just pointing out some of the things I've gleaned from reading between the lines of your e-mails. Whether willingly or not, you've revealed a darker side to the otherwise wonderful life that you lead.

Okay, now that I've had the courage to say that I hope you'll forgive me. From now on we should stick to the subject and discuss the upcoming chapters, shouldn't we? Anyway I hope you enjoyed your day off; what did you do? Did you go nightclubbing or what?

Yours
Mia

I turn off the computer and go to bed, it takes a while to fall asleep, so many thoughts crowd my mind. Is Mia right about me being melancholic and lonely? I feel stung, as though she's found me out. But maybe I'm judging by the day I just spent wandering through the woods, alone but for a dog and my memories from the past.

But no, that's a distortion; true, I was alone in the woods, but alone doesn't mean lonely. And revisiting the scenes of a carefree youth doesn't mean I'm melancholic. On the contrary, I've never felt in any way depressive or deprived after spending a day in my hills.

I started that day by having a long chat with Clara, then made some new and unusual friends in the afternoon, and basked in Mauro and Emilia's affectionate company at dinner. What else could I ask for? Would I have been better off nightclubbing in Florence, or seeking the love of my life on the crowded dance floor of some squalid disco? I'd never fit in those places as a teenager; now that I'm middle-aged it would just be ridiculous. Does Mia really believe I'd waste my spare time in that way? . . . I doubt it.

Anyway, tomorrow I'll provide her all the details of that most memorable day, but I will have to disappoint her with regard to Cristina; I simply don't want to mention her anymore. When she left me I fell into a deep, dark tunnel, and now that I can see the light at its end I have no intention of tormenting myself any further — delving back into that awful mire of trying to figure out why she is no longer sharing her life with me.

Maybe Mia mentioned Cristina to provoke a reaction in me; might she have been prompting me to send her an account that includes her as well? I can definitely understand Mia's curiosity and her desire to speak more intimately; that doesn't disturb me the slightest.

Except where it concerns Cristina.

Certainly Mia is a cunning woman.

Minutes later I'm asleep, embracing my pillow tightly.

∞

The last day of November has arrived.

I spend the better part of it writing about my walk in the woods. The most difficult part is trying to describe the strong sensations that overwhelmed me when I arrived at the Belvedere. It would be easier had I taken some notes when I was there but I hadn't brought any writing materials along. To help get into the right mindset I sip some Mecacci; and finally, late that evening, I am sufficiently satisfied with the text to reply to Mia's last e-mail.

From: Dario Castagno
To: Mia Lane
Subject: re Welcome Back!
Attachment: Una Giornata Particolare

Dear Mia,

Ciao! It's a pleasure to be back and yes, I must admit I missed your emails too. I'll advise Pietro and Alessio that they will be included in the book; I'm sure Pietro will be thrilled. As for Alessio . . . well, he won't have a clue what I'm talking about but it might provoke one of his hearty, infectious laughs.

I can understand your curiosity about my relationship with women. As a matter of fact, the situation couldn't be simpler: I have none. Since Cristina left me I have, as you well know, been living a very reserved life — almost monastic. I've retired to the great enveloping silence of my hills, where I listen to music, read, write, and drink red wine. Women, I've come to realize, are far too complex for me, and I doubt I can ever find a girl who would appreciate my simple way of existence. To be honest, for many years I loved women while never really understanding them; and whenever I thought I had gained some insight or seasoned comprehension, I was inevitably disillusioned again. I've been heartbroken too many times now even to think of starting any kind of relationship. Possibly because such relationships are not casual to me; each and every time I fell in love, I was convinced that I had found the partner of my life and, why not, the mother of my children.

You see, Mia, you may not have met me but you've managed to capture, as you describe it, the "darker side" of my character that comes through with greater knowledge of me, and that I'm certain is what eventually makes the women flee from me. My conscience however is clear, as my nature has always seemed to me to be rather the romantic, old fashioned sort. I'm one of those relics who finds satisfaction in sending bunches of roses and writing poems, or reciting excerpts of the Canticle of Canticles to my beloved in front of a romantic sunset in one of my favorite spots. Very seldom have these gestures been appreciated. I've always considered women to be as delicate as rose petals but in reality you are all far too complex and intriguing. The unavoidable conclusion I've been forced to reach is simply that women don't like me.

Attached you will find in full detail how I passed my day off yesterday, a chapter I've named after a famous Italian movie, *Una giornata particolare* with Sophia Loren and Marcello Mastroianni — because indeed it was a particular day. In fact I believe that I can classify it as one of my most intensely lived in the past several months, and you know what, Mia — I don't know what exact role you have in all of this but certainly part of the credit I attribute to you.

Regards
Your obscure friend
Dario

εσ

December already. The date stares at my from each page of the daily newspaper that is my sole company at the local bar where I've chosen to take breakfast.

When I return home I trip over the sacks of empty bottles at the door — what a quantity I've drained in the past several days! Clearly it's time to visit to the glass-recycling bin in the village. I drag the two sacks to the car, causing a clinking, clanking din with each step through the tight alleyways. When I reach the receptacle I open the sacks and extract the bottles one by one, feeding them through the opening and listening as each tumbles to the bottom with a jarring crash.

Suddenly I feel a prickle of guilt, as though I'm abandoning faithful companions who had supported me during days of difficult labor at my writing desk. I carefully examine the label of each bottle I take it up, bid it a fond farewell, then watch it disappear into the anonymous, imposing container. Somehow each of those bottles contains a tiny particle of inspiration. And now they're all gone.

I try to cheer up by telling myself that I'm giving them the possibility of a new life, that maybe in the future they will return to my hand again, and bless me anew with the gifts of their rich, red contents. Still, I'm a bit embarrassed because there are *so* many of them; the sack seems bottomless. And most of these bottles, I remind myself, I emptied all on my own. And it's only been a few days since my last errand here.

Maybe it's time to clean up my act a bit, and follow the rule *il pan finchè dura il vino a misura* ("The bread while it lasts, but measure the wine") and forget about *Dottor* Becchini's suggestions. Luckily, the only person I've encountered en route to the bin is the innocuous Giulio (who's shrunk another few inches since last I saw him), and compared to him I'm but an amateur; he could fill a bin all by himself, I think with a chuckle — and then I realize someone is observing me.

Emanuele appears wearing his characteristic look, which I've yet to be able to decipher; he has something in his gaze that might either be vaguely dreamy or vaguely idiotic.

He lives with his widowed, sickly mother though he is more or less my age; he lives off her meager state pension, having in all his life achieved nothing on his own. He's minute and curvy, with round, narrow shoulders. On his lower lip there rests, as usual, a tiny hand-rolled paper cigarette; perhaps it's because of his incessant smoking that his skin looks like second-quality leather, the kind sold by Chinese vendors at a street market. Certainly his teeth are blotched with nicotine and caffeine stains, and at the corners of his mouth are hideous frothy lumps of dried saliva that make me momentarily want to heave up the blackberry-stuffed bun I wolfed down with a cappuccino at breakfast.

The few thin hairs that sprout from his tiny skull don't have a defined cut and drastically want a trichological treatment. His sunken eyes are surmounted by a single thick eyebrow that crosses his forehead from side to side, and his eagle-beak nose has the same convex line as his back. When he speaks it's only to express scornful or racist remarks. I'm about as happy to meet him as I would be to find Bin Laden boarding an Alitalia flight with me.

I swiftly turn my head away so as not to meet his eyes —but as I feared, he saunters up and remarks, "Dario, congratulations, you'll win us the prize for the town that recycles the most glass," which is an acceptable jibe. Then he adds, "One more bottle and I think we can give the Guinness Book of Records a jingle," and this is passable as well. But then, as always, he crosses the line by adding, "If you continue like this I doubt your johnson will ever get straight," then throws back his head and howls a macabre laugh, his hand on his stomach and a frothy string of saliva dangling down to his T-shirt. Instead of ignoring the unpleasant freak, I stare at him with rage, and just as I'm about to snarl a retort at him Giulio, who has approached unheard from behind him, raises his walking stick menacingly in the air and brings it crashing down on Emanuele's head, producing an awful thud. Emanuele hurls a spate of vile epithets at the old man, then slithers away, massaging his smarting cranium.

To my amazement Giulio then actually speaks, declaring, "*Chi vuole un buon vino zappa le vigne d'Agosto!*" ("He who wants good wine must hoe the vines in August.") I pivot on my heels, mentally thanking him even though I have no idea why he's talking about August in December, and return home laughing.

When I get back Orazio is waiting for me, seated on my doorstep with a magnum of wine in his hand, and I get the sinking feeling that my day is over. I like Orazio well enough, he's a nice fellow, but he's also an endurance test. As soon as he sees me he stands up and says, "Dario, eh . . . eh . . . eh . . . you know that guy? The guy that . . . come on" — and here he pauses to remove something between his teeth with his fingernail — "I mean the one that bought the farm on the road to" — an epic pause; a pause you could fall into — "the road that once was rubble and now is paved, and that heads for, uh," — pauses to scratch his hairy nose — "you know close to, to, to . . ." — pause to snap his fingers — "I mean, not those, the others, the ones that, that" — pause to adjust his underwear, which has ridden up into his sphincter. After twenty-two minutes standing with the key in the door waiting for Orazio to conclude his greeting, I figure out that he's come because he'd like me to taste the wine a friend of his has made, and that he thinks excellent.

Orazio stays for a couple of hours during which we empty the magnum, and I feed him a plate of pasta with a sauce I make out of *olio novo* and a fresh *buffalo* mozzarella. I manage to tune him out by using a technique I perfected when taking boring clients out on my tours. I simply look him in his eyes and smile and nod every now and then, but my mind is elsewhere, thinking of the things I'll write about over the following days. Of course I can't avoid the spray of particles of mashed-up pasta that end up in my face — and on my plate.

After he leaves I'm horrified to find in my toilet bowl a giant menhir he evacuated after lunch. To be able to send it down the pipe I need to throw three buckets full of water that I release energetically together with the flush.

I spend the rest of the day jotting down some anecdotes that Mia might be interested in, and decided to reward my labors by opening an important bottle of Vino Nobile di Montepulciano Vigna Asinone that soon will join Orazio's depleted magnum in the recycling sack. I put Joni Mitchell on the stereo and sip the fine wine while I download the day's e-mail. As usual, I find numerous requests for tours so I roll up my sleeves and summon my guides. Once that's finished, and there being no missive from Mia, I decide to write her a note while finishing the last of the wine, despite feeling a notch or two above plain tipsy.

From: Dario Castagno
To: Mia Lane
Subject: None

My beloved Mia,
Ciao! I'm drinking a bottle of Vino Nobile Vigna Asinone

— truly a great wine — and listening to a CD, "Blue" by Joni Mitchell. The soft December light is waning and enchanting me with all its might and magic. I'm happily alone now, taking in my usual elements without getting annoyed as always in my daily consuetude. Maybe I'm simply getting old, and just as for the elderly the monotonous routine affords me a sense of security.

I've been meaning to ask you why you don't scold me for not asking anything about you, about your life. Maybe it's my ego that's impeded me from doing so, or maybe it's my narcissism, or maybe I've simply been a misogynous fool. Anyway, I beg your pardon. You know Mia, in this very moment I'm drunk and forgive me if I have already quoted *in vino veritas* but it is inevitable. There is no way that I'm going to bed now, I want to walk in the woods and breathe some fresh air, I feel like I'm an integral part of this sweet land and that even the wild animals perceive it; I've noticed they no longer fear me or shy away from my presence. I even manage to caress the lizards on their heads and steal the honey from the bees without getting stung.

I think I'm falling in love with you Mia . . .

෨

I am awakened by the sound of thunder punctuated by stroboscopic flashes of lightning that intermittently illuminate the room. I must have fallen asleep in the chair in front of the computer. There's a terrible taste of nausea in my mouth, and the first thing my weary eyes catch sight of is the message I wrote to Mia the night before which, fortunately, I never actually sent. I can't believe I wrote such bullshit. "The animals no longer shy away from my presence, I even manage to caress the lizards on their heads and steal the honey from the bees without getting stung." Who was I thinking I am, Saint Francis or the Lord of Chianti? When I see what I wrote next — that I was falling in love with her — I immediately delete the entire text. She is, I remind myself, a literary agent with whom I'm working, not a girl on a silly chat line.

I slap my face to wake myself up, and am slightly repelled by the odor of oxidized wine released by the empty bottle and glass next to me. And outside I can hear the sound of the car tires on the wet asphalt made by the local commuters hurrying to work. So at least some of my senses are back in good working order.

As I am sitting there, pausing for thought, and waiting to be reconnected, I see that Mia has sent me a message.

From: Mia Lane
To: Dario Castagno
Subject: Re: A Giornata Particolare

Dario! Today I made myself a *bruschetta* and realized what an amazing color your oil has; it glows in the light. Amazing! Also amazing was your "Giornata Particolare"; you turned a simple walk into an extraordinary chronicle. I'm starting to believe that you live in a wonderland and maybe it's your deep sensibility that's responsible for transforming every small gesture into a special event. Please remain the person you are; I'm convinced that your simplicity, mixed with the joy you take in your surroundings, combine to inspire these stories. Some higher power may be trying to communicate something to you by continually providing you with such remarkable meetings and situations. In any case I'm certain you're an integral part of the world you live in.

I pause a moment to make sure I never sent her the e-mail of the night before.

Now Dario, I don't want to make your head swell so I'll stop right now and change the subject. Yesterday I opened a very special bottle of Vino Nobile di Montepulciano that I drank with some girlfriends who came over for dinner.

I'm shocked; it's the same kind of wine I myself drank last night! Am I *really* sure I never sent her the e-mail? Another quick check: no, I definitely didn't.

I bought it some years ago when I visited Tuscany; it's produced by Avignonesi.

Okay then, not Vigna Asinone as I'd thought.

I promised to open it when I turn forty on December 31.

So you're my age, Mia!

Instead I opened it last night in your honor, while reading aloud the story of the Truss to my friends. They clutched themselves and laughed helplessly, like college students. I hope you won't be crazy with me for having done this, Dario.

No Mia, why should I?

I was sorry to read about your terrible history with women, but have faith, your girl is somewhere out there waiting for you. You've just been disillusioned by your recent experiences.
But now let's talk seriously: my boss has read the first few chapters and is very enthusiastic; he really wants to publish this book. Do you have an agent? If so please forward me his/her address; if not I can easily enlist someone who can look after your interests.

Ciao
Mia

I stand up and instinctively peer out of the window to see if a girl is out there waiting for me, as Mia suggests. I look carefully in the fields and vines as well as underneath the wet olives, but can't detect anyone, alas. If this hypothetical girl is really out there, she's going to have to stop being so coy about it. Either that, or send me a postcard telling me where to come to collect her.

I head downstairs for a cup of *orzo*, then take a quick shower and I'm ready to reply to Mia. I already have a new chapter in mind, inspired by her message.

From:	Dario Castagno
To:	Mia Lane
Subject:	Your birthday

Dear Mia,
Ciao! Of course you have my approval for reading the Truss chapter to your friends. Possibly I've inspired you all to undertake the experience yourselves one day.

You know that I trust you, and I'm sure you'll make good use of the material I'm sending you. I'm so happy that you're enjoying the extra-virgin oil; if you run out I'll send you more, no problem — I have a decent personal supply. By the way, your choice to accompany it with a Vino Nobile was perfect.

I have included the info regarding my manager Laura Grover, who like you lives in Los Angeles. I'm sure you'll get on well together. Believe me, she's used coping with me so she's extremely patient and will forgive me for not having informed her about this project, now so far along. So you also were born on December 31! I say "also" because I once had a girlfriend with that birth date; it was torture for me as I have always despised going out on New Year's Eve, and for a few years I couldn't find a way out because she, of course, expected to be celebrated. But as we've mentioned New Year's Eve, I'll write to you soon about a very particular year's end that occurred in 1988, and which I'd nearly expunged from my memory. I'm enjoying our correspondence also for this reason: retrieving distant memories, even unhappy ones, and giving them new life as stories.

Just give me leave for a short run through the forests, as it is no longer raining; that will give me time to reassemble the events in my head. Then I shall open a bottle of the great Chianti Classico Ispoli — because *se vuoi ubriacarti ubriacati di vino bono* (which means, "If you want to get drunk, do so with good wine") produced by my brother, who I seldom see despite us living so close to each other.

Until then, Mia . . . !

22

CRAPPY NEW YEAR

One early December night in 1987 I was curled up in the fetal position on a wrought iron-bed, submerged in a pile of eider-downs and blankets in a decrepit farmhouse I had recently rent-ed. This old colonial house was only just barely habitable and in urgent need of repairs. It lacked any kind of heating beyond a rudimentary wood stove that needed to be fed constantly if it were to give off even the most minimal warmth; and since I lived there alone and was out working all day at the winery, it was con-sequently almost useless. The best tactic I'd found to stave off the biting cold was to go to bed early wearing various layers of woolen garments, and lie beneath a mountain of bedclothes.

On this particular night all was well until I was jolted awake by the trill of the phone in the living room. Instinctively my eyes sought the clock on the bed stand. It read 3:28. Afraid that something serious had happened, I threw back the thick layer of blankets and, shocked awake now by the instant embrace of frigid air, got out of bed. In a state of semi-unconsciousness I lurched barefooted across the icy terracotta tiles that had been worn away by hundreds of years of being trod on by my prede-cessors. I passed underneath the arched entrance of the living room and with numb fingers lifted the receiver from the phone.

The cold had now penetrated my bones and my heart beat frantically. The last thing I was expecting was a casual call from a friend.

"Davio, its Mavco, can you heav me?"

Even if he hadn't announced himself, I would have recognized the characteristic French r's. "Marco, what is it? Are you okay?"

He was a recent acquaintance of mine, about ten years my senior, whom I had met while guzzling down some wine in a rundown *osteria* in Siena, around about closing time. As I was the only other customer, he drew closer to me and we bandied words to kill time. Since that day he'd attached himself to me like a tick on a mangy dog; to define him otherwise would be euphemistic. Possibly because of my chronic curiosity, or maybe because he provoked in me a mixture of piety and compassion, I hadn't yet rid myself of him like the rest of the world seemed to have done.

But when he told me the purpose of the call was to find out — at almost four o'clock in the morning! — if I had any plans for New Year's Eve, I decided the rest of the world had the right idea; I told him to go to hell, slammed the receiver back into its cradle, and returned to bed, the heat of my anger somewhat countering the bitter cold.

When I awoke the following morning I gave a quick glance at the world out the window; it was Saturday and I had the entire weekend before me. With any luck, the weather would allow me to spend at least part of it outdoors. It was an unusual meteorological situation: the sky was the soft color of burned olive-wood smoke, but as soon as a ray of light managed to pierce the dense sheet of clouds, the tops of the chestnut trees suddenly glowed a bright coppery brown. Cheered by the sight, I decided on a stroll in the woods to fill my lungs with fresh air.

On my way out of the door, I grabbed a straw basket from where it hung on a rusted nail on the porch. If I found some *giallarelle* mushrooms, I could add them to the tomato sauce I had planned for lunch; but the chances of this were slim, as the mycological season had almost ended.

An hour or so later, as I returned home on the country road with my thoughts as empty as my wicker basket, I heard behind me the sound of a car horn. I whirled and found myself facing Marco's old Renault 4. It was a complete wreck, reduced to a mass of rot and rust; you could just vaguely perceive by a few traces of paint here and there, that the body had once been bright red.

He shifted down to first gear, then kicked the brake and stopped a few meters ahead of me with a sinister rattling, the sound of scrap iron grinding against itself. Marco opened the door, which didn't come away in his hands only because he'd affixed it to the rusted hinges with a length of wire.

"Ciao, Davio come on boavd!" he said, grandly waving me inside.

I took my place in the passenger seat, shoving aside a pile of crumpled beer cans, empty bottles and cardboard boxes containing mold-encrusted slices of leftover pizza. The car was thick with the rank stench of petrol, tobacco, fried chips and garlic — the latter of which Marco so craved that he kept a head of the stuff in his pocket, and every now and then would peel off a clove and pop it in his mouth like a stick of gum. He was listening, as always, to the music of a French teen-pop band of the 1970s called Les Rockets, who during their concerts dressed up as aliens with their heads shaved and painted silver. Their lyrics were exclusively space-themed. The music came from a large portable stereo he had modified which was powered by tiny solar panels. He was in certain ways quite ingenious, and this contraption, which he christened his "ghettoblaster", proved his ingenuity.

We drove on to the chords of "In the Galaxy," a somewhat unusual soundtrack for a cold, clear day in the rolling Chianti hills. When we reached my house he parked his wreck in an uncultivated field in front and, not wanting to seem impolite (did I have a choice?), I invited him in.

As usual he was wearing leather sandals, worn, ripped jeans on which he'd scribbled all his important phone numbers in black ink, and a T-shirt with the image of one of Les Rockets' most recent albums, "Plasteroid" — topped off with his ever-present green print jacket, rife with tiny pockets that contained all kinds of contraptions, screwdrivers, fuses, electric wires, torches, and — inevitably — garlic bulbs. In fact he extracted a clove right now, as though it were the most normal thing in the world to do at eleven o'clock on a Saturday morning. He offered me one as well, but I declined with an eloquent flick of my wrist, upon which he popped this second clove into his mouth and started crunching away.

Physically he appeared older than his twenty-eight years. His belly was as distended as a forty-year old couch potato's, and he'd lost many if not most of his teeth. His frizzy hair was bound in a red elastic headband that reminded me of Jimi Hendrix at the Isle of Wight concert.

Officially he was a student at the University of Siena — of what discipline I had no idea as he skirted the subject whenever I asked. He was the only child of a fallen (but economically well-off) noble family who had marginalized him, obviously disillusioned by his bohemian ways. Yet they allowed him to remain in their high-class home within the historical centre of Siena, in the Turtle district to be precise, on condition that he confined himself to the attic. This cramped space he shared with Priscilla, a big, black tarantula for whom he cared as though she were his daughter.

This alcove was off-limits for his family and accessible only to his friends — of whom he had none. His parents had tried to reintegrate him in society, but after having spent a fortune on the most exclusive analysts and behavioral therapists, they had with extreme reluctance admitted defeat and resigned themselves to being stuck with such a son.

I opened a Mecacci and passed him a glass while he contentedly munched a third clove, chewing with his mouth open and obliging me to put a hand over my nostrils to thwart the toxic emission of his breath.

"So, Marco," I said, "do you mind explaining why you woke me at three in the morning just to ask about my New Year's Eve plans?"

"Sovvy, I didn't vealize it was so late, I was watching TV and at a cevtain point the pvogram started talking about the poovest town in Italy."

"Continue," I said now curious to hear what this possibly had to do with me.

"Well, they said it was a village down south somewheve in the Sannio mountains."

"So?"

"It's called Castel Pagano and I've decided to go theve fov New Yeav's Eve."

"Uh-huh. And what have I got to do with this, Marco?"

"I was hoping you'd come with me."

I immediately declined, thanking him for the invitation but pleading a long list of prior engagements I was obliged to keep that made it completely, utterly, unarguably impossible for me to spend any time at all with him on New Year's Eve. Alas, he was stubborn, and possessing no social graces he simply refused to accept my refusal. Rather he persisted in pressing his case with an enthusiasm you could read in his beaming eyes, while he detailed the route we would take and the marvelous sites we'd visit along the way.

In fact I had no prior commitments for that evening, but had no intention of being part of this harebrained project. However, I *do* possess a modicum of social graces and couldn't quite bring myself to hurt him with an absolute rejection. So in desperation I made the excuse that I had no car (I possessed only a motorbike), and I wouldn't risk the ride in his junker. I told him I would go with him only on condition that he came and picked me up in his father's car. I really thought this guaranteed my safety. His father was the proud owner of an extremely expensive and fully equipped Mercedes coupé, and knowing how obsessive he was about it I was sure he'd never lend it to his dilettante son.

Marco abruptly stood up from my tumbledown sofa, gulped the last of the wine and shook my hand energetically, saying we had a deal and that come December 30th he'd be here to pick me up. Having obtained what he wanted he turned for the door, tossing me one last tooth-challenged smile (and the accompanying shock wave of garlic breath) as he waved goodbye.

His confidence in the plan caused me a moment's anxiety; but no, it was impossible, his father would never allow anyone else behind the wheel of his custom-built car. I had nothing to worry about. I topped off my glass and watched out the window as Marco climbed back into his disaster-on-wheels, and offered me one last wave through the rear window — which I almost couldn't see because of a Rockets sticker affixed to the glass (which may have been the only thing holding it in place). In a few moments he'd be gone, and I'd be happy.

But no. As was often the case, he couldn't get the ignition started. I felt obliged to go out and help him. Donning my coat, I left the house and gave him a push; the engine made a wheeze, then a groan, and then coughed into life. From the driver's seat Marco gave me a thumbs-up as he sputtered away; I watched lest the car conk out and once again require my aid; but soon enough it passed over the horizon and out of sight.

I returned to the living room and turned on the TV, and settled in to watch an old episode of *Charlie's Angels* — but my mind wasn't on the show. Instead I pondered the reason I seemed to attract all these dregs of society. I leaned back on the sofa and observed the wooden beams that held up the roof, which were full of holes made by voracious woodworms, and I came to the conclusion that I probably wasn't all that normal either.

∞

The 30th of December was cold but dry. I was in the kitchen preparing a *ribollita* for dinner, and had chopped up most of the vegetables before I realized that I had no black cabbage — a fundamental ingredient. I went outside to the vegetable garden where Porfirio Mecacci (yes, my historical wine supplier) was busy hoeing the surface. I loved this old man, with whom I was in the habit of exchanging a few excruciating puns. He was born and raised in Chianti and had always worked the fields, despite which he had the refined, elegant posture of a broker in the city of London. In fact he reminded me vaguely of David Niven, what with his slim moustache and all; chubbier, but still David Niven. He was very happy to give me a few cabbage leaves and even added a flask of his wine (the original Mecacci), and I returned to the stove to finish off my soup.

Just as I placed the pot on the fire I heard a faint knock on the door. I wasn't expecting anyone, and wasn't at all pleased to recognize Marco's silhouette through the glass — unmistakable despite his profile being distorted by a woolen ski hat pulled down over his eyebrows. When I opened the door he raised his hand like a native American and said, "Ciao." Before I had a chance to ask what he was doing here, he said, "Well, ave you veady?"

And that's when I saw, to my horror, the silver Mercedes parked in the barnyard, gleaming in the full, bright moonlight. Somehow he'd managed to keep his part of the bargain — now I had to keep mine. I felt panic rise up inside me; then I quelled it. I reminded myself that I had no actual obligations on the docket, so maybe I could endure a couple of days with Marco — who could say, it might actually turn out to be good fun after all.

I invited him in and together we wolfed down the *ribollita* and the Mecacci; then I packed my rucksack with a few necessities and off we went. I stopped long enough to say goodbye to my chubbier David Niven, who was busy storing his tools in the shed; minutes later I was comfortably seated on the white leather seats of the Mercedes, cruising south in style and listening to a cassette titled "Astral World" by (who else?) the Rockets.

When we left the provincial road for the state highway we soon came upon an official roadblock and we were ordered to pull over. Of course it was Iuzzolino — at the time a young officer wearing the beautiful blue-and-red winter uniform of his branch of the *carabinieri*. He asked Marco for his license; then, noticing me for the first time, nodded in my direction, visibly surprised to find me the passenger in such a luxurious car.

"Glad to see you're acquiring some more respectable friends, Dario," he said, while handing the license back to

Marco. "Okay, *Signor* Tommaso Crociera, you're free to go."

Marco pulled away and we had no sooner cleared the area than he actually produced a joint from one of his many pockets and lit it.

"Marco," I asked him, impressed by his sheer bravado, "who the hell is Tommaso Crociera?"

He released a puff of smoke, immediately inundating the car with a sweet scent of Jamaica, and replied, "I have a tvial soon, and so as not to make more pvoblems I fovged a fake license. I made it while they vhere bvoadcasting *Top Gun* and since I couldn't decide what name to choose . . ." He shrugged as if this were no big deal.

"You translated 'Tom Cruise' into Italian?" I asked, incredulous.

He shrugged again, and merely grinned.

I decided not to ask for any further details — such as what he was going to be on trial for — and sank deeper into the plush seat, while Marco flicked away the butt and popped a clove of garlic in his mouth. I had the impression that I was in for plenty more surprises.

When we reached the outskirts of Siena, instead of taking the main road for Rome he told me he had to stop at home to pick up a few things first. "Shan't take a minute," he promised.

Then he parked the car in front of his parents' villa and told me to follow him and to take my rucksack with me. He led me towards his dilapidated Renault Four, plopped himself in the driver's seat, flung open the passenger door and gestured me in.

"Come on boavd!" he said cheerfully.

"What are you talking about?" I protested.

"You told me you'd come with me if I picked you up with my babbo's Mevcedes. Well, I did, now lets get moving."

"Marco, I meant to take the entire trip in that car, not just the first ten miles."

"Then you should've made that cleav," he said. "What's the matter, you don't tvust my Venault?"

"Not as far as I could throw it," I replied. "Which is probably farther than you could drive it. Take me back home right now. And you know me well enough by now, to know that when I say no, I mean *no!*"

Minutes later I was seated in his passenger seat, almost buried in crushed beer cans, cigarette butts, greasy take-away cartons and an appalling mass of other junk he had accumulated over the years. I also noticed that beneath my feet some slim green blades of grass were actually sprouting. "The only car with an ecological floor mat," I thought.

Marco tried to calm me down; he told me to relax and take it easy, that once we picked up Amanda the four of us would have a smooth ride to Castel Pagano.

"Who is Amanda?" I asked annoyed. Before he could reply, I added, "And pardon me, maths has never been my strong suit, but unless she's twins she'll make *three*, not four."

"You've fovgetting Pviscilla."

"What? . . . Your tarantula? There's a tarantula in the car?" I looked anxiously over my shoulder.

"Well, I couldn't just leave hev alone, could I? . . . She's in the back, in hev glass cabinet." He spoke as if it were the most normal thing in the world to spend New Year's Eve with a poisonous spider in the trunk.

"And this Amanda," I said with a sarcastic sneer, "exactly how many legs does *she* have?"

He chuckled. "Velax, Davio, only two."

"And are they human or insect?"

"Human. Please, she is a sweet young maiden, you'll like hev I sweav. And anyhow Pviscilla is not an insect, she's an avachnid." As if this detail was of any importance to me.

Amanda was waiting for us in front of her house. The "sweet young maiden" was a girl with a very apparent weight problem; perhaps it was to draw attention from this that she'd dyed her hair Granny Smith apple-green and styled it into a voluminous rockabilly-style pompadour, that could only have been held in place by enough bottles of hairspray to finish off the ozone layer. It looked immobile and invulnerable; it might have repelled bullets.

She was dressed all in black; her ears, nose and lips were pierced, and later I would discover her tongue was as well. Her breasts were truly enormous, and despite the bitter cold she was wearing a micro-miniskirt with no tights, leaving her doughy, snow-white legs naked; they were also, to my horror, covered with tiny black hairs.

She scampered up to the car in shiny plastic boots with incredibly high stiletto heels. Without them — and if her hair were flattened out — she would have been a good deal shorter, but even with these artificial boosts she didn't quite reach five feet. She threw open the back door and leaned in, and I could see that her makeup was thickly layered and heavily accentuated — Kabuki makeup would look subtle in comparison — with coal-black lipstick and fake eyelashes so long they might have been Priscilla's younger sisters sitting on her face. She tossed her luggage into the car (her fingernails were as black as her lipstick), then climbed in after it — and any hope I might have had that this mini-aircraft carrier was at least good company was shattered when she immediately began bitterly complaining about how she'd been waiting for over an hour. Then she produced a flask of red and gave a long gulp, and passed it up to Marco — while shooting me a menacing look with her little black eyes, as though I were an intruder who had better watch my step around her. I got the distinct impression that she hadn't been informed of my part in this journey — just as I hadn't been informed about hers.

Left to my own devices, I started drinking my personal stock of my own Mecacci. The first half hour was agonizing; we listened to "Plasteroid" in total silence, with Amanda's mouth more or less affixed to her bottleneck like a lamprey; though every now and then she'd remember to pass it up to Marco, who in the meantime had devoured an entire head of garlic. I continued to consume my wine as well, but to no avail; not even a Mecacci could dampen the depression and agitation I was feeling, so that eventually even Marco picked up on it.

"Davio, *velax*," he said cajolingly.

I tried to comply. I told myself the situation wasn't really all that bad. And really, it wasn't. If I could just ignore that I was seated next to a mentally disturbed freak who was soon to go on trial for God only knows what kind of crime. And that he had essentially shanghaied me and was taking me against my will to an unknown town dubbed "the poorest in Italy". And that he was driving with a forged license, while carrying marijuana. And that there was a hairy black tarantula in the trunk — and another larger one in the back seat who looked like she'd rather kill me than speak to me. And that we were all speeding along in a completely hazardous wreck of a car whose tires were slick as Parmesan cheese, and whose sputtering, decrepit motor might at any moment burst into a fireball.

Other than that, it wasn't really so bad.

Marco then outlined his plan: We were heading south

towards our final destination, Castel Pagano, about 320 miles away. Ordinarily this would take about seven hours, but after we passed Rome we would be taking a "small" detour to attend a reunion of Les Rockets' fan club, after which we would sleep in the car and recommence driving in the morning, arriving in time for the New Year's Eve celebration — if in fact there were any, considering that the poorest town in Italy might not be able to muster much in the way of a party. Then, on New Year's Day, we would return to Tuscany.

This was the first I was hearing about any Rockets fan club or sleeping in the car, and I wasn't wild about either idea. But at this point the only option open to me was to lift the bottle and take another long swig.

After a few hours of continued silence (broken only by the sounds of "Electric Delight," performed by — who else? — the Rockets), Marco pulled up to an Autogrill and parked, then turned over his shoulder to Amanda, who was extracting something viscous from her nose with her middle finger, and said, "Is evevything all set, Amanda?"

Amanda nodded, and I felt a sudden surge of panic as I had no idea what this "everything" might be. A flurry of possibilities whipped through my mind, including that they would pull nylon stockings over their faces, grab a pair of machine guns from under the seats, and charge into the restaurant, slaughtering the clientele and making off with bags of cash like Bonnie and Clyde. My anxiety increased when Marco took a large duffle bag from the trunk, slung it over his shoulder, and strode up to the Autogrill entrance. Amanda followed him, and I reluctantly did the same, though I decided it best not to make any inquiries; the less I knew, the safer I'd feel. Instead I headed for the counter and ordered a sandwich and a quarter liter of Chianti. Meanwhile Marco and Amanda disappeared into the restroom.

I waited. And waited. I finished my sandwich and ordered more wine. I was feeling the need to go to the bathroom myself when I heard a strange hum of excitement arise, and then just as suddenly the hundreds of travelers in the place all fell silent. Seconds later I saw why.

All eyes were turned towards Marco, who had finally come out of the rest room. His jeans had been replaced by shiny black lycra tights, which were tucked into a pair of varnished-silver high-heel space boots; his intimate parts were covered by tiny silver glittered underwear, while cinched around his waist was a silver holster containing a toy (I hoped) laser gun. His torso was enveloped in a skin-tight black silk jersey, augmented by silver epaulets that curled upwards as in a Japanese space cartoon. Pinned to his back was a shiny silver cape that fell all the way to the floor. But the biggest shock was his head, which was completely shaven (which explained his woolen hat) and *painted silver*. He was, in short, the spitting image of Alain Maratrat, the Rockets' lead singer.

He casually made way through the speechless crowd, as though strolling through an Autogrill with a shaved silver head, a cape and high heels were something he did several times a week. Jaws fell open as he passed, and some people started giggling. I felt ashamed for him, but my larger problem was that *I was with him*. I deftly turned towards the exit and tried to get through the door as quickly as possibly while seeming as indifferent as possible. I would have asked the first truck driver I saw for a lift, never mind what his destination was; but alas Marco and Amanda (who was hot on his four-inch heels) followed me outside.

Amanda was busy fussing with Marco's cape and adjusting his costume; despite this she saw the look of desperation on my face and tried to calm me. This was the first time I heard her put a full sentence together, and I was shocked to hear that she had significant trouble stringing two words together in a way that made any sense at all. It was Marco who now explained to me that it was "novmal" to turn up at a Rockets event dressed this way, and if anyone would be out of place there, it was me.

And so it was. During the last few miles of the drive Marco and Amanda sang "Galactica" at the top of their lungs; I gathered it was the Rockets' biggest hit, but I will be more than content to live the rest of my life without hearing it again. Given their wild singing, crazy high spirits, and Amanda's inability to speak coherently, I started to think that their visit to the Autogrill bathroom hadn't been solely to alter Marco's costume. Probably they'd taken something to alter their mood as well.

Finally we reached the site of the gathering. It was a large, gray concrete building, utterly anonymous, but judging by the numbers of cars in the lot the club must have been pretty popular. As we got closer to the entrance, however, I realized something was wrong; the place was full of middle-aged couples, all of whom were coming *out* of the place as we were trying to make our way *in*.

Suddenly it became apparent that we were in the wrong place. This was no Rockets fan club reunion, but a simple *liscio* dance night for seniors. Marco immediately went to the cashier — startling the crowd as he swept through their ranks, his cape flapping behind him and his silver head gleaming; it's a miracle none of those old people had a coronary. When he reached the counter he placed his fists on his hips and stood with his legs wide apart, like a Marvel Comics superhero, and bellowed, "Vhere are the Vockets fans?"

The somewhat abashed clerk explained that the Rockets event had been cancelled for lack of ticket sales, and that in any case it had been scheduled for the 30th of November, not December; none of which did anything to improve Marco's mood. But before he could protest further a pumped-up security official appeared and strongly suggested we depart the premises. "You're terrorizing our clientele," he said, "and if you don't leave I'll be forced to call for the police."

By this time, however, the people in the lobby no longer seemed terrorized; in fact they'd started to laugh. Clearly this idiot in a space costume prancing around in a huff, must be part of the show — or a silly advertising promotion of some kind. As the chuckles and giggles filtered through to Marco, I could sense that under his layer of paint he was beet red with embarrassment. It was as though he'd turned up for a wedding in a pink rabbit costume; he couldn't have looked more ridiculously out of context.

All we could now was go back to the car and find someplace for Marco to change back to his clothes. A nearby pub served the purpose. While he was in the men's room I found myself for the first time alone with Amanda. I tried to initiate a dialogue; I asked her, now that Marco was out of earshot, if she could see the funny side of the situation, as I certainly could; but my only reward was a tremendous yawn right in my face, without any attempt to try cover her mouth (fortunately she didn't share Marco's affinity for garlic). After several more minutes of equally unsuccessful conversational gambits, I gave up. I'd have better luck talking to an amoeba.

Marco eventually reappeared, back in his street clothes, but his head still covered in paint. He was a bit worried as he hadn't been able to get it off. All we could do now was to find some-place to park the car and sleep; then in the morning we'd seek out a hardware store and buy some solvent.

We weren't anxious to go back out in the cold so we had a few more glasses of wine; then the bar closed and, droopy with exhaustion, we headed back to the car.

Before Marco could retire for the night he had to tend to Priscilla. He opened her habitat and she crawled onto the back of his hand; he fed her a moth (I won't describe her eating it), then cuddled her a while before kissing her goodnight and replacing her delicately in the glass case.

Finally, all was quiet. Marco rested against the steering wheel, Amanda sprawled out across the back, and I curled up in the passenger seat, trying to find the warmest and most comfortable position possible. Amanda removed her boots, and immediately the odor of her damp, fungal feet began competing with the acrid stench of garlic. Fortunately I'd had enough wine to dull all of my senses, smell included, and soon I was fast asleep.

The sun roused me at dawn. Marco was already awake, though Amanda was still snoring; her tiny skirt had ridden up during the night, and it was a bit of a shock to have, as my first sight of the day, her fleshy, hairy legs exposed right up her black pantie line. Certainly it jolted me awake better than even the strongest espresso.

Marco decided it was time for breakfast, so he broke open a new garlic head and munched a few cloves, washed them down with a swig of wine, then leaned back and lit up a joint. His head was still solidly silver, and in the morning sunlight it was some-thing to see.

He then checked to see that Priscilla was all right; then, without saying a word he turned the key in the ignition, shifted into gear, and set off.

In the light of day I could see that we were in a squalid indus-trial sector, God only knows where — somewhere on the far outskirts of Rome, was all I knew for certain. After having dri-ven around the area a while we found a hardware store that was just opening, and Marco sent me in to purchase a bottle of tur-pentine — which he then actually poured over his head, with the help of the newly awakened Amanda. The paint dutifully dissolved, but half the container's contents soaked into clothes, triggering some kind of reaction that made his skin go rash all

over. Also, need I add that we now had the pungent sting of tur-
pentine to add to our medley of foul aromas?

The drive proceeded unremarkably for a while longer, but
when we reached Montecassino the inevitable finally occurred.
Dense, black smoke began to seep through the hood of the car,
and the engine began to shudder and to jerk. Marco beat his
fists on the steering wheel and shouted, "Jesus Chvist!"

He pulled off the road to the emergency lane. We all disem-
barked.

End of the tour.

Marco and Amanda fell into an immediate quarrel, hurling
abusive phrases at each other and even occasionally descending into a shoving match. Meanwhile, each car that zipped past
formed an air pocket that made the flimsy Renault rock gently
back and forth, giving it a deceptive semblance of life. I stood
to one side, observing the whole mad sad scene beneath a
cloud-choked gray sky.

Suddenly I felt an urgent need to withdraw from this farce,
so I jumped over the guardrail and went in search of a bush
behind which I could hide myself. When I found one, I
crouched down and had a brief spate of angry, frustrated tears,
and cursed myself for so passively allowing Marco to corral me
into this disastrously stupid adventure.

As I was returning, I noticed a flashing blue light and so
ducked down behind another bush and peered out at the scene.
The highway patrol had arrived, and as I watched, my two idiot
traveling companions were shoved inside the squad car and driven away, leaving the Renault in the company of an agent who
had apparently remained behind to guard it.

I felt the onset of panic: my rucksack was still in that car! But
after mentally taking stock I realized there was nothing in it that I
truly needed. My identification and cash were safely tucked in my
inner pocket. Maybe this was the best thing that could have happened to me. All I needed to do was trek across the fields; sooner or
later I would reach a town, and with a bit of luck a train station, and
I could return home. I thanked Providence for giving me my nervous attack at exactly the right moment. I set off on my journey.

About twenty minutes later it started to rain and the field
became a muddy swamp. With each step I took, I sank further
into the slime. Still, I had freed myself from those two halfwits,
and this was enough to hearten me.

Finally I did indeed come upon a small village, and even better, it had a small railway station. As I walked through the streets, kids were already out of doors, exploding bangers and cherry bombs, their enthusiasm apparently too great to wait for evening, or even late afternoon. I smiled as I passed happy families leaving the stores with bags full of *cotechino* (a large, stuffed, minced-pork sausage), lentils, bottles of *spumante*, and all the other goodies people traditionally consume on the night of Saint Sylvester. The streets were alive with colorful banners wishing onlookers a Happy 1988, and a group of workers was setting up a small stage on which, I gathered, there would be some kind of performance before the midnight countdown. There was a sense of collective euphoria in the air, its spirit was infectious; my step was brisk and cheerful as I entered the small station. The teller put down the pink daily sports paper he was studying to serve me.

"Siena," I instructed him.

He issued me the ticket and explained the various changes and connections I needed to make.

I had a bit of time before the departure so I went out for something to eat, and entered the first *osteria* I came across. As I was in Lazio, I ordered a pasta *con la pajata* (served with the intestines of a suckling veal) and a liter of wine from the Roman castles.

I thought about Marco and Amanda and wondered what their fates had been, and whether the forged license or the marijuana had been the cause of their arrest. Either way, I thought it possible that the police might turn a blind eye to the offense because it was a holiday, and release them with a warning. As for the car, I was sure it was definitely kaput and destined for the auto graveyard.

I paid my bill and returned to the station in good time for the train to Rome, and just as easily made my connection to Chiusi. I always like traveling by train; I like the regular, monotonous cadence; it relaxes me. In fact, as is often the case, the rhythm gently soothed me to sleep.

When I opened my eyes I had a very pleasant surprise, as I was no longer alone but sitting across from a splendid young girl. We darted a few furtive glances at each other until I broke the ice and introduced myself.

Her name was Caterina. Not a beauty, exactly, but she had an indefinable quality about her. Her hair was bobbed with a nice fringe suspended above two lively hazel eyes, which in a certain light seemed to hint at melancholy; I found this frightfully attractive. She wore a pink turtleneck angora sweater, irresistibly feminine.

We started talking. She told me she was on her way to see her family; then I related my entire misadventure, telling her all about Marco, Amanda, even Priscilla. She listened attentively, giggling every now and then, while the landscape flowed past us. Soon we were out of Lazio and into Umbria; Tuscany would be next.

Before she could tell me more about her, I asked if I could get her something to drink, and she accepted. I took some cash from my jacket where it hung on a hook, opened the sliding door, and proceeded up the corridor. In the compartment adjacent to ours there was a nun reading the Vatican newspaper, but after that the train appeared to be almost completely deserted. I had to wonder why a young girl like Caterina had chosen my compartment rather than one she could have had all to herself. Possibly she was afraid to be alone; but I was sleeping when she came in, so I was scarcely good company. Also, my jeans and boots were covered in mud and I was scruffy and unshaven; one might think I'd be exactly the type she'd be afraid of.

The train stopped briefly at a station while I was choosing a bottle of Bardolino at the bar. I asked for a couple of plastic glasses and headed back. On the way, I encountered a very large ticket inspector striding up the aisle, wearing the typical worn-out uniform with the FS badge stitched on the jacket pocket and the plastic cap, and like all ticket inspectors on the Italian railway in the 1980s, he sported a thick black moustache. He had an annoyed look on his face, as would anyone compelled to work on New Year's Eve, and he asked to see my ticket. I explained it was in the compartment with my "girlfriend." He told me to go on ahead and followed me; we passed through a few cars until I once again saw the nun who was my point of reference — and so in the next compartment I should have found Caterina. Instead I was in for a terrible surprise: both Caterina and my jacket were gone. She had evidently stolen it and skipped the train at the last station.

As if prompted by my sudden black mood, the train now entered a tunnel and the noise level rose to a truly sinister racket; a moment later the lights went on automatically. I felt the urge to smash everything in sheer rage.

I faced the ticket inspector, who was staring at me very dubiously, but because of the din I had trouble making him understand what had happened, until the train exited the tunnel and I could be heard again. His doubtful look did not alter. To prove I wasn't making up the story I waved the two plastic glasses before him. "I wouldn't have brought back two glasses if I were drinking alone," I said desperately.

He raised his cap and curled the tips of his moustache thoughtfully, then said in a very pronounced Roman accent, "Because its New Year's Eve I'll be magnanimous and spare you a fine. But you must disembark at the next station."

I tried to protest but it was hopeless; he didn't believe my story. When the train stopped in Orvieto I again pleaded with him, but he threatened to call the police. I tried to dart away but he got hold of me by the collar, dragged me to the door, and threw me out on the concrete platform. Fortunately I landed on my feet and managed to save the bottle.

The doors closed and all I could do was stand aside as the train departed with a whistle. I watched as each car slowly passed in front of me — and then I spotted through the window *another* nun reading a newspaper. And in the following compartment, there was Caterina, staring at me with her mouth agape — and my jacket hanging on the hook just beyond her!

What were the chances of there being *two* damned nuns on a nearly empty train? I cursed myself for not having noticed the second one earlier, but reasoned that she'd probably got on while I was buying the wine.

I watched as the train picked up speed and finally receded into the distance, and a faint "Caterina" escaped my lips, accompanied by a single bitter tear. I stood alone on the platform for a few moments longer, my face twisted by self-loathing and regret, the bottle of wine still gripped in my hand. I must have looked like an idiot.

All I could do was buy another ticket — fortunately I had just enough cash left over to cover it — and drink the Bardolino all by myself, because *contro i pensieri un gran rimedio è il bicchiere* ("To unburden your thoughts a great remedy is the glass") — but alas it didn't work because *il dolore profondo è quello che il vino non colma* ("Profound pain is that which wine cannot ease"). And need I add, without my jacket, I was quaking in the cold.

I got home close to midnight. I went straight to bed and

thought about Caterina, I couldn't get her out of my mind; how true it was that *il vino e le donne fanno perdere la testa* ("Wine and women make you lose your mind"). I wondered if I'd ever see her again. If only I'd left some identification in the jacket she might have been able to track me down. I hoped at least she'd gotten the story from the ticket inspector and wouldn't spend the rest of her life wondering why I'd apparently fled her.

While I cursed New Year's Eve and whoever invented it, outside the window I saw the first bursts of fireworks over the villages and scattered around Chianti. "Happy 1998, Dario," I uttered sarcastically; then I buried myself under the covers and hoped to find at least some measure of forgetfulness there.

ᔕ

I read the story through a couple of times and am quite satisfied; it needs only a few touches. It's a job well done, which of course means it's time for a *self-brindisi*.

After toasting myself I send the story to Mia, then head upstairs for the night. I lie on the bed with the lights off, gazing out at the sky. The stars are hidden by thick clouds, and further obscured from me by the light rain whose drops streak the glass of my windows. Minutes later, lulled by the soft patter of the rainfall, I am fast asleep.

23

THE POOLIO

From: Mia Lane
To: Dario Castagno
Subject: Re: Crappy New Year

Dear Dario,
Thank you for the chapter on your worst New Year's Eve. I think it needs to be revised a bit since, as you antici-pated, it does tilt slightly away from the original theme — though only slightly, as the characters are as ever pic-turesque and wine does play a pivotal role. (Which reminds me, I have to ask, where the hell do you put all that vino? You're just a normal-sized human being, to judge by your author photo.)
Did you ever encounter Marco and Amanda again? I can't help wondering what they may be up to now. You know as well as I do that *la curiosità è femmina* (curiosity is female), don't you? See, you're not the only one who can drop Italian quotes; that's one from my grandmother, who was originally from Puglia. Alas she's my only ancestral thread to your country; but at least you now know that I have *some* Italian blood running through my veins.
I must sign off now as I'm looking at an extremely busy day. Speaking of which, thank you for contacting your manager about our project; she emailed me afterwards. She seems very sweet and is not by any means upset with you; at least that's the impression I get.
By the way, I finished my first bottle of your oil yester-day. I will have to ration the second, otherwise it won't make Christmas dinner and that would be a shame.
Finally, a request: I'd like to read something sooner or later that includes the Palio; I'm sure you have plenty to share on the subject.

Ciao, my friend
Mia

From: Dario Castagno
To: Mia Lane
Subject: Re: Crappy New Year

Dear Mia,

Ciao! You wonder where I put all that wine? . . .
Sometimes I ask myself the same question. But I simply
do as I'm obliged — like we say over here, *il vino è metà
nutrimento* ("Wine is half nutrition").

I'm happy to learn something more about you and that
you have some Southern Italian roots. By chance do you
have a black moustache as well? Kidding, kidding —
actually southern Italian women are well known for
their Mediterranean beauty.

I went back through the chapter I sent you yesterday and
found myself laughing out loud. I'm always surprised,
whenever I read what I've set down a day later, to realize
that I actually possess a style, and that I can tell a story
not just coherently but with some spirit. I do think an
appreciative audience helps bring that out – so I must
thank you, Mia.

I never saw or heard of Amanda again. I think at the time
she was just studying in Siena and probably ended up
returning to her hometown. Marco however continued to
pester me until he came up with the bizarre idea to go and
pick apples in Israel; I haven't seen him since, though I
have read about his pranks in the local paper. Once he
was arrested for somehow rigging his phone line so that
it tapped into his neighbors' line; they became suspicious
when they started receiving astronomical bills.
Apparently he spent hours chatting on a hard-core sex
line. His mental health worsened after that, and I read
that he was arrested in Florence for preaching to the
winds in a public square while completely naked. He was
locked up in a hospital and for all I know remains there.
In his way Marco was a misunderstood genius; a bit
crazy, certainly, but on the whole innocuous.

Regarding the Palio: well, Mia, right next to where I'm
sitting the Caterpillar flag is unfurled, with its simple yet
elegant crowned Caterpillar against a yellow and green
background bordered with blue. The colors are faded

but that is actually a good sign; it means that recently we've won often — which entitled me to keep the flag waving on the pole outside on the terrace.

I do have many stories regarding my Palio experiences that I would love to share with you, but I think it best to do so in a future book entirely dedicated to that amazing, passionate event. Everyone lives the feast in an extremely intimate and personal manner — so personal that never does one citizen's recounting of a race tally with anyone else's, no matter if they are from rival districts or members in the same one.

I might, however, have a couple of Palio episodes that fit the theme of our project. Maybe subconsciously I was waiting for you to broach the subject. When you wake up tomorrow you'll find something waiting in your in-box. I promise.

Yours
Dario

I decide to go out and buy a special bottle of good wine for lunch, because *la vita è troppo breve per bere del vino cattivo* ("Life is too short to drink bad wine") — and also to keep me company while I write. But before heading out to the store I do raise a single toast of Mecacci in honor of the Noble *contrada* of the Caterpillar.

I return with a bottle of Chianti Classico Volpaia. While enjoying my plate of spaghetti carbonara, I think of the words of Brillat-Savarin: *Un pasto senza vino è come un giorno senza sole, un giardino senza fiori* ("A meal without wine is like a day without sunshine, a garden without flowers"). Certainly I agree with him and also agree with whoever stated that *il vino è la parte intelettuale del pranzo ("Wine is the intellectual part of the meal")*

After lunch I sit down and check my old journal to find out exactly what day it was when I met those crazy, fun-loving people from Wisconsin.

෨

The 16th of June, 2002. The sun was intensely blue, with nothing cool about it, and indeed we were in the grip of an unusual and unrelenting heat spell. Not a breath of fresh air disturbed the parched, suffering trees.

185

I was driving through the arid hills south of Siena, better known as "Le Crete." Everything around me was immobile, almost asleep, as if suspended in time — or quietly holding its breath for the end of the dog days and the return of rainfall to restore the country's natural rhythms.

At lunch I had cooked myself a bream *all' acqua pazza* (literally, "crazy water"), which is a recipe consisting principally of tomato and white wine. I only use white wine for cooking because I believe in the saying *Chi beve il bianco è vicino al pianto che beve rosso ha la gioia addosso* ("He who drinks white is near to tears, he who drinks red is close to joy"), and in fact I paired the soup with a light Chianti that was now swashing and swishing in my stomach on the bumpy road.

I was on board my little Subaru van which lacked air conditioning, and the open windows sucked in a mix of warm air and dust from the white road. I was heading for an old renovated farmhouse that had been rented by five American couples who had read my book and wanted to meet me personally, especially requesting that I lecture them on the Palio of Siena. I agreed, as I always enjoyed meeting people whose interest was sparked by my book.

When they sent me directions to the place they were staying, I recognized it as a place I knew from my teenage years. I was looking forward seeing it after all this time, as I hadn't laid eyes on it since the early 80s, when my friends and I would spend our spare time scouring the countryside for abandoned houses on our mopeds and Vespas. I recalled that we had only visited this particular house once, because it too tumbledown and dangerous to host one of our big feasts; the very paving threatened to cave in. And besides, the surroundings were too bleak and deserted; we always preferred the more lush landscapes of the Chianti hills to the lunar-like landscapes of the Crete. Suddenly a memory flashed to my mind, of Giorgio quipping in his pronounced Tuscan accent that the place was so isolated even the Jehovah's Witnesses would have trouble reaching it.

I'd been on the road just twenty minutes and the dashboard was completely covered in dust. The national radio was broadcasting coverage of the Alpine stage of the Tour de France and the announcer was delivering an update on the umpteenth achievement of the legendary cyclist Marco Pantani, who had left the rest of the competitors far behind and was on a solitary flight. His voice was rather metallic, as he was reporting from the passenger seat of a motorbike.

Minutes later I listened as Pantani arrived at the finish line, arms upraised, and almost simultaneously the farmhouse appeared on the peak of the hill. It seemed I also had reached my own winning post, and like the legendary Pantani I was drenched in sweat, even though my endeavor compared to his superhuman feat was next to nothing.

I took the turning and started up the road to the estate, now lined on both sides by cypress trees — young ones, that would still need many more years before becoming the splendid, towering icons that ennoble so many of our roads, and which distinguish Tuscany so particularly. At this stage they were only minuscule, half-dried shrubs; I could almost hear them imploring for water.

The gate was wide open and I parked on the gravel drive next to five Mercedes that were identical both in color and model. As I approached the colonial house I could tell it had been very recently restored; even the stone walls had been sandblasted back to their original splendor.

The heat was nigh on unbearable, and the sun beat so cruelly on my head that when I ran my fingers through my hair I almost scalded them. It was indeed a torrid, scorching summer. I imagined the headlines on display at the newsagents the following day; they would be all about the fierce temperatures. And if someone happened to die the phrase "killer heat" was inevitable, even if the victim were a ninety-year-old cardiopath who probably would have died soon anyway. I also anticipated the usual common sense, if not ridiculously obvious, safety tips provided by medical luminaries: stay inside during the hottest hours, eat fruit and vegetables, drink water, don't drink alcohol.

I thought about my friend *Dottor* Becchini, who would have strongly disagreed on the last point. As he was fond of saying: *Bevi, morrai! Non bevi? Morrai lo stesso! Perciò bevi* ("Drink and you will die. Don't drink? You'll still die. So you might as well drink!") — and let me just add a quote from Charles Baudelaire: "He who only drinks water has something to hide."

When I reached the entrance silence was sovereign. The front door, carved from expensive chestnut, hung wide open, and I poked my head inside and said, "Hello!" There was no reply, nor could I hear any sign of life within; but as I was expected I felt authorized to enter.

The living-room was well furnished with hardwood furniture, and the old fireplace where once I had roasted chestnuts with my friends had been rebuilt with care. It was difficult to find, in this luxurious country villa, any trace of the rundown ruin of my memory.

There were several filmy glasses left haphazardly on the table, and I counted half a dozen empty bottles that had apparently been recently consumed. I was once again on the point of calling out for someone, when I noticed a sofa with its back turned to me; reclining on its headrest was a mane of bushy silver hair. I crossed the room and placed myself on the opposite side and found myself looking down at a very large man, his body glabrous and pink, fast asleep with his mouth hanging open.

"Mr. Jameson?" I said, raising my voice slightly.

The man sputtered awake, then looked at me with an alarmed expression. I immediately calmed his anxiety by extending my hand and introducing myself. When he realized who I was, his face lit up with a large smile. He got to his feet and accepted my handshake with an energetic squeeze. I was slightly alarmed at this sudden lunge in my direction, because he appeared to be completely naked; but I quickly realized that his intimate parts were tucked into an almost microscopic Speedo swimsuit that had previously been hidden beneath his lolling, hairless stomach.

"Pete," he corrected me as he filled two glasses of wine, handing me one without inquiring whether I wanted it or not. "Call me Pete." He told me that everyone in his party was dying to meet me, and that the "troops" awaited us around the pool. With a wink he invited me to follow him, and when he turned I was shocked to see that his fleshy hind parts were almost completely revealed. The only nod to decency was a tiny patch of fabric stretched over his sphincter. I had seen many more attractive sights in my life. What made the whole effect even more disturbing was that his face reminded me uncannily of Pope John XXIII.

We went down a short flight of terracotta steps, each adorned by a pot of lavender that emitted an intense perfume and was, perhaps for this reason, swarmed by a startling variety of insects. I decided it best to focus on these lovely vases because the only other available option was Pete's gelatinous buttocks bouncing merrily before me.

The other members of the party were napping lazily under linen beach umbrellas, their bodies sunken into what were obviously very comfortable deck chairs, and sipping wine from bottles they kept chilling in ice buckets. When we were halfway down the steps Pete sang out, *"Look whoooo's heeere!"* Suddenly the entire party raised their heads, like a bunch of high-school kids copying papers during an exam. One woman promptly deposited her wine glass on the side table and managed in a nanosecond to touch up her face, deftly daubing a radioactively bright pink lipstick across her mouth and adjusting her hair with a rapid flick of her hand, after which she leapt up and cantered towards me with open arms. She sported a black bikini, but her panties, unlike Pete's, were very ample and actually covered her navel; on seeing them together my first thought was that maybe by mistake they had put on each other's swimwear.

"My wife Kim," Pete said, endorsing my theory of the swap.

Kim reminded me of the English actress Patricia Hayes; she embraced me, then kissed me on my cheek, thus gifting me with a good smear of the makeup she'd only just applied, as well as tinting my white shirt with her carroty sunscreen.

"Derrrrrrio, oh *Derrrrrrio,"* she trilled as though I were a new puppy who'd just been delivered into her care, "you are *so* cute, *much* better in real life than on that TV show." Her eyes actually welled with emotion, and she continued praising me while holding me in her vice-like grip. "Derrrrrrio, your book made me laugh *so* much, did you *really* experience all those crazy people?"

When I assured her I had — no, really, I honestly *had* — she finally let go of me. I did my best to keep a smile on my face after this rather unexpected assault. Like her husband, Kim was also rather puffy and had the same pleasant, friendly appearance. I began to relax; she was clearly harmless . . . or mostly so. She passed me a glass of frozen wine and proposed a toast to all the other guests who had now gathered around me.

After the toast I shook hands with a middle-age man who somewhat resembled Elvis Presley; but more of the late, bloated, dissolute Elvis. In fact, more like Elvis ten minutes after he died. His wife, for her part, looked like Brigitte Bardot . . . as she is today.

The third couple, also middle-aged, comprised a character who reminded me of a grizzled Clark Kent, with big black-framed reading glasses and a muscular, athletic body; and his wife, a minute woman with tiny bones and an extremely wrinkled face. She was the only female wearing a full swimsuit, festooned with big textured flowers. She somewhat resembled Goldie Hawn, if Goldie Hawn had spent about sixty or seventy years sun tanning; you might call her Oldie Hawn. But I must admit she did have a certain charm.

As usual, once I got into this mental game of finding celebrity resemblances, I couldn't let it go; so the fourth couple, I decided, were the spitting image of the secretary of a national workers' union (clearly I was stretching my definition of "celebrity" here), and a sort of Sigourney Weaver type with a more pronounced lower jaw — so much so that when it rained it must have caused her some problems.

The fifth and final couple were also extremely friendly, but despite my best efforts I couldn't compare the husband to anyone famous; and the best I could do for his wife was that she appeared to be a female version of my postwoman — yes, the female version, as my postwoman is almost entirely masculine. In fact, if she hadn't born both a female name and something roughly approximating breasts, I'd never have guessed her sex; the rest of her looked exactly like a stevedore from the Livorno dockyards. (Certainly she drank grappa like a stevedore; I know because I once offered her a glass. She downed it like mineral water, so I offered her a second, to the same effect, and then a third. After her fourth shot I just handed her the bottle to save time.)

The irony, of course, is that while I was trying to pin celebrity look-alikes on each of my new acquaintances, they were treating me like a genuine celebrity. I do occasionally find myself being fawned over in this way, almost always by Americans, and while it's certainly a gratifying sensation I never let it go to my head; this has allowed me to remain my own simple self over the years. But it was fun to indulge it on this occasion, with these lively Wisconsonites flashing cameras at me and continually refilling my glass and asking me question after question and laughing eagerly at all my silly puns. But I had, after all, been paid to be there and so at a certain point I decided to earn my wage; I invited them to move to the living room, where I would give my usual Palio lecture followed by a viewing of the video I had prepared for such occasions.

Minutes later I was speaking before my little audience, who paid as much attention as they could while continuing to pop open bottles, first red, then white. Inevitably, due to the effects of the alcohol and maybe also to my words, which had begun to slur a bit thanks to the amount of wine I myself had consumed, I realized they weren't really comprehending the complicated rules of the Palio. I tried to be more explicit, but slowly, inexorably, their eyelids began to droop; some of the hardier of the bunch (the grizzled Clark Kent look-alike, for one) tried heroically to snap them open, but after just a few seconds they began to fall again. I thought of inserting the video to regain their attention; but that would require turning the lights off, and that would just conk them out definitively. I needed some alternative plan, and I needed it fast, because my audience was dropping like flies . . .

Then it struck me. Maybe it was my native genius, maybe the inspiration of the wine; but I decided that my clients would learn about the Palio by racing it themselves. *That* would get their blood flowing. There were ten of them — perfect, the exact number of horses that participate in each race. It would be one Wisconsonite for each *contrada*.

But . . . *where* would we race? Around the pool seemed the most logical. I clapped my hands abruptly to bring them back to life, then asked for a sheet of paper that I tore into ten pieces. On each scrap I scribbled the name of whatever *contrada* came to mind. When I'd finished, I had the following:

Caterpillar . . . .my own *contrada*
Giraffe . . . . . . .it had once been our enemy
Tower . . . . .our ally
Goose . . . . .the enemy of our ally
Turtle . . . . .they had just won the last Palio
Snail . . . . .the enemy of the Turtle
Owl . . . . .the *contrada* of my ex-girlfriend
Unicorn . . . . . .the enemy of the Owl
She-Wolf . . . . .my ex-ex-girlfriend's *contrada*
Porcupine . . . .the enemy of the She-Wolf and our ally

To make it all more realistic, I took down the picture of the Madonna that hung on the stone wall and announced that this would be the Palio, the prize the winner would triumphantly claim.

Fortunately my clients seemed to find the idea exciting. They all stood up, shook themselves awake again, and anxiously retreated back outside, everybody armed with a bottle of wine. I took up the rear — rather literally, since once again I had Pete's enormous, buttery buttocks preceding me.

At the poolside, I took an empty glass and put the folded pieces of paper inside it, then gave it a shake and emptied it on a marble tabletop. I then invited each of my clients to take one of the slips, unfold it, and then read aloud which district they would be representing.

The female version of my postwoman unwrapped hers first; she had drawn the Tower. Then Pete — a.k.a. Pope Speedo XXIII — opened his (with difficulty due to his large fingers) and revealed the Turtle. Dead Elvis chose the Caterpillar, Patricia Hayes the Unicorn, Oldie Hawn the Snail, the former union leader the Porcupine, Sigourney Weaver the Giraffe, Clark Kent the Goose, Brigitte Bardot the She-Wolf . . . and last but not least Mr. Nobody, the man whose drab, ordinary features kindled no comparison of any kind, the Owl.

There were howls of excitement at each draw. Then I explained that the prize would go to the first contestant to complete three laps around the pool — and what's more, it was permissible and even advisable to obstruct and interfere with your competitors, to the point of pushing and shoving.

Now they really were getting the sense of the entire Sienese tradition. They started laughing like little children who had just been taught a new game — a game that actually rewarded cheating!

Before starting, they opened a bottle of Brunello Poggio Antico for good luck. While we were gulping down the wine I observed them with a keen eye, and thought how in the ordinary run of things they would never have allowed themselves to be involved in such foolery. But since they were on vacation in these desolate lands of the Crete, so far from home and their more buttoned-up, professional lives, they allowed themselves to let their hair down and be more than slightly ridiculous. And in my opinion there is absolutely nothing wrong with that.

Once again I drew lots, as in a real Palio, to see who was placed next to whom on the starting line — who would get the coveted inside track, and who would be the even more coveted final draw. When they were all thus lined next to each other, I purposely provoked them into jabbing and shoving each other, and explained that the race would commence only when the tenth in line decided to start. This place had fallen to the former union leader and he did a good job of it, because he purposely held back from making his approach, upsetting his friends who were literally pawing the ground in eagerness to get going.

Then, just as in a real Palio, off he went, without warning — and taking everybody else by surprise, so that they all came bursting forth at once. In the first lap Mr. Nobody took the lead followed by the Oldie Hawn, with Dead Elvis in third — followed by my postwoman, the former union leader neck-and-neck with Sigourney Weaver, Brigitte Bardot, Pope Speedo, Clark Kent, and in last place Patricia Hayes — who was perhaps slowed down by having to run in swimming trunks that were too big for her.

On the second lap the rumpus occurred; my postwoman (Tower) cut the turn and crashed against Elvis (Caterpillar), who in turn tripped and fell against Oldie Hawn (Snail), and all three fell with a heavy splash into the pool. Then Brigitte Bardot (She-Wolf) gave up because she stubbed her bare foot on the concrete base of the umbrella stand (I've never said the Palio wasn't perilous), leaving the field to Clark Kent (Goose), the former union leader (Porcupine), and Mr. Nobody (Owl), all of whom easily outdistanced Sigourney Weaver (Giraffe), Pope Speedo (Turtle) and poor Patricia Hayes (Unicorn) who now trudged far behind, dead last.

On the third and final lap it seemed it as though it was all between the Porcupine and the Goose, but the former union leader raised his elbow threateningly and Clark Kent responded by grabbing his waist, which allowed Mr. Nobody to sail ahead of them, going from third place into first and then right past the finish line with his arms waving triumphantly over his head. The Owl had won!

He grabbed the picture of the Madonna and made a victory lap around the pool, acknowledging the good-natured applause of his defeated friends. Despite a few abrasions and scratches, everyone was laughing, smiling, and panting from exertion; and when they caught their breath, to my amazement, they grabbed me and threw me, fully dressed, into the pool, then jumped in after me. We splashed about and sprayed each other mercilessly, like toddlers in a wading pool. Then the female version of my postwoman opened yet another bottle of Brunello and we drank it directly from the bottle, passing it around.

We continued chatting and laughing and reliving the "Poolio," as we had christened it, until we realized that dawn was drawing nigh. We couldn't believe it when Oldie Hawn pulled her watch from her purse and announced that it was 5:17 — and they had a plane to catch in Rome.

Suddenly the party was over — and their vacation as well. In a few hours they would be boarding a jumbo jet and returning to their daily lives, resuming the roles that society demanded of them, the physician, the professor, the lawyer, the judge.

They hastily pulled themselves together, threw on some clothes, and wheeled their luggage out the front door; I accompanied them to their car, all of us drooping and swaying both from exhaustion and from the effects of all that wine. We said a hasty but warm goodbye, and they insisted I remain at the villa and have a nap, as they were rightly worried about my blood-alcohol level. I reassured them I was fine and would have no problems getting home.

As soon as I began walking towards my van, though, I realized that I was indeed quite drunk; my head was spinning like a top. I turned on the radio and made a conscious effort to concentrate on the drive and keep the car moving in a straight line. The sky was now welcoming the crimson sun that was rising up from behind the mountains, and suddenly I noticed a flock of sheep crossing the road ahead of me and slammed on the brake in time to avoid making their acquaintance far too forcefully.

The wool of the docile flock, under the first fiery rays of the sun, had assumed a suggestive pinkish color. The Sardinian shepherd who drove them was small and dark, his features hard and grim and his cheekbones hollow. Over his shoulder he carried a leather sack with a flask of wine tied to its extremity. He was taking advantage of the comparatively fresh early morning temperatures to graze his charges on the grasslands, accompanied by three proud-looking Maremmano sheepdogs. As I sat staring at him, waiting for my heartbeat to return to normal, he made a slight nod in my direction which I returned.

When he had gone I shifted into first gear and drove on as the sunlight gathered strength. The radio began broadcasting Vivaldi's Four Seasons; I couldn't have asked for a better soundtrack.

Now the road descended with hairpin turns to the bottom of the valley, and in the distance I saw the church bell of what in my opinion is one of the most spiritual monuments in all Tuscany, the Abbey of Sant' Antimo, a masterpiece built some 1,200 years ago. Each time I stand in its presence it produces in me such strong and stirring emotions. Perhaps it was the beautiful daybreak, or maybe the lingering effects of wine and weariness, but it appeared almost more beautiful than ever. Sant' Antimo is one of a very select number of structures that manage to generate in me the kind of feelings only nature has ever regularly supplied me with.

A light early mist remained suspended a few inches above the ground, just enough to cover the grass; and I stared in awe at the stupendous, ancient olive trees surrounding the property in untidy formation, their wayward branches following no logical line. Then I realized I was drunk indeed, because Sant' Antimo was in the exact opposite direction of my home. I had taken the wrong road — or maybe, I thought, trying to convince myself, my unconscious had deliberately directed me here to this ethereal site. Despite not being a Christian, when I enter this valley and observe this church in its serene alabaster and granite glory — it is said that Charlemagne had ordered the church to be built and that it had been constructed overnight by fairies — I lapse into a strange mystical state. Many of my clients in the past have been similarly affected, some to the point of suffering sudden sweats, tremors, and even panic attacks when they passed the threshold.

On the whole I was happy to find myself there, despite a terrible headache and a longing for my bed. I parked the car beneath a cypress tree and climbed out onto the grounds. The sky was once again cloudless and it looked like the day would be another scorcher. I walked in the desolate valley; the mist was melting now, dissipating beneath my feet and revealing blades of grass covered in thousands of tiny cobwebs, all dripping with dew and glittering with the kiss of the sun.

I chose the shade of an olive tree to sit and rested my back against its trunk. With my gaze fixed on the splendid abbey I drifted into a doze. My sleep, though, didn't last long, as I was awakened by the plangent chime of the bells cleaving through the air. I opened my eyes in time to spot three monks clad in white come out of an oak forest in the distance and approach the church.

I decided to enter and I took a seat on the wooden bench closest to the altar. Seven monks now entered from a side door in single file. The first was surely the abbot, for he was very old; he was followed by six much younger monks. The third in line reminded me of John Belushi, but as soon as this thought entered my head I gave myself a little kick and said to myself, "Enough of that, Dario." The monks bowed before the altar and then divided into two groups of four, each filling a bench on either side of the altar, facing each other.

The abbot gave a knock on the bench to signal the beginning of the "Lodi" prayers, and a young monk stood up and intoned a Gregorian chant with a truly celestial voice, which thanks to the marvelous acoustics spread all around the church and into every hidden gorge. I felt honored to be the only spectator. The voice insinuated itself into the apse that, as in all Romanesque churches, faces Jerusalem; then it bounced off the alabaster columns, resounded through the three naves, skimmed the crypt where it is believed Saint Antimo himself is buried, and finally dispersed in the high vaulted ceiling. When he finished his prayer, the young priest sat back down on the bench and his brother across from him stood up and in the same algid voice, but with a smoother tonality, began reciting his verses. I got goosebumps when they all joined in the chorus, and couldn't prevent a few tears from trickling down my cheeks.

The sun, by now well in command of the morning, boldly sent its shafts through the full-length windows, illuminating the serene faces of the choir, making them look even more harmonious — in peace with themselves and with the God they so artfully worshipped; and in that moment I envied them and the life they led.

Minutes later it was all over; the abbot signaled the end of the vespers with another knock on the bench, and again they bowed at the altar before departing in as profound a silence as when they had entered, through the same tiny side door. And with that I was alone in the church.

I got up and walked down the aisle, each footstep echoing in that vast quiet until I was once again outside, where I was welcomed by storms of swallows diving into the valley, scooping up insects for breakfast. The sight of those greedy, gobbling birds reminded me that I myself had yet to break my fast; it was just after seven, so I drove back to my village, where I ordered up a cappuccino and a freshly baked bun from a local bar, after which I planned to spend some time nursing my hangover by sunbathing along the river Farma.

At the bar I met *Maresciallo* Iuzzolino, in uniform and swallowing a quick espresso before going on patrol. He ran his hand over his hair and lit a cigarette, through lips stained black by Arabic coffee he said, in a friendly enough tone, "Dario what an early bird you are today! If I didn't know better I'd suspect you've never even been to bed. Remember how you'd stay out all night with your friends and get into a dozen different kinds of trouble?"

"Eh, dear *Maresciallo*, don't remind me. What a freak I was then; how could I forget?" I dared not tell him how close to the mark his old suspicions would be, today.

The experience of the Poolio on that boiling summer night inspired me to propose it on several other occasions, when I happened to give my presentation in the vicinity of a swimming pool; but it never turned out as successfully as the first time. That, indeed, was a Poolio for the ages.

೮೨

I'm satisfied with the chapter, so I light the fire and grill up two chicken drumsticks, which I accompany with a radicchio salad dressed with abundant vinegar and a bottle of Santa Cristina Antinori. I finish the bottle without hurry, taking only small, appreciative sips, then fall asleep on the sofa watching the glowing embers wink and sizzle in the hearth. *Buon fuoco e buon vino mi scalda il mio camino* (Fine flames and fine wine warm up my hearth)

24

REQUIEM

For Andrea and me, the 4th of December has a particular significance, and now that the day has arrived I know it's only a matter of time before I hear from him. In the meantime, I replace the bed-settee to where I pulled it out the night before, only managing on the fourth attempt and as always nearly amputating my phalanges.

I decide not to check my e-mail; I don't have enough time to respond to it, because I'll be spending all day in my friend's company. Instead I water the plants in the terracotta vases scattered around the house, removing the yellow leaves from the ficus that's grown so much in the last year that it would no longer fit through the door should I ever desire to move it out.

The sky is grim and threatens rain, with one particularly unattractive black cloud suspended low over the vicinity and looking just about ready to burst. Despite this menace I feel the need for a run, and after having checked the time I realize it's feasible. I choose a more level, less demanding route than my usual hilly path, one that winds through the vines of the Borgo Scopeto estate. My choice is also determined by the fact that the forests I usually run through this morning echo with the sounds of barking dogs and rifle reports, indicating a boar hunt in progress — and I have no intention of finding myself anywhere near the crosshairs of a rifle. All it would take is one careless trigger finger and I'd end up being served in a casserole in some local restaurant.

I take my portable phone with me, inserting it in a money belt I tie firmly to my waist. And with that, I'm off and running — literally.

As I predicted, it does rain, but I continue at my regular pace, getting back to my village just shy of nine o'clock, completely soaked by the contents of the big black cloud, which seems to have followed me exclusively throughout my run.

At nine sharp my phone starts to ring, as I knew it would. I flip it open and without waiting for a greeting say, "Same place, same time?"

"Yes, old boy," Andrea replies, "same place, same time."

Before going home for a shower I stop at the bar for a hot *orzo*, and as usual Giulio is there, contracted and cramped on his trusty walking stick and drinking a big goblet of red. Out of courtesy I greet him, not expecting any response, and unexpectedly he smiles at me, revealing all of his gold-capped teeth, and observes that my sweat-streaked face is "as red as a sore ass." Then suddenly he darkens again and hobbles towards the exit, and I soon realize why: Emanuele with his idiotic gape has entered. As a result I too pivot on my heels, ignoring an offensive jibe lobbed in my direction, and follow Giulio out the door.

Soon I'm back home. After the shower I wrap my body in my sponge bathrobe, colored yellow, green and blue in honor of the Caterpillar. As I pass through the kitchen I notice a few flies busily feeding off the rings of crusted wine at the bottom of last night's glass; "What gourmands," I think. "In Chianti even the flies appreciate the gifts of Bacchus, unlike their counterparts elsewhere in the world who subsist on far less exalted fare." I rub my hair dry with a towel, and notice that it's no longer soft and silky as it was in my youth, but brittle and frizzy. To be honest I don't much care; I actually enjoy watching myself transform as the years go by. I've always considered aging a natural process, a venerable rite, despite living in a society that increasingly works to convince us of the opposite, making role models of desperate youth-seekers and setting absurd standards for dress to which middle-age people can adhere only at the loss of their dignity.

These days celebrities of a certain age actually boast of their plastic surgeries, even though the results are almost always obscene. I think of the *polisportiva* in my village, and imagine what the seniors there would look like if they'd all gone through facelifts and nose jobs and chemical peels. It would be like taking away their souls, like removing the dust from prestigious old wine bottles or ripping discolored pages from ancient manuscripts — in short, attempting to erase experience and falsify history, and all in vain, because time passes inexorably for everything and everyone.

I fill the kettle and bring it to a boil, then drop a depurative tea bag in the ceramic cup made by my friend Romano and sweeten it with a spoon of acacia honey. I cut a slice of cereal bread, toast it and add a drop of oil and a pinch of salt, then sit on the terrace with my feet on the wall, contemplating for the umpteenth time the hills whose majesty provoke in me the most intense feeling of my life. While I'm sipping my tea I again catch sight in the distance of a certain abandoned house in the middle of the forest, a house I've never figured out how to reach. At this point I'm not sure I ever really want to; it's almost comforting that there is still at least one structure in the vicinity that's unknown to me, that represents a final frontier, still to be explored.

After my frugal breakfast I linger awhile, observing the valley; meanwhile a light breeze kicks up, causing the branches of the olive trees on a terraced field below to sway gently. I don my boots, jeans and white shirt with an elegant tweed coat that covers my knees, and set out — purposely leaving the phone at home. No interruptions today.

Carrying a three-liter container of Mecacci, I walk to the bar. The bartender says hello for the second time this morning, then hands me the daily paper that has just been delivered. I immediately check the score of last night's Siena basketball game, and then turn to the front page — which is largely devoted to a rather unlikely incident in which an old pensioner erroneously administered glue instead of collyrium to his eye; and the ambulance sent to rescue the unfortunate man got stuck in the tight alleyway where he lived in the historical centre of Siena. Headline news in these parts isn't always as earth-shattering as it is elsewhere.

I replace the paper, which is then immediately snapped up by Orazio, who has in the meantime come in for a mid-morning break from the vines. He orders his usual *ciaccino* with mortadella and a glass of wine, and as I feared he begins to give me his opinion on an article he has just skimmed. I move a few meters away to avoid getting sprayed by his spittle, and off he goes:

"Eh . . . eh, the Arabs . . . no . . . the oil wells, you know the . . ." A pause to scratch his head. "I go to the gas station . . . the one, you know the one, it's . . ." A pause to rub his jaw. "C'mon . . . the one whose owner lives in . . ." He snaps his fingers. "Help me out. . . the one who got married." A pause to squeeze his primitive nose.

"Orazio, get back to the original subject," I tell him. Meanwhile I spot Andrea parking in front of the bar.

"Eh . . . the war in Iraq . . . no Kuwait . . ." He continues in fits and starts as Andrea enters, and keeps sputtering away through all the time it takes Andrea to wolf down three mayonnaise club sandwiches and as many glasses of wine, in which endeavor I assist him. Then Orazio finally ends his disquisition and goes back to work.

After he's left the bar, Andrea, the bartender and I all burst out laughing; we figure out that what he was trying to say was that they could start all the wars they want and raise the cost of gas as much as they like, he wouldn't be affected because he never put more than ten euros' worth in his tank.

That settled, we turn serious again.

"Dario, are you ready?"

"Yes."

"You've got everything, old boy?"

"I believe so."

"Let's go, then."

I tote the three-liter bottle of Mecacci out to his car and climb into the passenger seat. Andrea doffs his coat and folds it neatly on the back seat. The 11 a.m. bells chime, and we depart in silence. Andrea is more nervous than usual and bites his nails.

"Same as last year?" he asks, while inserting a CD of the Sicilian songwriter Franco Battiato.

"Yes, Andrea. Same as last year."

He takes the turn for Gaiole in Chianti. The wind is blowing harder than it was earlier this morning, sweeping the surface of the white road and depositing clots of mud on the broom that delineates the way. We pass an ancient parish and then return to the main tar road, while the chords of *Esodo* provide a soundtrack. We still haven't exchanged more than a few words, but that's how it always is on the 4th of December; for us, this is a solemn date.

A few miles later Andrea stops the car, turns to me, and says, "Courage, old boy!"

We get out of the car. I fill three glasses with the Mecacci wine and pass one to Andrea. We walk along the edge of the road and after a few steps reach a small wooden cross, now partly covered by bushes, but with its small plate still visible, the name and date engraved on it still legible. We make a toast, swallow the contents of our glasses, and pour the third over the ground of the tiny memorial.

It was in the summer of 1986 that Paolino — who had a passion for motorbikes and raced them as a hobby — missed the bend and crashed his Honda against this very guard rail and died on the spot. He was just twenty-two.

We stand in silence for a few minutes more, remembering him, then return to the car. At the 38-kilometer mark we once again stop at a small tombstone, this one erected in memory of Maurizio. A second *brindisi*, with once again the contents of a third glass offered up in honor of our lost friend; we watch as they are absorbed by the damp soil. Maurizio was killed here, while driving his small vehicle late one freezing night in mid-winter; he apparently skidded on a patch of ice and crashed into this very tree. His car was reduced to a mass of crumpled metal. Andrea and I had just seen him, we were all at the same party held in a local castle, but we only heard about the tragedy when we read the paper the following morning. I opened it to the front page and there was a photo of Maurizio embracing his girlfriend on the beach. When I read the accompanying article I lost my breath, as though someone had punched me in the stomach.

We switch to a new road to pay homage to Gianfranco, where we repeat the ritual. Gianfranco was the first friend to leave us, while riding a motorbike whose model was nicknamed The Coffin because of the numerous fatalities it was involved in. I remember that particular accident as if it happened only yester-day. He had arrived at the bar with his brand new set of wheels, and as soon as we heard the roar of the engine we all filed out and surrounded him with admiration. Then he invited Claudio for a ride; Claudio eagerly climbed on the seat and held on tight while Gianfranco departed with a wheelie. We all watched in awe as our two bolder, older friends disappeared in the distance — nei-ther one wearing a helmet — and muttered to each other in envy, as Gianfranco's father had purchased him a real motorbike while the rest of us were still riding second-hand scooters.

Eventually it became apparent that they weren't coming back, and we began to worry in earnest. The sound of sirens in the distance coincided with the first buzz of rumor to hit the bar — that there had been an accident at the almond tree on the road to Siena. We all fled the bar and jumped on our scooters and go and find out; but when we reached the road we found it blocked by the police. Looking past them, we were horrified by the sight of the motorbike lying on the asphalt in the middle of the road, in a pool of fresh blood.

We quickly cornered the young officer Iuzzolino, who with

pale face and trembling voice informed us that our friends had been rushed to the local hospital. And with that we were again in motion, a small convoy of Vespas, each with both a driver and a passenger, speeding around every bend, risking our lives, disdainful of helmets even after what we'd just seen, the tears in our eyes streaked across our face by the wind. And then we arrived at Emergency only to discover that Gianfranco had already passed away and that Claudio was in coma.

Claudio eventually recovered, though his legs remained paralyzed; and today each time I see him in his wheelchair I remember that the last use he put his legs to, was to swing them onto the seat behind Gianfranco that damn Saturday evening.

We perform the same ritual, then move on to another road, another friend — Giorgio, who had been so vigorous, so ambitious, so full of life. Kilied when a car careered into his lane and smashed into his Vespa. He died on the spot. Giorgio was a natural leader, destined for success in whatever field of endeavor he chose — but alas his dreams were crushed on the hood of a car driven by a drunken old man in the company of a prostitute. Again we raise our goblets in the same ceremonial fashion.

On to Roberto, further up the road. Poor, tormented Roberto, abandoned by his girlfriend and taking it very hard — soaking his desperation in hard liquor and possibly even harder drugs. We weren't very surprised to hear about his death, but grieved for him no less than the others.

Then Pippo, who didn't even own a motorbike because his parents were afraid to buy him one. But Fate is not so easily skirted. He was killed while riding his bicycle, run down by a car containing three boys on their way home from a disco at ten in the morning. Again Andrea and I stand in silence before the little wooden cross, now covered by moist green moss but still wrapped by two timeworn scarves: one from his *contrada*, the other of the Siena soccer team, of which he was a passionate supporter. At the first game after his death his companions asked for a minute of silence before the clock started, but the visiting team's fans disdained the request and filled the silence with a chorus of offensive slurs. Now the scarf is fading, though his memory is not; like all our lost friends he'll always occupy a special place in our hearts.

We have only one more loss to commemorate; but as is our tradition, we'll pay that visit after lunch. We decide to stop at

Gina's for a few quick dishes that include her specialties: *ribollita* and stewed rabbit in wine sauce. We park in the tiny hamlet nestled on the top of the hill and are welcomed with fierce hugs by Gina, an extraordinary woman whose powerful arms are the fruit of more than half a century working the fields. I feel her soft cheeks, which carry the fresh scent of our ubiquitous Chianti limestone, rub against mine.

Gina is a very intuitive woman and instantly senses that Andrea and I are not in the mood for jests or puns, so having accompanied us to our table and taken our order, she leaves us alone — though she returns just long enough to deposit a flask of Chianti Classico Rocca delle Macie on the table between us, together with a tray of hams and salamis brilliantly cured by her husband Oriano.

We sit under the porch facing the valley, observing the massing of gray clouds that every now and then release a tiny rain shower. We sip the wine in silence, as in the old saying *Come un tranquillo vino si pone il silenzio che è rimasto* ("Like a tranquil wine it evidences the silence that remains") . . .

&

It was the morning of December 4, 1984. Andrea arrived early to pick me up, accompanied by Giuliana, whom he had met a few months earlier. I was so happy for him, because finally I saw him bloom in company of a girl.

Giuliana was a robust young woman, the daughter of local farmers; but she was more than that, possessed of a disarming simplicity and a spontaneity I found adorable. She lived with her parents on a small farm tucked away in the Chianti hills, and she was studying agriculture in high school because she had a passion for living in the open air and wanted to continue to work the lands she loved so much. She had a marked folksy accent, and her ways were rough but somehow gentle; her character was bright and never grungy; she loved good wine and a good table. In some ways she was a bit old fashioned; she amused herself by knitting and cooking, and she dreamed of a large family with many children playing in front of a comfy hearth. I could tell that Andrea had completely lost his head for her and I didn't blame him.

On that morning Andrea found me in the company of Erica,

a young decorator with eyes the color of the sky and a very typical Etruscan look; I had been dating her a couple of months. We'd been invited to a party at the villa of a friend of ours out on the Tuscan coast. As was often the case at that time of year the sky was serene and the temperature mild, and at the seaside, some sixty miles from Siena, the temperature might be up to ten degrees warmer.

We departed early to take advantage of the splendid day; we'd go for a walk along the beach, take in some sun, and have lunch at a romantic seafood restaurant before going to the bash.

The beach was deserted when we arrived and the sand beneath our feet squeaked like violin chords. We walked the shoreline with our shoes in our hands, arm in arm as any teenage couple would be. Giuliana had brought a bottle of wine made on her family's estate, and when she handed it over said *"Non si cava la sete se non con il proprio vino"* ("You should only quench your thirst with your own wine") — a typical farmers' expression. We passed the bottle back and forth, sharing both the wine and the joy of the day. Our high spirits kicked in and we chased each other along the beachfront, trying not to get wet, but when the waves broke in front of us we collapsed in merry exhaustion, rolled on the sand and fooled around light-heartedly.

Later we had lunch at a *trattoria* recommended by a friend, a few miles inland on the Maremma plains. It was a gorgeous place, the walls hung with old fishing nets and other curious objects that once had belonged to an old cutter. We started with warm sea *antipasti, crostini* with crab pulp, a fish salad, then *spaghetti allo scoglio* (with squid ink), *cacciucco alla Livornese* (a thick fish soup), a tray of crayfish, grilled breams, boiled mussels, and for dessert a *tiramisu* and a lemon sorbet. Of course we paired the meal with a few bottles of Vernaccia, a Pinot gris, a *prosecco* and the unmissable Limoncello to clear our palates. To watch Andrea and Giuliana devour that Lucullan lunch was a joy; as each course was served, their eyes would light up, every tray was received with claps and ooohs and ahs. Erica and I laughed at how, between courses, they would unabashedly lean in to kiss each other with their greasy lips, and we exchanged a few knowing glances to indicate that indeed Andrea and Giuliana were a perfect match.

With all the wine we had downed we were soon talking over each other, proof that *la verità è nel vino dopo bere ognuno vuole dire la sua* ("The truth is in the wine, after having drunk everyone wants to give his opinion"). We were very loud and drew looks from the other diners as we hotly debated a wide variety of subjects that none of us knew very much about.

Finally, it was time to go to our friend's beach house. We found it full of friends from Chianti and Siena, but also with locals whose acquaintance we had yet to make.

A large bonfire was lit and we all joined in to sing the songs of Fabrizio De Andrè and Francesco Guccini, following chords plucked on a few of the more talented guests' guitars. There was a demijohn sitting on the veranda from which we might serve ourselves, and as *dove c'è il vino buono tutti accorrono* ("Where there is good wine everyone will flock") it was literally assaulted and emptied in record time.

Then we danced around the fire until late into the night, when a chill set in and chased all but the hardiest back into the house. There, another fire had been lit in the enormous living room. We continued talking and drinking until we drifted off, cuddling up peacefully on the sofas. I found a small space for myself where I could doze.

The following morning I woke up dazed and stunned from all the wine I'd downed. The house was still full of kids, all splayed across the floors and furniture in the most uncomfortable and impossible positions. The aftermath of the feast was visible everywhere, as well: empty glasses and wine bottles, ashtrays full of cigarette butts, debris strewn all about. I wobbled towards the porch and spotted Andrea out on the shore, his hands in his pockets, contemplating the ocean. I decided to go and join him. On my way out I disturbed a flock of seagulls who'd been canvassing the beach; they reared up their heads, chided me with their strident cries, then flapped angrily away and landed on an old fishing boat painted in red and blue horizontal stripes, where they settled down and sulked.

The bonfire on the beach was now just a sad heap of cinders and blackened trunks that released into the cold air a trickle of greasy gray smoke. The sea was flat, last night's undulant waves now napping. When Andrea sensed my approach he turned to greet me; his face had the numb look a hangover often provides, but he looked otherwise peaceful and self-contained, in a way I had never seen him before.

"Where's Erica, old boy?" he asked.

"Still sleeping. What about Giuliana?"

He smiled. "Gone. She slipped away while I was asleep, but left me this in my pocket." He passed me a slip of paper. "It's personal, but you can read it, Dario. You know, old boy, I think I'm seriously in love." He turned back to the sea again with a melancholic gaze.

I opened the note. It read:

Dear Andrea or Luca or whatever,
I've decided to return home because I can't wait to tell my parents the good news. I'm letting you sleep (you're so cute snuggled up on that sofa) and am returning with Sandro and Davide; you couldn't have chosen a more romantic moment to ask me to marry you. How can I ever forget your sweet words and your kisses, wrapped up together with the sea in our ears and the stars over-head. Call me as soon as you get back home; I can't wait to see you.

I love you
Giuliana

I folded the note with care and handed it back to him; he delicately replaced it in his inner pocket as if it were a precious Egyptian papyrus of inestimable value. Then I slapped him on the shoulder and congratulated him; I was brimming with happiness for him. Giuliana was perfect, I couldn't imagine a better match for him.

Knowing that his only desire was to return home to her, I went to wake Erica who was still fast asleep on a couch. I told her the happy news and we pulled ourselves together and got back on the road to Siena, happy and joyous. During the trip we teased *Andrea innamorato* and envisioned him in slippers, surrounded by howling kids.

Soon our stomachs began grumbling; we decided to stop for a *cappuccino* and jam *cornetto* along the main road. As is my habit, I picked up a copy of the local paper to read over my breakfast. Meanwhile Andrea went to the restroom and Erica lingered at the counter, unable to decide which pastry to choose.

I opened the paper. The headline screamed out at me:

MORE BLOOD ON THE SIENA-GROSSETO ROAD

My mouthful of food went down the wrong pipe and I burned my mouth with the boiling hot *cappuccino*. A fear I couldn't even name had taken possession of me, and when I read the first two lines of the article I knew why:

Last night three youngsters were killed while returning to Siena, in a head-on collision with a truck. The names of the victims are Giuliana P., Sandro F., and Paolo T.

I banged my fists on the table in denial, drawing the attention of the others around me, including Erica who immediately raced over to me. I couldn't speak but I pointed to the paper, which she picked up and read. She covered her mouth with her hands and stood silent and pale, then collapsed into a chair and quietly wept.

Now my thoughts turned to Andrea, who was just now leaving the restroom and was coming towards us, wearing a sweetly oblivious smile. I stood up, grabbed him by the shoulder, and shoved him brusquely outside; he was too astonished to resist. Then I embraced him, and with tears streaming down my face I told him to be strong, and begged him not to do anything foolish. He had no clue what I was talking about, but I had very much alarmed him; he freed himself from my grip, and I didn't do anything to impede him as he went back inside to Erica. She handed him the newspaper. I watched him through the window; he read for a few moments, then looked suddenly stricken. His eyes reddened, he sat down, and while I could hear nothing I read his lips: *Giuliana amore mio.* For a moment it seemed as if some kind of desperation might seize him, but then he lost all expression and sat as if in a trance, his gaze directed on something only he could see.

After leaving him thus for some forty minutes, we managed to convince him to finish the journey home. I took the keys from his pocket — he seemed to be unaware of me doing it — and drove, and it was only then that I realized our route would take us directly past the spot where the tragedy occurred. To avoid this I took a side road that was much longer, but preempted any addition to our already unbearable burden of pain.

∞

Twelve years have passed, and every 4th of December Andrea and I feel obliged to pay homage to Giuliana, and to all our other friends who were taken from us in so abrupt a manner. We're very aware that we're lucky to be still here, as we've so often been reckless and irresponsible; clearly it's only destiny that has spared us. A local saying goes *Vino dentro senno fuori* ("Wine goes in, reason goes out") and it's true drinking has played a large part in our troubles, but even so Andrea and I haven't changed our habits. Today is a perfect example; we've been drinking and driving all morning and now we're seated at the restaurant emptying a flask. Call it spitting in the eye of fate – a fate too cruel and unfair to respect.

We spend another good hour discussing those years of our youth, and the fate of our friends who are no longer with us. The casualties seem to have been so high — almost as if our generation had taken part in a war. Maybe even worse; in a war there is at least glory.

Of all those friends, however, Andrea and I will always reserve a special place in our hearts for Giuliana; and when we leave Gina's we go, as always, to the small country cemetery were she is buried and lay a spray of fresh flowers on her marble grave. The photo on the marker portrays her smiling round face, a young woman — eternally young now — whose only role in her own death was simple impatience; she was so in love she couldn't wait to break the news of her engagement. A few more hours — a few more *minutes* — and how different everyone's lives would have been.

Andrea has always been a rational man and he recovered from the shock after a few months, though I know he's never truly forgiven himself for falling so deeply asleep on the couch.

The investigation into the collision concluded that Sandro had most likely fallen asleep at the wheel, letting the car drift into the opposite line where it lodged under the carriage of an oncoming truck. Giuliana was probably dozing on the backseat, which means that her passage from light slumber to eternal sleep had at least been instantaneous and painless. Many times Andrea and I have fantasized about what she was dreaming in that single fatal instant. Even today at Gina's we tried out a few new suppositions, knowing that if she could hear us she'd appreciate them — that she'd be grateful to know she still mattered so much to us.

We finish the Mecacci while walking around the walls of a medieval castle. At sunset Andrea takes me back to my village and for the first time since I met him he looks me in my eyes and says, "I'm very fond of you, old boy."

I'd like to say, "So am I," but I just nod and give him a friendly pat on the shoulder.

I watch his car vanish in the distance. It's been an emotional day. At least he has a wife and kids waiting for him at home, to pull him back to the present.

I trek back to my own empty house. I'm tempted to stop by the *polisportiva* for a nightcap but force myself to pass its door. At home, I climb the stairs and lie down on the bed, my eyes moist with too much feeling; I have difficulty falling sleep. I'd like to share these emotions with someone besides Andrea, and Mia is the first person who comes to mind. It's odd, since we have only a cyber-relationship, but despite this she now seems the most intelligent and sympathetic listener I know. Which means I've found the subject for my next email to her. It needn't be material for the book, I know; we've moved beyond that. I find myself wondering what her voice is like; maybe I should call her and find out. But no, I decide against it; after all, if everything goes as planned, I'll talk to her soon enough, and even meet her in the flesh.

Thinking ahead to the day out of the blue an additional quote springs to my mind; *Quel che non va in vino va in lacrime e sospiro* ('What does not end up in wine ends going into tears and sighs') and then I phase into a deep sleep.

෪

The following morning I awaken very early. It's still pitch black outside, but I have to catch up with my work as I'm already a day behind.

I see that there are two emails from Mia. But it's become a point of discipline that I put off reading her messages until I've replied to all the others first. Her words are a kind of reward.

But after handling all my other correspondence I feel stiff and restless, so I delay opening Mia's emails even longer in favor of talking a short break. I trudge up to my Summer office and enjoy the sunrise. It's slow, steady, and serene; today will be a fine day.

Back home and, finally, time for Mia.

From: Mia Lane
To: Dario Castagno
Subject: Re: The Poolio

Dear Dario,
I think we need to register the trademark for The Poolio as well as The Truss. I'm absolutely positive they'd both be a huge success over here. What a stroke of genius on your part to improvise a game both to keep your clients alert *and* get them to understand the Palio by competing in one of their own! You are aware, I'm sure, that you'll have to change names of your guests for publication, to avert any risk of being sued. Actually, now that I think about it, you only mention Pete Jameson and his wife Kim by name; the others you just referred to be their lookalikes.

Seriously, Dario, do you truly reflexively pair each new person with a celebrity? I can understand it if someone's a dead ringer for a famous actor or pop star, but the female version of your postwoman got me on the ground.

I thoroughly enjoy waking up in the morning and reading about your life over coffee, what a great way to start the day! It's like I'm living a double life, a parallel reality. My days here in L.A. pass rather monotonously, but my computer screen has become a magic window onto Tuscany, and getting on-line is like opening the shutters and having your magical hills come into view, with all their history and beauty. I'm afraid I've become morbidly obsessed with your life. Do you realize that in almost no time at all, you've sent me almost enough material for a complete book?

When — if ever — you exhaust your stories I'll be obliged to close the imaginary window and frankly I'll miss you and long for our frequent exchanges. I realize this can't go on forever. Can it? The regularity with which I receive material from you is very gratifying. I hope it doesn't take you away from anything more important. But I won't complain and I won't dissuade you. In fact, you mention a second chapter regarding your *contrada* and the Palio — well, I can't wait!

                                         Mia

The second email followed the first by a full day:

From: Mia Lane
To: Dario Castagno
Subject: Another "Particolare" Day?

Dear Dario,
The fact that I didn't hear from you signifies another "Giornata Particolare," I'm sure. Will you tell me all about it? Please, Deeeeerrrrrio?

Mia

I smile, because I've already decided to tell her about it. And I proceed to set it all down for her, after which I undertake my reply, as follows:

From: Dario Castagno
To: Mia Lane
Subject: The Wine Roads

Dear Mia,
Ciao! Believe me, as long as you wish it your window onto my world will remain wide open. It is, after all, *your* window, and therefore your decision when to close the shutters. Until then I'm at your service.
In the attachment you'll find the entire story of what transpired yesterday. To be honest, the 4th of December has always been a very private day and if you were to consider publishing this, I would require the consent of both Andrea and Guiliana's parents.
Regarding the second Palio chapter, it will be a few days yet, as each Friday we organize a dinner in the *contrada* and I thought I would take the opportunity to start a conversation at the table, ideally provoking some of our more interesting characters to comment on the Palio. It should be fun. But to loosen their lips as much as I'd like, I'll need to refill their glasses very often and as it's only polite that I keep pace with them, I can anticipate a super hang over on Saturday.
I'm glad you appreciate my punctuality, because it's an attribute I thoroughly believe in. In fact, while we're

waiting for the Palio dinner to roll around, I'll send you an account of an episode involving punctuality that occurred many years ago, an episode that doesn't reflect well on me, alas. I'll need some wine to jog my memory — no problem, as I already have a bottle of Chianti Classico Santedame breathing in the decanter, just awaiting my attention.

I feel obliged to fill you in on a few facts regarding those years; and going back to the 70s can't help but afflict me with a mixture of unsettling emotions. Mia, you're causing me to trawl up many lost sensations. Anyway . . .

Italy in those years was still in the so called Prima Repubblica and I remember that it was normal to receive candies, bon bons and licorice sticks as change in the shops, because for some obscure reason there was a shortage of coins. It was a controversial period, the economic crisis had us in a stranglehold; the boom years of the 50s and 60s were long gone, and people finally stopped daydreaming and faced cold reality. To make matters worse, the entire country was a theatre of daily, vicious terrorist attacks. The tension in the cities was palpable, there was aura of fear in the air, and civil war seemed almost inevitable. Governments fell like ripe chestnuts and reformed with the rhythm of a banana republic, and the Italian Communist Party was the largest outside the Iron Curtain.

I spent my teenage years creating my own little world; I was aware of what was going on all around me and so, perhaps unconsciously, chose to escape from that reality. I worked as a laborer in a very large winery, and in the canteen and the locker room the only topics of conversation were political; there were heated calls for strikes, occupying the warehouse, and communist revolution.

Looking back I can see that while the country has changed drastically I really haven't; my passions are the same, I still live alone, I'm still single. Anyhow let's not veer too far from the subject. Just read this amazing story that I've narrated many times around the fireplace to my friends. It really is perfect for the book.

Your dear friend
Dario

25

THE IMPORTANCE OF BEING ON TIME

April 1983

It was a magnificent evening. A thunderstorm had cleared the air and lifted the cape of humidity that for most of the day had cloaked the hills and obscured the horizon. Now it was possible to see the peaks of the mountains towering powerfully over the Crete Senesi — and in fact the extraordinary light of the gloaming made it possible to make out even the palette of colors that comprised the distant fields. In the nearer distance, a flurry of sparrows was busy pecking at a drift of millet seeds, which had spilled from a truck that had probably been overloaded at the local mill. They quarreled joyfully over the unexpected meal.

I had just finished my shift at the winery, where I was employed in the warehouse, and was returning home on my Cagiva motorbike, concentrating on the lines of the curves I had to tackle. I brushed the arc of each turn using the weight of my body, swaying my torso to and fro, then exited the bend while lifting the bike, trying to maintain a regular rhythm.

The day had been particularly intense, as I had loaded by hand two containers destined for New York, a truck for a German supermarket, another for Northern Italy, and a rail wagon bound for Switzerland.

The fact that Ivo, the foreman and a severe man of few words, had personally praised me and patted me on the back, made me feel particularly proud of my labors. I couldn't remember him having behaved this way before with anyone else.

"One more big push tomorrow and we're done," he'd told me, while I shed my overalls and he lit what was probably his thirtieth Marlboro of the day. As I headed for a well-earned shower he reminded me to be rested and ready the following day as it would be another tough one. My biceps cramped from the fatigue of managing all those cartons, my back ached, and the calluses on my hands were hard and itchy. I planned an early night so that I could sleep off my fatigue and get an early start, arriving on time and and ready for whatever the day threw at me.

While I rode up from the valley towards Castellina in Chianti I thought how strange it was that all the wine I was loading onto those trucks was the fruit of the vines now surrounding me on either side of my road home. This reverie was interrupted by the sudden appearance of the medieval tower belonging to my friend Matteo; it was partially blocking the sun, now a flaming orb sinking slowly behind my beloved hills.

I downshifted a couple of gears near to a red-brick shrine which contained a tiny terracotta sculpture of the Virgin, partially hidden behind a vase full of wild flowers set there by some devoted acolyte. At this point the road branches, and I had two choices: I could continue straight home or take a small diversion that led to the castle owned by my friend. It wasn't yet seven o'clock, so I decided there was nothing wrong with stopping by to say a quick hello.

The wrought-iron gate was wide open, so I rode up the avenue, which was bordered by tall, elegant cypress trees, and parked the bike against an ancient stone wall. The massive wooden door was ajar and the inviting strains of music greeted me as I passed the threshold. Matteo as usual was playing his piano in the main hall, surrounded by portraits of his austere ancestors. But I was surprised to discover he wasn't alone: two girls were seated on the couch, each sipping a glass of wine. They seemed to be utterly absorbed both by the ambience of the castle and by Matteo's wizardly playing on his majestic grand piano.

My attention was immediately drawn to the shorter of the two, who turned with a light start, apparently surprised by my unexpected appearance. She smiled and I was struck dumb by her eyes: two precious, fire-flecked jade stones set in an alert, freckled face. Her head was covered by a mass of thick, ebony hair that contrasted with her milk-white skin as sharply as the keys on which Matteo was now playing.

She gently put her index finger to her lips — red as roses in spring, I thought banally if sincerely — and I knew I would honor her request for silence even if the roof came down around my ears. While she turned her eyes back to Matteo, mine remained on her; she seemed so soft, so velvety, and so ethereal in her simple white dress.

She was so enraptured by Matteo — who was thoroughly in the thrall of his immense talent, seated erect on his mahogany stool while his arms flew grandly across the octaves — that eventually I had to spare him a glance, if only out of jealousy; I had to determine what it was about him that had captured this girl's devotion, and whether it was something I myself might possess. I had always been attracted to diminutive girls, perhaps on the same principle as the local saying *il vino buono sta nelle botti piccole* ("Good wine is kept in small barrels").

When Matteo at last concluded his dalliance with Mozart, everyone broke into applause — myself included. When he stood up to acknowledge this he finally saw me, and motioned me over to an elegant cherrywood cabinet where he filled two glasses, one of which he handed to me.

"Ciao," he said with a smile so genuine that I knew despite the presence of the girls I was welcome; then he embraced me, and with his lordly but never cloying ways — very sophisticated for a teenager — he presented his guests.

"This is my new fiancée," he said, gesturing to where the girls sat, and my blood froze; I hoped he didn't mean the creature I had just fallen in love with. Then I sighed with relief as the taller of the two extended her arm.

I found myself shaking hands with a rather wiry girl named Marzia, who wore a sad, almost haunted expression. She was dressed very simply — in fact nothing more than jeans and a white T-shirt — which was in stark contrast to her excessively heavy make-up. She smiled weakly as Matteo explained to her who I was — and then it was my turn to discover the identity of the little beauty. "Simona," she said, presenting herself as if too impatient to wait for Matteo to introduce her, and then she shocked me by ignoring my handshake, instead slinging her arms around my neck and planting a kiss right on my lips. She had a sweet scent that reminded me of the musk in the undergrowth of an oak wood after a summer rain. I was extremely impressed by her forwardness, and by her magnetic eyes. If it's true that the eyes are the mirror of the soul, then hers must be crystal clear, a little sunburst of purity. I couldn't seem to tear my gaze from her, and was so tongue-tied that I couldn't manage a word. I felt as though I'd been knocked off my feet by a wave of happiness, the way a sudden gust of wind will suddenly fling open a door.

Matteo came to my rescue, breaking the silence by proposing that we go outside and finish the wine. He took some clean glasses from the cabinet, because the local dictate in these cases is clear: *In bicchiere non pulito presto il vino è inacidito* ("In a dirty glass the wine soon turns acidic").

We sat on the terrace sipping a sangiovese produced in Matteo's vineyards, and amused ourselves by playing the oldest game in the world: looking up at the clouds and naming the shapes they made, as the winds constantly altered and shifted their form. This endeavor lasted only as long as the wine did — as they say, *Il buon vino è come un bel gioco, dura poco* ("Good wine is like a fun game, it never lasts long") — and with the sun now winking its last on the horizon, I realized that it was past the time that I should have said farewell to the company. I absolutely needed a good night's rest for the following workday.

Matteo knew me well enough to have picked up on my infatuation for Simona; he also knew I was too cripplingly shy to ask to see her again. So he proposed that I give her a lift home, with the excuse that Marzia was staying at the castle for dinner.

And so I soon found myself not going home, but barreling down the state road towards Siena, tackling the curves with a marvelous young girl behind me, clinging to my thorax, her large, round breasts pressed against my back and her gentle breath caressing my nape.

The erotic charge of this emboldened me, and I managed to quell my shyness long enough to ask her if she'd like a pizza. "A quick bite," I thought, "then I'll drop her off and go straight home . . . I'll be in bed by ten thirty at the latest."

Simona accepted my offer and we decided to stop at Paola and Bianca's little pizzeria. The two sweet sisters greeted us joyfully, as was their habit, and as they accompanied us to the table I was surprised at how harmoniously they got on with Simona, who then explained to me that she often came here. I found it strange that I hadn't ever seen her before, as I was a regular.

Gaspare the waiter came for our orders, and without even asking me began scribbling on his notepad. "Pizza Dario and red wine," he said confidently, asking only "with or without the challenge?" I said I'd certainly take my namesake pizza, as always (it was a simple margherita with *buffalo* mozzarella and red hot chilly pepper) but would pass on "the challenge" because I didn't want any trouble sleeping tonight.

Simona ordered her own personal pizza (white with black truffle sauce and arugula). When Gaspare had gone, she used a paper napkin to wipe away the beer foam that had made a disarming little mustache on her upper lip, and asked what Gaspare had meant by "the challenge." I shrugged and explained it was a simple game I sometimes played with Ghigo the "pizzaiolo;" the gist was, if I managed to finish a pizza entirely swathed by his own home grown *peperoncini dinamite*, it was on the house.

I discovered Simona had many attractive qualities apart from her stunning beauty. She was extremely convivial and told me about her dreams and ambitions, which were basically those of any bright young woman; she talked about the countries she longed to visit and as she spoke of them her jade green eyes lit up. She was studying to become a goldsmith, she loved the hills of Chianti and the lunar landscapes of the Crete, which she painted in her spare time. It was easy to see that she loved life and embraced it with real energy and spirit.

I learned she was the younger sister of Susanna, with whom I used to go to school, and that we had many friends in common. This led to even more intimate conversation as we compared notes on our acquaintances, and I really began to wonder how it was we'd never met before. I also wondered where she was putting all the beers she kept ordering; there just didn't seem to be enough room in that tiny little body.

Later, as we were having an espresso, Giacomino, a friend of mine since primary school, spotted me and came over to our table. I was surprised to hear him greet Simona first; it was evident by their gestures and easy, free way of speaking to one another, that they'd known each other for some time. It really was astonishing that I had never encountered this girl before.

I glanced at the clock on the wall and saw that it was past ten thirty; I still had time to get Simona home and be back in bed in time to be fresh for work in the morning. But Giacomino ruined that plan by excitedly informing us of a party a friend was having at Poggio ai Pini in the wild boar hunters' shack; he'd been enlisted to round up as many people as possible. There was to be a local rock band performing, and of course drinks galore. Before I could say anything Simona piped up to say we'd certainly be there, then she ordered a round of grappas for the three of us and made a toast to the evening ahead.

Not wanting to be the spoilsport I pretended to be enthusiastic, and downed my shot in one gulp.

At 11:17 I parked the bike on a rubble road in the midst of a good number of cars, mopeds, Vespas and other motorbikes. The band was already in full swing, performing old beat classics to a crowd of unbridled dancing teenagers who were exchanging bottles of wine, beers and grappas, as well as embraces and kisses on this lovely Chianti night.

Simona immediately slipped off my bike and hurled herself towards the fray, pausing only to grab my wrist and drag me along behind her. She started flailing to the rhythm of the music, and her enjoyment was so infectious I followed suit. The last time I checked my watch, it was 11:48.

I was transported by the music, overwhelmed by the fumes of the alcohol, and buoyed up by the general enthusiasm. I switched off completely, shedding any and all inhibitions, freeing my mind from any conscious thought. I recognized many friends: Nicche, Peo, Stina, Teo, Pampocchia, Stiego, Tabacca, Verro, Shorty, Macca, Fanala and Cuzza, among many others.

While I was draining a flask of Chianti directly from the bottle, I met Matteo, still accompanied by Marzia. He plucked the flask from my hand and helped himself to the last swig. We had to raise our voices to make ourselves understood in that open-air din. With a malicious grin he asked why I wasn't in bed. I told him to get lost, adding that *quando Bacco trionfa il pensier fugge* ("When Bacchus triumphs, the thought flees"), and went back to pogo-dancing with the other scruffy youngsters following the beat of The Clash's "Should I Stay or Should I Go".

Simona approached me and unexpectedly took my hand and squeezed it; my heart started pounding like a jackhammer. She led me out of the crowd, across a vine, and stopped beneath a mulberry tree. I stared into her eyes a few seconds and simply couldn't resist her any longer — I was utterly undone by this extraordinary gem of a girl — and I clasped her firmly to my chest. She wrapped her arms around my neck and while she caressed my long hair, I pressed my lips to hers and kissed her passionately. She returned the kiss, and for several minutes I wasn't able to detach myself; I felt like a limpet on a rock. When we finally broke away, we gazed at each other; I was completely lost in those glittering jade eyes. Somewhere during this encounter the music had faded out and now we could hear the roar of many engines — though these too eventually faded, as if swallowed by the night. We remained entwined beneath the fruit tree, staring up past the moon at the celestial vault that hung over our young heads. Then the rustle of leaves in the trees made us realize that we were immersed in near-total quiet; there was no other sound of life to be heard.

Simona broke the silence by asking if I was happy, and I whispered that I was, because I had met her. We were both under the influence of wine, beer and grappa, and the romantically charged words we exchanged were slightly slurred; my head was in a whirl. "Dariolino," she cooed, while I lovingly twirled a lock of coal-black hair around her ear.

"I think we ought to go," she said finally. "It's almost three, and I have school tomorrow." These words were sufficient to break the spell; I realized that I had at best three hours of sleep still available to me —two, actually, since I had to take Simona back to Siena and then ride all the way back to Chianti.

We brushed the grass and the dust from each other's backs and returned the way we'd come, treading across a carpet of empty bottles and cigarette butts. My bike was just where we'd left it, but now it was the only vehicle left on the hill.

Bracing myself for the drive, due to my alcoholic intake being much higher than I'd usually have allowed, I escorted Simona to her home on a steep street in the She-Wolf district. We said goodbye with another endless kiss, promising to meet again very soon, and when she closed the door behind her my heart sank in my chest.

I turned to go. Now that Simona's stimulating presence was removed from me, I could feel my forehead pulsing — no, it was spinning like a mill paddle in full activity — and no wonder, I had not only drunk a fair amount of wine but also mixed in a variety of hard liquors. I had to really concentrate on keeping my eyes open on the drive home; I longed for my bed and the few scant hours' sleep that separated me from my shift — even though I was well aware of the mammoth hangover I'd have at the end of it. *Una buona ubriacatura nove giorni dura* ("A serious boozeup continues for nine days") On the other hand it was to be expected; there's a famous Tuscan proverb that warns *non si può pretendere di avere la botte piena e la moglie ubriaca* ("You can't demand a full barrel and a drunken wife") — meaning you can't have everything in life.

But if a silly headache was the price to pay for having met Simona, it was certainly worth it. I smiled as I went back over the night in my mind, while kicking up speed now that I was outside the city. I decided to remain on the main road instead of the short cut through the woods, in order to avoid crashing into a pack of wild boars. I couldn't take my mind off Simona; her green eyes and heavy eyelids gave her such a sexy, rakish, street-scamp appearance.

Suddenly at the start of a tight curve my thoughts went blank as I was blinded by the lights of an oncoming vehicle that suddenly swerved into my lane. To avoid impact, I instinctively released my grip on the handlebars and threw myself to the ground. The bike skidded on the asphalt and I rolled into a ravine covered by bramble bushes and thorns. My brief life passed before me as I kept tumbling down, tearing my jacket and ripping my jeans, till finally I reached the bottom and came to a halt.

The first thing I did was to pat myself all over, checking to make sure I was in one piece. I was covered with abrasions, bruises and sores, but nothing seemed broken. I looked up at the road above me; all was silent, but I could see the lights of the car that had nearly hit me arcing over the edge of the curve. I scrambled to my feet with extreme difficulty and managed to climb back up on my hands and knees, even as I trembled in fright.

When I reached the top there was the car — a Fiat, its engine still running — with a tiny woman in a nurse's outfit weeping, her forehead on the steering wheel. I went over and opened the door, and the first thing I noticed was a bulbous nose that resembled that of the actor Karl Malden. Then she cried out; she was evidently more traumatized than I was. She spilled from the car, shoving me aside, then looked towards heaven and started invoking the names of a series of saints to whom she was obviously devoted. She was crying hysterically, and I tried to comfort her — as though she were the victim and I the one to blame for the accident. I tried to bring her back to reality; "Signora, are you okay?"

Suddenly a nearby window lit up, its shutters flew open, and an elderly woman — who'd obviously been awakened by the sounds of the brakes and the impact — called out that she had phoned for an ambulance, and that the *carabinieri* were on the way, and was anyone injured? I assured her we were all right and thanked her, even as I cursed her under my breath; all I needed now was the police charging in and breaking my balls!

The nurse with the Karl Malden nose kept on weeping, trying to justify herself. Between a sniffle and a sob she explained that she'd just come off a long duty and had fallen asleep at the wheel momentarily and simply hadn't seen me. To be honest, I couldn't have cared less about her version of the event, all I wanted was to pick up my bike (scratched and dented but still working) and go home to bed. But she pulled out an insurance paper, saying that it was her fault and all I had to do was sign it; then she put a handkerchief to her sizeable schnozz and blew a few trumpet-like notes. The ambulance promptly appeared, as though this had been its summons — and as I feared, the *carabinieri* were right behind it.

The ambulance was sent away since it wasn't needed, but the *carabinieri* , alas, were not so easily got rid of. A very young officer stepped out of the van and asked to see our licenses. He looked them over and handed them back; then he looked at us — the tiny, middle-aged nurse, and me in my leather jacket, crash helmet, ripped jeans and bleeding knees — and asked which one of us had been riding the motorbike. (This is why in Italy we make so much fun the *carabinieri*.) I was about to tell him to stuff it when I spotted the arrival of *Maresciallo* Iuzzolino, whom I already knew very well. I thought, *Uh-oh*.

He let the nurse with the nose go home and ordered me to sit in the van. Then he took off his cap and offered me a stick of gum, and when I refused it he handed me a bottle of disinfectant and some cotton wool from a First Aid kit. While I ministered to my scrapes and cuts he, as usual, started in on a paternal lecture that seemed have no ending. The usual points were covered: when would I grow up, *chi del vino è amico di se stesso è nemico* ("He who is friend of wine is an enemy of his own self") he would ruin me one day, and so on. When at length he finished his spiel he asked if I could drive back home, and I assured him with a confident nod. He had me sign some document — I don't remember what it was or what it said — and let me go.

I rode home with a world-class, brain-banging headache — whether from a hangover or from my fall into the ravine, I don't know. I rested my dented Cagiva on the stone wall and swooped and stumbled up the steps to my front door. On the third attempt I managed to get the key into the lock and I lurched into my house. It was dawn.

Under the door I spotted the morning newspaper; and my sight fell with dismay on the front page, which bore a reminder that at 3 a.m. we were to move the clock ahead an hour. So it wasn't 4:49 now, but 5:49. I had less than fifty minutes before my alarm would go off.

I threw myself on the bed without even brushing my teeth, and while thinking about Simona's jade eyes I fell into deep sleep.

I woke up without the aid of the clock; I had set it for 6:30, and it was 6:28. I was surprised because I felt fresh and rested and in great shape. I went to the bathroom and looked in the mirror, expecting to see a drawn, fatigued face staring back at me; but no, I looked remarkably good.

I took a shower, taking special care to rinse my wounds; my arms were bruised and I had a swollen black hematoma on my knee — but apart from those minor infirmities I felt fine and fit and eager to get to work. I whistled merrily as I rested the coffee pot on the burner, so proud was I that I'd recovered so rapidly from my grueling night; again I looked at myself in the mirror and gleefully said aloud, "Who can beat you, Dario?"

I repeated the phrase several times as I descended the stairs pumping my fists, as though I were in a boxing match with an invisible opponent. I skived a punch and knocked out my adversary, then hopped on my motorbike — which in the light of day wasn't as badly damaged as I'd feared — and started the engine.

During the ride my thoughts inevitably returned to Simona; I longed to see her again. Tomorrow would be Sunday;

I would certainly call her, hoping to arrange a date.

I reached the warehouse, where I expected to find the yard full of trucks waiting to be loaded; but none was there. There were no cars in the parking lot, either; in fact the whole scene was inexplicably desolate and silent. Even the gate was closed.

I waited around another few minutes, trying to imagine what might have happened. A last-minute strike? The sudden death of the owner? A bomb scare? Some kind of colossal joke on me? An invasion by space aliens? Each seemed less plausible than the last. Finally I decided the best course of action was to go the closest village and ask around; surely someone would know what was going on.

I had just entered the town when I passed a newsagent's stand; one of its billboards trumpeted, "BASKETBALL TONIGHT — SIENA VS. PISTOIA." I pulled the brake and the motorbike came to a sudden halt. I rubbed my eyes in case I had misread it. Was it possible? . . . This was *Sunday*, not Saturday. I hadn't slept fifty minutes, but *twenty-four hours* and fifty minutes! *That's* why I'd awakened so refreshed this morning. So much for the theory that I was a superhuman; the sad truth was, I was just another stupid jerk. I actually punched myself in disgust.

When I recovered from the shock I realized I was in big trouble. On Monday the foreman was going to kill me — or worse, fire me. I didn't know whether to laugh or cry, so I did a little of both.

"What the hell," I concluded with a sigh; it was a beautiful day, I might as well enjoy it. I'd go to Matteo and tell him the story over a couple of glasses of wine; then maybe I'd call on Simona and take her on a ride through the shimmering hills.

€Ɔ

"*Magnifico,*" I think as I conclude the chapter. This has always been one of my best stories. I perform a *self-brindisi* with the wine remaining at the bottom of the bottle.

The sun has set, I've been in front of the computer all day. But I don't regret it; it's been time well spent, thinking about Matteo — to whom I dedicated an entire chapter in my last book — and Simona, whom I still see occasionally and who is still as beautiful as ever. And about Mia, who I'm pretty sure will enjoy this one.

26

THE BOLSHEVIK

I sip my steaming hot *orzo* while listening to Ruggero Leoncavallo's immortal opera *I Pagliacci*; I've raised the volume so that I can hear the music seated here in front of the computer.

From: Mia Lane
To: Dario Castagno
Subject: Two new chapters

Thank you, Dario!
Yes, you took a day off but I wasn't the slightest bit concerned, as I feel through our correspondence I've gotten to know you very well and I was pretty sure that a message would show up in my in-box today. I was right, and wasn't I pleasantly surprised to find *two* new chapters.
The first was of course was infinitely sad; agonizing, actually. I couldn't help biting my lips while scrolling down the text. When I was halfway through it I had to get up and fetch a Kleenex to dry my eyes, and while I was on my feet I filled a glass with Merlot to cheer me up. If Andrea agrees then yes, I would like to include this chapter in the book. In fact I believe it's a necessary one, because it represents the other side of the life you're describing — a life that can certainly be sweet and affords us many opportunities for laughter and joy, but often leavens it with doses of bitterness and regret.
The other chapter about your hilarious lost day was extremely entertaining; it seems no matter how hard you try to be a good boy, you always ended up compromised somehow! I was fascinated by your reference to the Communist period Tuscany went through, these political facts intrigue me. Can you tell me more? Maybe you might even write an episode of some sort that refers to that bizarre period. I'm sure you can, Dario.

Finally, it was very moving to read again about Matteo, with whom you concluded your last book so memorably. Just curious to know if the castle he owned still belongs to his family, and if the statue of the little angel still exists in the garden?

I hope you have a great day. Keep up the good work!

Mia

I log off without replying, because I've promised myself to prune the lavender bushes in the garden and really can't delay the task any longer. The stems are all sadly drooping and it's been weeks now that they've been urging me for a drastic cut.

Even when I finish in the garden I don't immediately return to the computer, but change from my overalls to my running gear. I need to meditate on Mia's most recent request. I find it odd that she's so interested in the Tuscan political situation of the 70s. But there is also something else in her message that's left me uneasy, and I can't quite figure out what it is. Maybe a kind of subliminal phrase hidden between the lines?

During my run I give some thought to the problem while making the steep climb that leads towards Misciano. Along the way I spot two splendid English Setters lying miserably on a muddy field outside the abandoned house. One of them pricks his ears and stands up as I approach, and seconds later starts to howl desperately, his tail tucked between his legs in fear. The other doesn't move an inch, but seems to recoil in shivering terror. My first guess is that they've been abandoned by some ruthless hunter, but then I noticed they're both wearing collars with copper identification tags attached — the kind that are engraved with the name and the number of the owner. They're not abandoned, then. My next guess is that they were lost during a boar hunt.

I stop a reasonable distance from them and crouch down; I extend one hand and creep forward, speaking to them in the most reassuring tone possible, trying to gain their confidence. But I soon realize it's useless; their demeanor doesn't alter. Their eyes remain wide open with alarm, one barks frantically at me and the other gone nearly fetal, trembling like a leaf in the wind. I'm able to get close enough to decipher the phone number, partly covered in mud; then I pull out my portable and dial it. After a couple of trills I hear a brash voice on the other end: *"Pronto!"*

Still panting, I ask if I'm speaking to the owner of two lost hunting dogs.

"No, why?" is the answer.

I explained where I am and describe the look of the two canines before me.

"Oh, them," he replies. "They're not lost, I left them there yesterday; they're being punished. I told then not to move an inch till I came back for them, and judging by what you're telling me they haven't; good." After a pause, as if to reassure me, he adds with an unfriendly grunt, "I'll go and pick them up tomorrow."

Now I'm curious to find out what the dogs did to deserve such harsh punishment.

"The *stronzi*," he snarls in disgust. "They ate the pheasant I shot yesterday morning instead of retrieving it. So I ordered them to stay put, right at the scene of the crime. That'll teach them."

"I see," I reply, and I hang up. All I can do is to continue my run; but I promise myself that I'll bring them a plate of food as soon as I return home.

At the end of the run I've realized not only the physical benefits jogging has on me, but also once again I've gathered sufficient material to respond to Mia. I've also recalled a long-lost prank that I and some friends had prepared specifically for special occasions, an act we christened "The Bolsheviks."

But first I prepare a bowl of steaming hot pasta mixed with minced meat for the two dogs, and return to Misciano to give it to them. They shy away from it distrustfully, but as I'm leaving I look over my shoulder and see that they are tentatively approaching it. I'm satisfied that they won't go hungry. I also make a vow to check on them tomorrow in case their neglectful owner forgets to come for them.

Back home, I crack open a bottle of white — but then I recall the time *Dottor* Becchini scolded me when he caught me sipping a Vernaccia of San Gimignano at the bar. He gravely explained that drinking white wine was a bit like making love in a canoe: "It's hopeless, as it's too close to water." And so, not wanting to contradict my esteemed *dottore*, I replace the wine in the refrigerator and from the rack choose a more appropriate Chianti Classico Poggio Amorelli. I pour the wine into a goblet and after my usual *self-brindisi* I scribble down the following:

Dear Mia,

Ciao! I must say, you are a surprising woman. Don't take it personally, but why for God's sake are you interested in Italian politics? The subject couldn't be more tedious . . . Even so, to please you during my morning run, I thought hard about the period you find so interesting. I realized that I lived the "red" period marginally and rather passively; together with my rene-gade friends we actively ignored the meetings, debates and assemblies that the Partito Comunista tried to interest young-sters in. This doesn't mean that we abstained completely; we did take part in the various feasts of the left-wing parties, but with a completely different spirit and purpose. We just wanted to have fun.

There are many reasons that Tuscany and its neighboring regions experienced such a radical move to the extreme left after the war. I believe that the end of the *ventennio fascista*, cul-minating in a dramatic war that obviously brought nothing but destruction and countless deaths, is by far the main factor. The reasoning was simple: if the extreme right brought about such unrelenting misery, its antithesis must produce the opposite effect. To this we must add the natural aversion towards the landowners and noble families, who for centuries had main-tained an ancient system of sharecropping that had kept the region rooted in near feudalism. True, this system guaranteed survival, but it could promise nothing in the way of comfort, prosperity or anything remotely resembling modern conve-nience. Even the clergy must claim their share of responsibili-ty for the leftward swing, for having always tacitly supported the old regime and playing a fundamental role in maintaining it for their own personal benefit. Both the Church and the landowners had also shamelessly supported the Fascist regime, and as a consequence of the post-war economic boom of the 50s, the farmers emigrated *en masse* to the cities, where they were employed in the thousands of new industries that sprang up like mushrooms after an autumnal rainfall. The proletariat for the first time gained a measure of power thanks to the rise of the left-wing trade unions, which guaranteed not only edu-cation, but also the kind of social assistance programs that until then had always been denied.

The Communist party never won elections at national level, but took the merits from its electors for those assistance benefits, while at local level they dominated the scene — gaining up to eighty percent of the consensus not only in Tuscany, but in other central regions such as Emilia-Romagna and Umbria. The *Partito Comunista* owed its success to two major groups of supporters: first, the laborers employed in the industries and the peasants who still worked the lands; second, the intellectuals, who came from the universities imbued with Marxist ideology and were firm admirers of the Soviet and Maoist models. Many became outright fanatics, organizing themselves into subversive groups that terrorized the country and whose principal aim was the overthrow of the center-right government by a military coup. Italy inevitably dissolved into chaos and became a theatre of disorder, kidnappings, and attacks targeting the heart of the state. This strategy of terror wasn't a trademark of the left, however; the far right organized themselves similarly and responded with the massacre of innocents — chiefly by the cowardly means of setting off bombs in public structures. We were perpetually at risk of a bloody civil war, and that era, far from being a golden age, will be sadly remembered as the "leaden" years.

When I first moved to Tuscany as a child, my family and I quickly realized that everything surrounding us was politicized; there were supermarkets where left-wing voters would shop, and nearly identical stores selling the same items that catered exclusively to a right-wing clientele. There were bars and recreation centers managed by the *Partito Comunista* where entrance was allowed only to *compagni* who produced a membership card. It spiraled into absurdity when even the medical emergency organizations split, so that if you were a Communist and needed urgent attention you would summon the *Pubblica Assistenza*, and if you had different political views or were a Catholic you would call the ambulances belonging to the *Misericordia*. But it was the left that dominated in Tuscany, and many streets were named not only after heroic members of the national party, but also after Marx, Lenin and even Stalin. Squares were built and monuments erected in honor of the Soviet Union; churches were abandoned by the once-faithful who now preferred ideology to theology, and began frequenting the bars managed by the left. Many local families adapted to this "mini-revolution" and christened their children with more fashionable Russian names, and thus an entire generation of

Igors, Yuris, Rudys, Katiuscias and Olgas appeared. Even the Catholic sacraments were forgotten and many families turned atheist, disdaining even to baptize the newborn. I personally attended funerals at which the departed were buried with a copy of the local Communist newspaper, *L'Unità,* tucked under their folded arms. Local feasts, always called *Festa dell'Unità,* were annually organized in each Tuscan village, with the red hammer-and-sickle flag raised high. Debates and meetings with important political figures were highly attended, and the latter were announced like celebrities from the loudspeakers that also pumped forth the notes of the *Internazionale Socialista* and other propaganda.

And Mia, it was during such feasts as these that we enjoyed playing one of our favorite pranks.

I was in the company of a small gang of friends from my village who, like me, were completely apolitical and hadn't been remotely persuaded by the ubiquitous Communist propaganda that brainwashed so many teenagers into joining left wing federations and youth associations. It was summer, sometime in the seemingly endless expanse of the 80s, and we were sunning on a smooth rock on the banks of the river Merse and listening to psychedelic music. The temperature was scorching, and when it became too much for us, we took advantage of the crystal clear waters to soothe our young, sweat-streaked bodies.

There wasn't much need to talk; we all knew each other too well and had been through quite a bit together. For instance, one famous night we'd dressed all in black and marched back and forth in front of the Communist recreation center, performing the Nazi-Fascist goose step and at the same time whistling a Fascist tune. Inevitably we got chased away by some hotheads who screamed *"Sporchi Fascisti!"* at us, and we were banned for good from entering that bar. We eventually realized that stirring up trouble in our own village wasn't a very smart thing to do because the most passionate *compagni* took their beliefs extremely seriously, and you never knew what kind of reaction you would spark in them. But we were teenagers and it was impossible for us to take anything seriously for long; our main desire, as it should have been, was to have fun — and our pranks were light-hearted and designed simply to provoke. So now, whenever the urge to pull a prank struck us, we were smart enough to pull it somewhere else; sometimes we even crossed the borders of other provinces, where we could be certain no one would recognize us.

Back to the gang at the rock. Foffo, his feet dangling in the water, was sipping from a fiasco of wine and browsing through the daily paper while the rest of us discussed plans for the evening. We were restless and eager for fun but none of us had any ideas on what to do. Foffo raised his head and while passing the flask to Peo informed us that according to the paper a village close to Arezzo was holding a *Festa dell'Unità*.

"How long has it been since we last played the Bolshevik?" he asked.

"I don't think we've done it at all this season," Dindo replied.

"Let's do it, then," I said, and after having agreed and raised a *brindisi* to the Bolshies, we finished off the flash; then we all dove for our final dip of the day.

Our rendezvous was at the local bar that evening, and after a couple of *gottini* we filed into Dindo's Deux Chevaux and drove across the Chianti hills, entering Valdarno at sunset. We headed straight for the Casentino area where the village was located. Its park was all dolled up with red flags and tables and chairs, and groups of volunteers were busy serving abundant portions of sausages and beans and red wine for the glory (and the cash registers) of the *Partito Comunista Italiano*.

We parked outside the village on a side road and started rehearsing the roles we had perfected over the years. Then Peo and I split from Foffo and Dindo. Peo had changed into a collarless shirt buttoned on one side, and was sporting typical Russian plus-four pants tucked into a pair of black leather boots with a busby hat resting atop his blond head. Thanks to this and his amazingly blue eyes and fair skin, he really could have fooled any native Soviet into mistaking him for a true Bolshevik.

At the entrance of the open-air festival sat an elderly farmer with a plump, friendly appearance and a red foulard around his neck. His chore was to affix all comers with a hammer-and-sickle pin. He welcomed us now with a hearty *"Benvenuti, compagni!"*

I politely replied by raising my left arm and clasping my hand into a fist, in emulation of the popular Communist salute. *"Grazie, Compagno!"* I said before introducing Peo. "I have the pleasure of accompanying a civil servant of the Soviet Communist Party named Serghei Peoski who has traveled all the way from Moscow to write a series of reports regarding the Feste dell'Unità we organize here in Tuscany, and he would greatly appreciate being introduced to the *compagno* responsible for this feast."

The old man could barely contain his excitement; he'd probably never dreamed of encountering a genuine Russian. Beaming, he invited us to follow him. He then proudly commandeered a table for us, shooing a bunch of kids out of their chairs in favor of his "special guests." Then with an enormous grin plastered on his face (which was now the color of his foulard) he invited us to sit down. He summoned one of the young boys to bring us a generous supply of sausages and beans and a liter of the best wine while he went off in search of some *responsabili*.

In the meantime Foffo and Dindo had gone roaming around the feast, visiting the stands that sold sandwiches and wine and inevitably ended up drinking while waiting for their turn to join the prank.

Minutes later two middle-aged men, accompanied by our elderly friend, came scurrying up, visibly excited and honored by our presence. They obviously were the *responsabili* and to them I introduced myself as the interpreter of *Compagno* Serghei Peoski. Peo then said, *"Vojvodina koskov, dinaminski tuskov jijinski,"* which doesn't mean anything at all, but that I pretended to translate as "*Compagno* Serghei would like to propose a toast to you and to your beautiful feast, and with your permission he would be delighted to say a few words to all the *compagni* participants."

The two *responsabili* were really just simple farmers dressed up for the feast; they seemed itchy and uncomfortable in their ill-fitting tuxedos. Their strong country accents, their rough calloused hands, and their sunburned napes were dead giveaways that they were really most at home working in the field. It was comical and yet somehow moving to watch them as they tried to raise their cups for the toast, but found their reach impeded by their tight suits. We pretended not to notice and raised our own drinks, then tossed them back dramatically. As soon as he'd swallowed Peo released a hearty belch, wiped his lips on his sleeve and tossed the glass over his shoulder; it nearly hit an elderly lady seated at one of the tables behind us before shattering loudly on the pavement. The two *responsabili*

exchanged a quick glance; then, not wanting to appear as igno-
rant country bumpkins who were unaware of the Russian traditions, they did exactly the same thing (omitting however the
burp) as if hurling glass receptacles through the air were something they did every day.

Now it was Peo's turn to fill up the glasses. He took a fresh
one for himself, filled it almost to the brim, drained it dry in a
single gulp, then again launched it over his shoulder.
Immediately he found a third glass and did it all over again.
People behind him had begun quietly getting up and moving
themselves out of his firing range.

The two *responsabili* again followed suit, and by now this
bizarre drink-and-destroy ritual was attracting a crowd of
onlookers — all of them taking care to keep a safe distance.
Then Peo mumbled another nonsense phrase which I, as trans-
lator, explained meant he was now ready to talk to the *popolo*.

Serghei Peoski was dutifully introduced over the loudspeakers, and everyone was invited to gather round and meet a
true comrade who had come all the way from Mother Russia.
Meanwhile I spotted Foffo and Dindo in the crowd, drinking
wine and trying very hard to keep a straight face as they
observed the scene.

To make the event as solemn as possible the organizers
played a recording of the *Internazionale Comunista* anthem
that echoed all over the village in honor of the unexpected
guest. I accompanied Peo to the small stage, which had originally been set up for an orchestra; now the musicians were
asked to stand aside until we had finished. I mounted the stage
and looked out. We had an audience of at least fifty simple
farmers, each one eager to hear all about the Soviet Worker's
Paradise from an honest-to-God Bolshevik.

It fell to me to introduce Peo. Taking the microphone, I told
the crowd he was the sixth of eleven children in a family of
farmers, that he was a nuclear engineer with a degree from the
University of Leningrad, and that he was employed as a potato selector in a company that produced trifled canned potatoes. Because of his talents he had been chosen by the
Communist Party to go and meet his fellow *compagni*
throughout Italy, and to write a report on what life was like on
the other side of the Iron Curtain.

There was a long round of applause, with some people

shouting *"Viva la madre Russia,"* and Peo, who was a natural-born performer (today he's a famous actor), stood up and saluted the crowd.

I asked if anyone had questions for the distinguished visitor. Many raised their hands but, as rehearsed, I singled out Dindo, who began, "Dear Compagno Serghei, welcome." As he spoke I pretended to whisper the translation in Peo's ear, but I was actually asking whether he fancied the girl in the fourth row in the green T-shirt with the big boobs. "How is it possible," Dindo continued, "that an atomic engineer has been assigned the job of quality control in a potato company?" Peo took a deep breath, then again gave forth with some remarkably Russian-sounding babble.

"Dear *compagno*," I said, pretending to translate it into Italian, "the control of quality of potatoes is an extremely delicate and noble task. You must realize that we consume potatoes at breakfast, potatoes at lunch, and if we are lucky potatoes at dinner too, and as it is our only source of nourishment you can well imagine the importance of my job. Certainly it is not the kind of task just anyone can perform."

As we had predicted there was a slight buzz of consternation among the spectators. Our cruel little hoax was working splendidly.

To allay any suspicion, for the next question I chose a woman in the front row wearing a lively flower-pattern dress who seemed particularly depressed by Peo's previous reply. Fortunately her question was innocuous: "How come, *compagno*, were you chosen to represent your country abroad?"

Again I pretended to translate what Peo said quietly in my ear (he actually whispered that he fancied more the girl in the second row, whose face reminded him of a Maltese whore) and keeping a perfectly straight face I said, "My dear *compagna*, it's simple. There was a worker who was always complaining that his daily ratio of potatoes wasn't sufficient to feed his large family, and one day I caught him stealing some extras from a sack meant for export, so I denounced him to the KGB for the glory of the National Communist Party. He was sent to Siberia to work in the mines and I was rewarded with this trip to educate Westerners on the miracle of the Soviet system."

This time very few applauded, even if a few fanatics did raise their voices to proclaim that this had been the right decision to take. The two *responsabili* were by now wringing their cal-loused hands and looking at each other desperately; they were obviously very ill-at-ease. I continued to "translate" as Peo explained how he shared a room with other three families, and as the only bathroom was located outside, his buttocks would freeze against the seat in winter; but that really didn't matter so much since due to a curfew nobody could use the toilet after nine o'clock anyway. The risk was to be shot on the spot. "But we are patriotic *compagni*," I continued to "translate", "and for the sake of the revolution we have trained our bladders to peaks of superhuman endurance!"

Some eyes began to brim with tears, as we were systemat-ically destroying the dream of the Soviet Workers' Paradise these poor peasants so fervently believed in. One of *respons-abili* now jumped on the stage and snatched the mic from my hand, announcing that the adderess was now concluded as they didn't want to tire their honored guest. He thanked us for our time while his companion mopped his sweating forehead with a handkerchief.

Now it was Foffo's turn to deliver the grand finale. From the back row he stood up and in an angry voice declared, "*Compagni!* They told us the Soviet Union was a garden of Eden, a paradise of social equality . . . words! Only words! *Compagno* Peoski has shown us the reality is far different. We have been conned!" As the tumult of the crowd grew louder he shouted over them: "The heads of the party are liars and enrich themselves by taking advantage of us poor farmers and workers!"

Now the crowd erupted with a mixture of boos, whistles, and scattered applause. Peo rolled up his sleeves and leaped down from the stage, throwing over chairs as he propelled him-self towards Foffo. When they met, they put on an extremely realistic mock fistfight. I played peacekeeper, trying to inter-vene and separate them, while one of the *responsabili* shouted into the mic that everyone must calm down, while his comrade ran around the stage with his hands waving in the air, as though he were the Pope.

It seemed as though some members of the crowd might get involved in Peo's and Foffo's brawl, but for real, so they now quickly broke apart; Foffo melted away, while Peo darted towards the exit. I followed him, shouting over my shoulder that everyone should feel ashamed for having offended such an illustrious guest from Mother Russia. The two *responsabili* ran after us with extremely pitiful looks. One of them grabbed a carton of red wine from the stands and shoved it into my hands, insisting we accept the gift.

"No hard feelings?" he said in a broken voice.

"None at all," I reassured him while accepting the carton with great pleasure. We were more than content to have hoodwinked some bottles from the local Communist party, so we bade them farewell with the excuse that I had to take Serghei Peoski back to the Russian consulate in Florence.

We met up with Foffo and Dindo by the car, and now that we were safe we all burst out laughing and exchanged high-fives. On the long drive home we kept reliving the questions and replies we'd given the audience and decided it had been our best performance by far.

At one in the morning we were back in our village. We decided we deserved a final *brindisi* for the success of our traveling Bolshevik act, and so filed into the local bar that was preparing to close. We were surprised to find Iuzzolino among the customers. He was obviously off-duty because he wore baggy khaki shorts and a black T-shirt, and leaned on the counter twitching his black moustache as if waiting for someone. When he saw us he broke into an enigmatic smile, then summoned the bartender to pour him a double Smirnoff vodka. "Well, boys," he said, "just before getting off duty for the day I got a call from one of my colleagues in a small village in Arezzo. He told me that four youngsters with a deux cheveaux — the same color as Dindo's, and like Dindo's with a Siena license plate, and even more curiously with a sticker on the rear window of our village soccer team — had been fucking about at their local *Festa dell'Unità* this evening. Obviously you know nothing about it. Hm? Dario? Foffo? Dindo? Peo?" He raised an eyebrow and added, "Or should I say *Compagno* Serghei Peoski?"

Peo had changed out of his Soviet costume in the car, but even so we knew Izzulino had enough evidence to give us a seriously hard time. We began to stammer out excuses and explanations, but we were in for a big surprise when he just smiled and gestured for us to be silent. "You're aware of my political sympathies, aren't you? No? Let's just say I'm definitely no Communist, and as I'm off-duty for the night I can respond personally instead of officially. So, personally, I raise this vodka to you and your hoax, and I will tell my colleagues they must have been wrong as you never left town all evening."

"Thank you *Maresciallo*," we replied in tandem.

"But," he said with a hint of menace, "let's pretend for a minute that I'm wearing my uniform again. I know that you are aware of that place in town that some lazy souls have turned into a kind of garbage dump; you know what I'm talking about, don't you? The spot close to the almond tree. Well, I have the strangest hunch it's going to be all cleared away this weekend. And my hunches are never wrong. What do you think?"

He finished the contents of his glass, wiped his lips with his hairy forearm and smiled broadly at us, revealing his gold-capped teeth. Then he pivoted on his heels and left us standing alone in the bar speechless. We had just enough time for one final *brindisi* that we dedicated to Iuzzi; in spite of everything, we wouldn't trade him for any other *maresciallo*.

ಞ

I send the chapter to Mia, with a note telling her that yes, Matteo's family does still own the castle and that the statue is still standing.

I'm tired but I also feel the need to talk to someone. I watch the sun set from the window; it's beautiful, indescribable — the kind of intense sunset you only get on certain nights in winter. I have the sensation it's not only saturating the valley with its vibrant colors, but pouring into my soul as well. I'm suddenly overwhelmed by a strange feeling, and my eyes flood with sudden emotion. What's going on? . . . I sit in front of the crackling fire and try to figure out why I'm suddenly so depressed.

"What's the matter with me?" I repeat several times as sadness swells my heart. What is it that's moved me so? Is all this digging into my memories to blame? . . . No, I'm certain there's something else tormenting me. When I feel completely overcome I open the front door and stare at the stars, and suddenly I'm taken by the strong desire to go for a walk.

As I set out my thoughts turn to Mia and our . . . well, at this point, I can only call it a relationship. I can't shake the feeling that she's tried to communicate something to me . . . that there was a subliminal message in her last e-mail. I trek up to the monument and sit on the wooden bench of my office, and drop my head into my hands. Then I again look up at the sky: the moon is pink, a bright, simply marvelous pink, and I'm struck by a sudden thought as I dry my eyes on my wrist:

Mia mentioned the little statue of an angel in Matteo's garden. How did she know about it? I'm pretty sure I never referred to it before. I wonder about this as I rest on the grass, observing the stars above me glittering in the winter sky.

"Mia, who are you?" I ask myself, repeating the question as if it were an Indian nenia. It's obvious this woman is trying to tell me something. What am I supposed to do now? . . . I'm wracked by a series of shivers that pass through me like a tube train, right up my spine, forcing me to get up. I decide the best thing is to go to the doctor — a specific doctor, one who I'm sure to find at the *polisportiva*.

As I enter the place, the same old men are busy playing the same old cards games, cursing at each other and exchanging menacing glances. Giulio is in his place, Dino is asleep in his favorite corner, and Becchini, as I'd hoped, is on a stool at the bar counter, emptying a bottle of red. When he sees me he waves me over to join him and fills a glass from an unlabeled bottle whose contents, he tells me, were produced by Maso, who is behind us playing *briscola*. "What's up, Dario?" he asks with a serious look. Obviously my feelings show in my face.

While I collect myself, he lights a cigarette and hands it to me. I take a deep breath and begin, "*Dottore*, I . . ." I can't get any more words out — even though it was specifically to speak to him that I've come here at all.

I empty the glass and he fills it up again; then he takes my hand and holds it tight and says, "Dario, don't worry, there's no need to say anything, I can see that you have been tormented these last years; you can't go on like this. I have been observing you lately, and to be honest, you are worrying not only me but everyone in the community. We have been gossiping about you in the village. You're never around, you no longer take part in the local feast, you never show up for the assemblies or dinners, and we haven't seen you in the company of anyone for years now. You haven't been to mass for a while, either. Look at you, you dress like a bum, your hair is down to your shoulders and you haven't shaved for days. Your happy expression has faded far away. The only time I see you smile is when I pass you with my car and find you torturing yourself under the scorching sun on your bicycle. Why do you do that? I saw Emilia and Mauro, they told me they miraculously managed to invite you to dinner, where you confessed to them that you spent the entire day alone in the woods scouting for old ruins. Tell me, have you spoken to anyone today? Don't bother to reply, I know you haven't. What about yesterday? You were always so friendly, so ready to socialize with everyone. Truly, I haven't recognized you lately. I've always been fond of you, Dario; I want to see you enjoying your life. Why not go and find a nice girl and build a family? Time passes inexorably and you . . . well, you are no longer so young. I also met Duccio in Siena, he said you seldom even go to the Caterpillar *contrada* any longer. Is this true, Dario? I gather by your red eyes that something happened today. Do you wish to tell me? Do you want to come to dinner tomorrow? My wife and my grandchildren will be happy to have you there."

I empty another glass and then another, until he blocks my hand and says, *"Il pan finchè dura ma il vino a misura,* Dario" ("The bread until it's gone, but ration the wine").

I stand up and embrace him. All I can say is, *"Dottore,* tonight the sunset deeply affected my soul; it could be because I believe in something, but it made me cry and sigh because I have something yet to discover. It could be something that illuminates my life but so far it has only made me shed tears. *Buonanotte, Dottore."*

I depart the *polisportiva,* leaving Becchini on his stool looking very worried; I'm sure he has no idea what I was talking about. But in truth, I'm not quite sure myself.

&

I return home in time to see the last flames die in the hearth. I pour a glass of Mecacci and shout, "Mia, who are you? What is it you're really asking? Is there a reason you simply can't come out and say it? Okay, then, you want to play? Let's play!

I hobble up to the second floor, risking a stumble at every step, my hands clasping the wall. Without brushing my teeth or even getting undressed I fall with a thud onto the unmade bed.

"Becchini was right," I tell myself. "I really need to straighten up my life." Even as I'm falling asleep I manage to smile, recalling that Becchini also announced his imminent retirement and that *Dottore* Bevilacqua (literally, "waterdrinker") will be the new village medic. What an irony! Maybe a new era is about to begin. How I wish . . . oh, Mia, how I wish you could descend from that pink moon and appear before me! *Come sei bella*, Mia!

27

THE MADRE OF THEM ALL

I awaken with a pleasant sensation, and feel somehow light-hearted. Maybe talking to Becchini last night helped me shed a weighty burden. I notice also that I've overslept — it's mid-morning — and this may explain why I'm so relaxed, so ready to face a new day.

I decide not to check my emails immediately but first to tidy up the house, round up the empty wine bottles scattered seemingly everywhere, and pay another visit to the glass recycle bin. Having done so, I open all the windows wide on my return, allowing the fresh Chianti air to take possession of the house. I change the bedsheets and the towels in the bathroom, do the laundry, sweep the floors and mop the terracotta tiles — all the while whistling a formless tune like a twerp. Then I pick up the phone and call Duccio, and ask him if there's to be the usual Friday *cenino* in the *contrada* and if so to reserve me a place. Then I call Viviana and Andrea and invite them both to dinner.

With that done, I drive to Siena while loudly singing Umberto Tozzi pop songs. After a stop at the car wash I head to the super-market (the left-wing Coop) and fill an entire cart with delicacies. Then on to the fishmonger where I select some fresh hakes, clams and mussels. And finally I pick up a carton of *prosecco*.

I return home and eagerly placed the shells under running water. Then I close the windows (the fresh Chianti air has now got the place rather chilled) and pile fireplace with logs, open a bottle of *prosecco* because *una buona bevuta ti fa vedere più bello il mondo* ("A hearty drink makes the world look more lovely") and light the fire. When the flames are blazing I insert a CD of 70s disco music and dance before the crackling hearth till I wear myself out.

I take a long shower, shave off my beard entirely for the first time in weeks, and even add conditioner to my hair before rins-ing and brushing it thoroughly. Then, finally, I sit down and reply to my emails — and am relieved for once not have any from Mia.

Back in the kitchen I remove the mussels and clams from the running water. I shell most of the clams, leaving just a few intact to place atop the serving dish, then cook them in a pan with olive oil, white wine and chili peppers, and finally finish them off with a sprinkling of parsley. I have to say, they look very appetizing.

Now I gut the hakes and stuff them with rosemary, salt, garlic, sage and pepper. I wrap them carefully in aluminum foil so that they're ready to grill over the fire. Finally I place the mussels in a stainless-steel casserole and let them boil in their own water while I set the table, which I've moved in front of the fireplace for the evening. I'm pleased with my progress, and with myself. All I have to do now is await my guests. I kill some time watching the olive wood logs burning, and while it's inevitable that my mind snaps back to the matter of Mia and Matteo's statue, I immediately banish the thought; tonight I refuse to torture myself, and I turn my mind to something else.

At eight-thirty the doorbell rings. Andrea has arrived, with Viviana whom he's given a ride. I welcome them in and pour each a glass of *prosecco*.

"Andrea," I remark, "you seem to have gained a few pounds since I last saw you."

"Not quite so," he says. "As a matter of fact I wanted to gain fourteen but I only managed to put on eight, so it's as if I lost six, right?" His same old jest; yet his inflections keep it funny. Then he places his hand on my forehead, pretending to gauge my temperature. "Are you okay, Dario? . . . I mean, you've actually invited other human beings to dinner. Have you not been feeling yourself lately?"

Viviana gave him a friendly slap on his bald head, and we laugh aloud; the ice is broken.

I watch as Viviana doffs her heavy coat and warms herself in front of the fireplace. She's still a very attractive woman. Her voluminous curly hair looks soft and silken in the firelight; it hasn't yet turned gray and assumed that dull, wiry consistency.

I serve a tray of antipasti and invite my friends to take their places at the table while I empty a box of Barilla spaghetti no. 5 in the boiling salted water, then serve the mussels that now are done to a turn *a puntino*.

"How's your little kick-boxing cousin, Viviana?" I ask just to keep the conversation moving.

This is sufficient reference to our final Truss to cause Andrea to burst into laughter again, and to kill Viviana's smile. She crosses her arm and gives me a playfully annoyed look. Then she tells us that her cousin is now the Italian champion and is training to challenge a Rumanian for the continental title. For a while we remain on the subject of the Truss, and even though Viviana seems less than comfortable she clearly harbors no more resentment. I take advantage of the moment to return the key to her apartment — a gesture of atonement.

She smiles and changes the subject, asking what I've been up to lately, apart from terrorizing her cousin.

I reply with a phrase I read in an archaic text a few days ago: *"Io sogno e scrivo, io bevo vino rosso e leggo ed il tempo passa"* ("I write and dream and drink red wine and read, and time passes").

"Now I'm even more convinced you're not feeling well."

"Don't worry, Andrea; I'm actually writing a book. And the subject, as a matter of fact, is my biggest drunks."

"And how many volumes will it be?" he quips. "Considering the material you've spent your life building up, old boy, you could spend the rest of your career on this one." He gives a hearty laugh and adds, "But if you're still on the lookout for some local proverbs, here's one: *Tutti dobbiamo avere un credo, io credo che avrò un altro bicchiere di vino*" ("We all must have a belief; I believe I'll have another glass of wine").

I thank him and give him the glass he's requested, and propose that for each additional quote I'll reward him with a refill.

"While we're on the subject," I tell him now as I amble back to the kitchen, "you might as well know that you appear in quite a few of the chapters as a supporting character." I strain the spaghetti in the colander and pour them into the pan with the clams, and as I stir the mixture I call out to both Andrea and Viviana, asking if either of them recalls the *madre* of all our booze-ups?

"Not off-hand," Andrea replies. "I mean, there are so many."

Viviana runs her fingers through her hair and says, "Neither can I. Are we forgetting some important date we should have etched on our brains?"

"I'll give you a clue," I say, as I bring the pasta to the table. "February 1994? That terrible blizzard?" I set the bowl on the table and start serving my guests. "I'm a little murky on the details myself, but if you can help me recall the events, I'd like to add it to the book."

Both Viviana and Andrea suddenly turn thoughtful and

begin digging through their memories, but largely in vain.

"Okay," I say, sitting down to join them. "I'll start, and you jump in when you're ready. Do you remember my mad crush on that girl with the jet-black hair and the walnut eyes shaped like raindrops ? She had a French nose that tipped skywards and a smile like strawberries and cream, and her neck was as delicate as a flower stem."

"Why not simply say Chiara," says Andrea, "instead of boring us with your silly poetry? Stop showing off. And speaking of 'French nose,' how's this for a quote: *Liberté, egalité, Beaujolais?*"

"Andrea, leave him alone," scolds Viviana. "It's rare enough a man uses such sweet terms to describe a woman. Dario, please continue."

"Thank you, Viviana. As for the quote: sorry, Andrea, that one definitely won't make the book, or earn you a glass. However, you're right, it's Chiara I speak of. She was so elegant; she had the gait of a supermodel, like she was on a perpetual catwalk. And she seemed both aware of the way she turned heads wherever she went, and blasé about it — she had both supreme self-confidence and lofty nonchalance. It was a very attractive combination."

"Now I remember her," says Viviana after swallowing a mouthful of pasta. "It was when we went to that nightclub — the one that closed down a few years ago. You never liked going to discos and we had to drag you there; you didn't want to leave the solitude of these boring hills." She smiled. "Well, *that* hasn't changed, has it?"

"Not really," I'm forced to admit. "Well, anyway, I knew at once I wasn't going to get her off my mind, that I'd spend days and nights thinking about her, and that my chances of taking her out were close to zero."

Viviana interrupts me while refilling up her wine glass. "You know what, Dario? I can confide in you now, after all these years, that I was very upset about your infatuation with Chiara, because the whole reason I insisted you come with us that night was that you intrigued me so much. I was very attracted to you. I may tease you about it, but in truth it gave me such pleasure when you expressed your passion for the Chianti countryside; your eyes would sparkle with enthusiasm. And I admired how you had turned your passion into a career, escorting tourists to the places you so adored. I longed to date you but I suppose you were too friendly with me to be really interested in a relationship; it was inevitable that we would be close friends and nothing more. I knew Chiara well, as it happens, but I never told you, did I? And I also knew she had a boyfriend."

Somewhat embarrassed by this confession, I get up to take the hakes from the grill, and while I unwrap the foil and delicately place them on a tray, Andrea polishes off a glass of *prosecco* and says, "Well, as long as we're all confessing, Dario, I must admit" — and here he mimicks Viviana's voice — "that I was in love with you, too."

He roars with laughter and Viviana balls up her napkin and throws it in his face. "Can't you ever be serious, Andrea?"

"All right, all right! I'll try ... Anyway, we'd known each other for years, old boy, our friendship was rock-solid and we could understand each other with a simple look or a nod. I must admit I often took advantage of our friendship, and will always be grateful to you for letting me use your house as a retreat from my squalid life as an insurance broker. You met Chiara during the period when our mutual friends would mock me for spending my vacations at your place; that's why I christened your house 'Rio,' so that when they asked where I was spending the holiday, I could make them think I was going someplace exotic, when really I would only be ten miles outside of Siena. But getting back to the subject: yes, I well remember how you gawked at Chiara when you first saw her; I could actually see you fall in love at first sight." He smiles at the recollection, then smothers his fish in mayonnaise.

I'm happy because I've succeeded in getting them onto the subject. But the conversation now changes to the food; I accept their compliments, and for a while we remember some other memorable meals; and it's not until the main course concluded, and I serve a lemon sorbet and open the third bottle of *prosecco*, that we move to the more comfortable sofas and I am able to continue my story. "Viviana, I was extremely thankful to you for introducing Chiara to me, but I was devastated that the first thing she told me was that she was engaged. But on second thought I decided that wasn't such an insurmountable problem because I've never been the jealous type. And she did let slip her address, which I memorized; and I promptly made a vow to send her a bunch of roses the following day. She was, to me, the essence of a real woman: sweet, feminine, mother and girl rolled into one. When she left me to return to her friends I was happy just to have shaken her hand. I guzzled red wine and flung myself around the dance floor like a maniac."

"I must say, Dario," Viviana interjects, "I was feeling some high emotions too. I was happy to see you dancing, as you seldom did, but I was jealous because you never acknowledged what I felt for you. Also, knowing Chiara, I was also well aware that she would fool around with you until she got tired of playing the game, then drop you cold. To be honest I was rather hoping this would happen, so that I would have chance to step in and win you on the rebound."

I'm very surprised to hear this from Viviana; I ask if she really was in love with me all those years ago.

"*Sì*, Dario!" she replies without a hint of embarrassment.

"Quando il vino rende lieti non si tengono segreti" ("When the wine makes you merry you can't hold onto secrets"), says Andrea — ruining the lovely rhythm of the quote by punctuating it with a hearty burp.

"I told you to cut that out," says Viviana, screwing up her face in disgust. "And enough already with the mayonnaise."

I am ecstatic to be in company of such good friends, and the evening is turning out to be perfectly enchanting. Why haven't I done this more often? I reward Andrea with another glass for the very fitting quote.

"Well, Dario," he says, "I do remember you getting drunk that night, but as usual you only drank wine while I downed a great deal of *amari* and *grappe*. Then you started tormenting me about Chiara so I got bored and decided it was time to take you home."

I nod. "I spent the next few weeks at the flower shop having red and pink roses delivered to Chiara's house. I chose the most beautiful blooms, the ones that were imported directly from Venezuela, and eventually I broke down her resistance: she agreed to let me take her out. And she must have enjoyed my company because we ended up spending many evenings together, even if the topic of conversation was usually her boyfriend and how selfish and abusive and even violent he was. But occasionally she'd tell me that no one had ever treated her like I did, I made her feel special and she liked being with me. I was positive it was only a matter of time and she would dump her boyfriend for me."

"You were completely out of your head," Viviana says. "Going around in a tuxedo, all clean shaven and perfumed like a high-board *gigolo* . . . now that I think about it, not too different from tonight."

"You were really ridiculous," Andrea agrees, putting the boot in. "And you didn't even call me for weeks, until suddenly out of the blue you invited Viviana and me for dinner with her."

"You're right, you're both right; I was out of my mind. I know many years have passed but would you accept my apologies now?" I put on what I thought was a terribly pathetic smile.

"Maybe if you open another *prosecco*," Viviana says with a radiant smile, and she turns her glass upside-down to demonstrate how empty it is.

I immediately pull the cork from a new bottle, refill all our glasses and then explain that when I invited them to that dinner with Chiara I was hoping that, as both Viviana and Andrea were single, it was a good occasion to start a *storia* all together.

"You must have been insane to even imagine such a thing." Viviana replies, looking askance at Andrea. "Though I must admit I was surprised that you got Chiara to agree to come to dinner. I was worried she'd dumped her boyfriend, and I had no idea why Andrea and I had been invited too; now it starts to make sense!"

"To be honest," says Andrea, helping himself to another dish of sorbet, "I was curious to meet Chiara, yes. But my real reason for coming — and now you're in for a surprise — was that I'd always been in love with you, Viviana."

"What?" Viviana exclaims, almost jumping out of her seat. "Andrea! Stop it!"

"I'm utterly serious," he says, completely straight-faced.

Viviana is rendered speechless; she blushes and starres at him incredulously. "You mean while I was secretly in love with Dario, you were secretly in love with me?"

"Looks that way," he says, and for a little while the only noise is the crackling fire I've just finished feeding.

It's suddenly turning out to be a pleasantly awkward dinner, and I'm enjoying it to the full. I end the little pall of embarrassment hanging over us by revealing that the occasion of our dinner with Chiara I spent the entire day cleaning and cooking, just to impress her.

"Oh, sure," Viviana says sternly, "but if I hadn't arrived early to help you, you would have accomplished exactly nothing."

"Are you sure, Viviana? . . . I don't recall you doing that."

"Of course you don't, you're a man! I even cleaned the toilet and the bidet for you, because God knows you'd never have thought of it. The state those fixtures were in . . . well, let's just skip over that. I will admit I was stunned to find roses in the vases, incense burning in strategically hidden spots, and the table well laid *con gusto* — and when I opened the refrigerator I was staggered to see it so full of goodies. You must have spent a fortune."

"That explains it then," says Andrea, twirling his near-empty glass in between his thumb and forefinger. "I thought it was strange you'd done all that housework; it looked as though it had a woman's touch. I also remember how visibly nervous you were — biting your nails and breaking out in a cold sweat."

"All I noticed was how quickly you pulled out your mayonnaise tube," says Viviana with a giggle. "Which was immediately, as usual."

"Speaking of which," Andrea says, and he squeezes a blotch of mayonnaise on a piece of bread and pops it in his mouth, swallowing it in a single mouthful.

"But poor Dario, Chiara never arrived," says Viviana with a sympathetic pout. "How long did we wait before she phoned? Nine o'clock, wasn't it? You took the call in your bedroom, I remember, while Andrea and I just stared at each other helplessly. What did she tell you, exactly?"

"To be honest, I can't remember the literal words — but the gist of it was that she couldn't string me along anymore; yes, she thought I was a wonderful person, but she was still in love with her boyfriend . . . you know, the normal bullshit women say."

"No, I certainly *don't* know, Dario . . . geez, Andrea, how can you eat mayonnaise after lemon sorbet!" She sticks out her tongue in disgust.

"Come on, Viv!" he says while mincing his mouthful. "Of *course* you know what Dario means. Anyway, old boy, I remember you came out of your bedroom with a positively desperate look and grabbed a bottle of wine from the table, and as we watched you threw your head back and drank it dry in just a few gulps. Thinking of which, as Fosco would say, *Para via la malinconia, bevi vin qualunque sia"* ("To rid yourself of melancholy, drink wine no matter the quality"). He pushes his glass forward with a smile, waiting for the refill he's just earned. As I pour for him, he continues, "I've never again in my life seen an entire bottle disappear that fast; it was incredible. I wanted to applaud you. But then you took your car keys and whooshed out the door, slamming it behind you. Not even saying goodbye!"

Viviana adds that she, too, was completely bowled over by my drinking performance that night. I shrug. "What can I say? . . . I was in rage, crazy with grief; I wanted to drive all the way to India or Nepal and become a Buddhist monk. But when I reached Radda in Chianti I'd cooled down enough to realize that wasn't such a good idea after all, as in Nepal they probably don't produce much wine; so I stopped in a bar that had just recently opened. I remember that I was the only client and the bartender was eager to show off his skills".

"So what exactly happened?" Viviana asks. "I've always wanted to hear the whole story."

"Nothing much. I just asked him to serve me his specialties."

"We were extremely concerned, you know that, don't you? We tried calling you on your portable but you ignored us. We had no idea where you were, and we were almost frantic. Well . . . I was, anyway. You weren't worried at all, were you, Andrea?"

"No, I knew the old boy too well. And since I was starving I helped myself to the *ribollita*; you ordered me to wait for Dario, but I knew he was out drowning his sorrows in wine. And we'd already waited so long for Chiara; I wanted to eat while the food was still warm." He rubs his tummy, remembering the meal.

"The barman actually poured me a Negroni," I say, resuming my story, "and I tossed it back like a shot. I thought it tasted good so I ordered another one; then he asked if I wanted to try a Mojito, and I did. Then I sampled a Martini and a Bloody Mary, and then something called a Cachaca. Then, inevitably, I started telling him about Chiara; I told him her belly resembled a goblet of wine and that her breasts were like two plump bunches of grapes, and her breath was as delicate as the perfume of wild apples."

"You were basically reciting verses from the Canticle of Canticles," Viviana points out with a smile.

"Was I? . . . Well, why not, they were true. Anyway, I ended up ordering a Stravecchio Brandy, which he didn't want to serve me because he was getting worried about my condition. It seems I was having problems speaking coherently; also I'd turned white as a sheet. I even fell off the stool at one point; but luckily I was the only guest. He helped me back up and somehow I managed to convince him even then that I was okay, and persuaded him to serve me the brandy. I wondered what I told him; I'm sure I spoke very badly about women; as Plutarch said, *Ciò che sta nel cuore del sobrio è sulla lingua dell'ubriaco* ('What lurks in a sober man's heart leaps from the tongue of a drunkard"). I imagine I let loose a whole misogynist spiel before my head started to spin like a top."

"I was furious with you," Viviana says. "How could you have just left your guests like that? And now that I think about it, I was a little fed up with you too, Andrea, because you started getting friendly with me, rubbing up against me and making doe eyes at me."

"C'mon, Viv, you were just too nervous. I told you I knew the old boy would be fine, so why not take advantage of the *ribollita*, and if the candles and roses inspired a little flirting, why not do that too?"

"I'm glad the ambience worked on you, at least," I say. "As for me, I was feeling very different; in fact I ended up wobbling to the men's room and crouching over the toilet, tossing up all the gunk I'd poured into my stomach. Then I splashed my face with cold water, and when the bartender came to see if I needed help, I asked him to get my wallet from my inner pocket and take whatever money I owed him, then to find your name on my portable and dial you up."

"I remember when you answered the phone, Andrea; you were, as usual, busy spreading some mayonnaise on a slice of bread. At first you looked worried but then you started smiling, then laughing out loud; so I knew everything must be okay. "

"Well, I saw your name appear on the Caller I.D., Dario, so I was expecting to hear your voice; but instead I found myself talking to a complete stranger, I had no idea who; he told me that you'd downed an immoral amount of alcohol, which was particularly worrying because it seems you were drinking cocktails instead than wine. Then he said you couldn't talk because you had your head in the toilet, and that's when I had to laugh."

"I can't tell you how miserable I was feeling. I kept thinking of Chiara even as I was watching the puke slide across the ceramic tiles. I was slick with cold sweat while cursing the bitch, the flowers, the boyfriend, fuck them all!

"Whoa," says Viviana, "are you still upset about it?. . . Because it's starting to sound that way. As for you, Andrea, I'll always envy the way you never take things too seriously. I was so frustrated with you when you were recounting what the bartender had told you, and laughing as if there was nothing to be worried about!"

"But what else could I have done? I know the old boy well, I knew he could take it. Though, as I said, I was alarmed that he'd been drinking actual liquor instead of wine. That's why I agreed to go fetch him. I knew he must be flat-out sloshed."

"I certainly was. But I did manage pull myself together, get to my feet, and face myself in the mirror. I was horrified by my appearance. I even thought, 'What if Chiara should see me now,' but then I thought 'Fuck that bitch' and I went storming out; only I couldn't see straight so I ended up in the ladies' room, and after that a supply closet, before I finally found the right door. On my way out I purchased a bottle of red wine to prove I was myself again, then headed for the exit."

"And you Andrea, donning your ridiculous beret and saying that it was your 'mission' to go and save him; but not such a crucial mission that you couldn't pause for one last shot of red for the road. Even so, Dario, I hoped he would return soon so that I could comfort you."

"Aw, c'mon, Viviana!" I can't get used to hearing her speak this way.

"Dario, what do you say," Andrea asks, eyeing the grappa on my counter, "should we open another bottle or pass directly to the heavy artillery?"

"No, let's stick to *prosecco*," I say while opening the fourth bottle. "But if you want another glass, I'll need a quotation."

"Hm," he says thoughtfully. "How about, *Mi ci vuole solo un bicchiere per ubriacarmi, purtroppo non mi ricordo se è il tredicesimo o quattordicesimo?*" ("All I need is one glass to get me drunk; alas I can't remember if it's the thirteenth or fourteenth.")

"Okay, I'll accept that, even though I already have it. George Burns, if I'm not mistaken."

Then Viviana pipes up, "How does this one sound ? *Ne annegano più nel vino che nell'acqua!*" ("More drown in wine than in water.") "My *nonno's* personal motto," she adds.

"Now *that's* a very appropriate addition," I say while pouring both my guests a refill. Then I settle back and continue my narrative. "I remember that I turned my head skyward, took a deep breath, and then realized that the sky was pitch black but — also white."

"Yes," says Viviana. "Remember, I walked you to your car,

Andrea, ordering you to bring Dario back immediately, and as I watched your taillights disappear in the distance, I too noticed that the sky was both dark but white."

Andrea takes a mouthful of *prosecco*, then says, "Okay, I'm no poet and I can't remember the color of the sky, but I do remember it was almost eleven o'clock and it was goddamn freezing cold and as I shivered in my car I couldn't help giggling, anticipating the condition I'd find you in, old boy."

"I was ashamed to be in that condition! My mouth tasted awful, but I took a big gup of red to cover the foul flavor."

"Anyway," Viviana interjects, "there I was, alone in that desolated house of yours, wondering how you could bear to live so isolated from civilization. I added a couple of logs to the fire and coiled up on the sofa in front of the hearth, and sat there sipping some wine and reflecting on how stupid men really are — when I happened to glance outside and saw that it was snowing! I watched the flakes come spiraling down, and it was beautiful; but then I thought about you two out there and I started to worry."

"I was halfway to Radda in Chianti when it started coming down," Andrea says. "Big, thick flakes that suddenly started blanketing the road."

"I remember," I tell him. "My windshield immediately filled up, the wipers could barely keep it clear, and I had problems keeping the car straight. Also, my head was banging; I felt like I had a pneumatic drill chipping away at my brain. I was in trouble. Then when I was sure matters couldn't get any worse, I spotted a bear. Now, I was well aware we have no bears at these latitudes, but I was convinced. God only knows what it really was. Then my mind doubled back to Chiara and once again I was tormenting myself over her behavior and wondering why she wasn't with me. Then suddenly I saw a car approaching in the opposite direction, and I was temporarily blinded by its headlights and I found myself swerving into the oncoming lane — it was only a fluke that I avoided a collision."

"That is exactly what I was worried about," says Viviana. "I was looking out the window, watching the blizzard get stronger and stronger, and hoping you had chains on your tires. I kept looking for headlights in the distance, hoping it would be you returning home. But no one came, and now it was really belting down"

"Tell me about it," Andrea says. "I was still far from Radda when a car in the other lane blinded me with its high-beams, and I slammed on the brakes and skidded over the snow sideways — I couldn't prevent the car from sliding dangerously towards a ditch." He pauses a moment, then narrows his eyes and says, "Hang on a second . . . Dario, that was you!"

I blink. "You know what, Andrea — it might well have been me. Funny we never thought of that possibility before."

"*You* might think it's funny; I was terrified! Anyway, the car eventually slid into a tree, and when I opened the door and looked out I realized that if that tree hadn't been there I'd have rolled down into the ditch. I somehow managed to get out and slipped on the asphalt and landed on my butt. The only thing I could do was call you, Viviana."

"Meanwhile," I say, picking up the story, "I was almost home; I have no idea how I made it so far. I was drunk, I was cold, I was upset, and I had difficulty recognizing where I was. Even the curves seemed tighter. I was 'out as a terrace,' as we say in Tuscany."

"I didn't know that when I called Viviana. When I finally reached her, instead of giving me sympathy she started shouting abuse at me — don't give me that look, Viviana, you did! — calling me a *cretino* and instead of asking if I was okay, demanding to know why I hadn't found Dario. I didn't care about Dario anymore — I was furious with him. And with myself. And with you too, Viviana."

"All right," she protests, "I may have been a *bit* unsympathetic; but I did come to your aid, didn't I?"

"Okay, okay," I say, quelling the nascent argument, "let's not quarrel, guys . . . As for me, I remember I kept drinking from that bottle of red, and when I was a couple of miles from home I almost collided with a car coming in the opposite direction. The windows were all steamed up and I couldn't see a thing."

"As for me," said Viviana, "I was on my way to help Andrea, and the only thing on *my* mind was how stupid men are. In fact I was so busy fuming about that, that somewhere along that snowbound road a car came barreling right at me, and I had to swerve to avoid it — I skidded against the guardrail, and the car died and wouldn't start again." She raises an eyebrow at me. "Dario, that can only have been you."

"Possibly . . ." I say.

She stands up and slaps me hard on the head, then we all

burst out laughing and finish off the bottle before tackling the next. While I'm opening it, Andrea chimes in: "So I waited and waited, but of course you never arrived, Viviana, and I really thought I was going to freeze to death out there till I heard an engine approach."

"That must be about the time I finally got home," I say. "I hobbled up to the entrance and somehow managed to get the door open on the umpteenth attempt. The lights were on, the fire was crackling, but no one was there. I was too sloshed to formulate any logical explanation. I just took it for granted that you had both gone, so I collapsed on the bed and passed out — as they say in Chianti, *il vino è un buon cavallo ma spesso getta a terra il suo cavaliere* ("Wine is a good horse but often throws its rider.")

By now we are all speaking at once, almost overlapping each other. "I just wanted to die," Viviana says, "I hated both of you and was asking what the hell I was doing on a deserted road in a blizzard somewhere in the Chianti hills. I sat on the icy guardrail and started to cry like a child, and began cursing one by one every single male in the entire world, but especially that idiot driving on the wrong side of the road." She again glares at me with mock menace, but fortunately Andrea is already talking over her.

"I jumped into the center of the road," he says, "and waved my arms frantically; and soon I recognized the car approaching as a *carabinieri* jeep. The driver saw me and came to a halt. Of course it was Iuzzolino. I was saved, even though I knew I'd have to endure his sermonizing all the way back to Rio."

"I say I passed out," I corrected myself, "but really I was still feeling a bit turbulent; and in fact I soon woke up again because the foul mixture in my stomach kept surging up, and I ended up getting sick all over the mat."

Viviana tucks her feet beneath her as she continues reflecting. "Finally the silence of the snowfall was broken by the sound of an engine approaching. I stopped sobbing and raised my head; I was safe! When the jeep pulled up I recognized Iuzzolino, and also your idiotic grin, Andrea."

"I can't help it, Viv, I just couldn't stop thinking of the irony of the situation. You should have seen yourself sitting there alone on the guardrail looking so forlorn, you'd have laughed too. I was sure we'd come across Dario next, and the picture would be complete."

"I wish we *had* found Dario. I wanted to ask about him, but

Iuzzolino kept droning on and I couldn't get a word in. Then I realized that since you weren't saying anything about him, Andrea, maybe you didn't want Iuzzolino to know about him; so I kept my mouth shut. When Iuzzolino asked what we were doing out so late I simply said we were on the way to your house for the weekend, Dario. I was so relieved to see your car parked outside."

"I thanked Iuzzi for the lift and told him we'd have our cars towed the next day, after the snow stopped — *if* it stopped. I'm sure he suspected we were lying, but there wasn't much he could do about it."

"When we entered the lights were still on. All I wanted was to climb in bed with you, Dario, but when I got a whiff of the smell in there I opted for the sofa."

"Leaving me no choice but to get in bed with you, old boy! Thanks a lot!"

The story has wound up and so, it appears, has the evening. "Look at the time," says Viviana, glancing at her watch. "We should really get going, Andrea; I've got a plane to catch tomorrow. Thanks for the exquisite dinner Dario; promise you'll phone more frequently from now on."

My friends linger another ten minutes to help empty the last bottle of *prosecco*; then they depart, and as soon as I close the door behind them I go and switch off the mini tape-recorder I hid behind a pile of books. I have a new chapter for Mia! Then I sit on the sofa and recall the final events of that episode.

When I awakened the morning after all the commotion, I was resting on my side. I felt as I though I had a nail driven into my temple, another one in the parietal bone and three in my forehead. My mouth tasted as if I had devoured an assortment of decomposing cadavers, and my breath could have peeled wallpaper off a wall. I could hear my innards gurgle and groan, as if I was about to give birth to the creature from the Alien films. I looked at the mess I had made on the mat and I cursed myself soundly, but I was in no condition to do anything about it now. I rolled partly over to rest on my back, and had a heart attack when I realized I wasn't in bed alone.

Now it had happened a few times previously that I woke up to find myself in the company of some wreck under the blankets after a mammoth booze-up, and I had justified it to my friends by saying that after 3 a.m. and four bottles of wine, as long as they're breathing anything is fine. But this time I had gone over the top, as beside me was the glabrous corpse of a huge, pink, fleshy *man!* Then I realized it was Andrea and relaxed.

I gave him a little shove but he didn't even wince; I slapped him repeatedly on the face until he jolted awake with a scream and sat up with his back against the headboard. He was as pale as a phantom, his face swollen and his eyes gummy; he was obviously, like me, suffering from a historic hangover. He mumbled that he had been on his way to fetch me but his car hit a tree by a ditch, and that Viviana came to the rescue but that she also ended up the same way and that Iuzzolino had rescued them both while on patrol and brought them back here. Despite the pain I couldn't hold back my laughter as the story continued, heaping one disaster on top of the last; but I had to control my mirth when I saw how serious Andrea was. He told me to shut my mouth and let him sleep.

I got up and went to the bathroom but the pipes were all frozen, and on top of that there was no electricity either. I took off my sweater — now encrusted with last night's intestinal regurgitations — and was reminded of how, as a child, I would return from school and my mother could tell exactly what they'd served us for lunch simply by examining the stains on my shirt. I kept my jeans on and donned an old jacket and my fireman boots.

In the living room there was a pleasant aroma of burnt firewood. Viviana was coiled up on the sofa. She looked a bit chilled so I covered her gently with an extra woolen blanket. I added some logs to the fire and got it going again. Then I was distracted by a blinding light that penetrated from the veranda; the sun had risen and was reflecting on the thick layer of immaculate white snow covering the adjacent valley and hills. This reflected light now inundated the room, and it was quite a spectacle.

I had difficulty opening the front door — it was wedged in place by the heavy snowfall — and once outside I saw that the vines and olives were coated with snow. My head was still hammering with pain, but I felt like walking in that fairytale ambience. The sky was such an irresistible shade of blue and the silence was absolute; everything was mute and immobile, as if frozen in time, and I was caught by the lure of so much stillness and beauty. It was amazing and at the same time intriguing to observe that my beloved hills had so suddenly changed color; I actually had difficulty recognizing them, as if I'd just awakened on some unknown planet.

Suddenly I was suffused by a strange contentment; somehow, being completely cut off from the world, with no water, lights, and telephone, it felt stangely safe — and liberating. I felt flush with enjoyment as I walked down to the valley, leaving my footprints in the virgin snow. I reached the petite pond and found it well frozen; I dared to put my foot on the surface and was surprised that it easily held my weight. I dared to shuffle cross it, then started mock-skating, amusing myself as only a child would.

While sunning my face in the cold, clear rays of morning, I suddenly heard like a sound like cracking glass — and a heartbeat later found myself in freezing water up to my waist. Immediately all the poetry of the moment vanished and I was shocked back to reality. My angry curses echoed in the valley, shattering the stillness I'd only just been treasuring, and I trudged home cold and angry, and with my headache returned more poundingly than before. I found Viviana now awake and heating some milk on the fire. She got up and hugged me and it was then that I realized that there was more in that tight embrace than simple friendship. I took off my jeans and she dried my wet legs with a towel and massaged my feet, then handed me a cup of milk she had sweetened with a touch of acacia honey.

Andrea came in, announcing himself with a long groan and rubbing his swollen eyes with his fists, and we made a tentative attempt at piecing together the facts of the terrible night we had all just experienced. How curious that we didn't draw the obvious conclusion that I had been the pirate who'd caused both their accidents. Camaraderie and laughter slowly returned, and we decided the best course of action was to put the chains on my car (which was all-wheel drive) and try to reach Siena, where we could hire a pickup truck. Then, until water and electricity were restored, it was best that I remain at Viviana's place.

Driving at a very low speed, we realized once we neared the city that the road was a virtual cemetery of wrecked cars; and once we reached the outskirts the roads were free of snow but congealed in a muck of black filth.

We left Andrea at his parents' house and walked to Viviana's apartment, which was located on the top floor of an ancient building in the Wave *contrada* of Siena. I swore to forget Chiara, no matter how hard that might be, and took a good, long look at Viviana: in the crisp, clear light she was really beguilingly pretty, with bouncy Shirley Temple curls and a disarming smile.

We drank a chicken consommé and went to bed early. I cuddled up next to her and started stroking her hair. We were safe and warm and together, and the moment seemed ripe. She rolled over to face me and just as I was about to press my lips against hers we heard a snap, then a screech, and then a deafening roar as a wooden beam in the ceiling gave way. Fifty hectoliters of ice-cold water came cascading down onto the bed. The roof hadn't been able to hold the weight of all that snow and had buckled, tipping the water tank in the attic on its side — and plunging its contents right through the ceiling onto us.

Viviana was truly traumatized and started to weep. I called the emergency number and then tried to comfort her. We ended up renting a room in a small pension. It was the perfect epilogue for a truly crazy two days. We decided to lay all the blame on Chiara!

It all seems so long ago now; and yet having Andrea and Viviana here tonight, it also seems like no time at all has passed. I shrug and get up to wash the dishes; after which I decide to sleep on the sofa in front of the fire, sipping the final glass of the day and recalling the pleasant dinner with my two dear friends . . . and also Becchini, to whom I owe the inspiration for this evening . . . and also, obviously, Mia, because as Rabelais once wrote, *quando io bevo penso, quando penso bevo!* ("When I drink, I think, and when I think, I drink.") In testament to which, I help myself to one more.

Just before falling asleep I hear the trill on the phone meaning that I've received a text message.

"Old boy! Thanks for the great fish dinner. On the way home I happened to think of a phrase that could be useful for your book, but probably more useful to us personally: *Se il bere interferisce con il tuo lavoro con ogni probabilità sei uno che beve molto. Se invece è il lavoro che interferisce con il tuo bere in questo caso sei un alcolizzato.*" ("If drinking is interfering with your work, you're probably a heavy drinker. If work is interfering with your drinking, you're probably an alcoholic.")

I chuckle appreciatively and eventually drift off to sleep to the sweet strains of Kerri Sherwood's piano.

28

MIMÌ

I'm awakened by the church bell echoing in the valley. Unhurriedly my numb fingers peel the heavy woolen coverlet from my inert body. My first thought is, Why are the bells chiming *a festa* as if it there were a village feast? Unless I've overslept a full day, as in that anecdote I sent Mia, it's Friday. Then I glance at the wall calendar my cousin Guido sent me, but my attention is distracted from the date by the photo above it. Guido is a world-renowned photographer who recently enlisted my aid for a *Playboy* photo spread entitled "Beauties Under the Tuscan Sun." Aside from scouting locations, my job was to entertain the models between shoots — a grueling job that I obviously accepted with little enthusiasm. Anyway, this calendar had been Guido's acknowledgment of my efforts. I manage to tear my gaze from the half-naked babe lying on a deserted beach to examine the dates laid out so prosaically beneath her . . . and that's when I realize it is indeed a religious feast day.

I don a tailored suit I had made specifically for a book tour in the U.S., and after breakfast I summon my will and settle on going to mass.

At the ancient village church I push open the heavy church door and find that the service has already commenced. I can only find room at the very back, next to an elderly woman I've never seen before whose powerful garlic breath reminds me of Marco — maybe a relative? As usual I have enormous difficulty concentrating on what Don Aldo is saying. Actually, a number of positively obscene thoughts creep into my mind, so much so that I have to wonder if it's the vestiges of my teenage rebelliousness; I regularly used to subvert the services with this kind of lascivious thinking, whenever I was dragged to mass against my will.

To divert my dirty mind I have a look around to see who's here. I spot Clara, sporting one of her Queen Mother hats with a brightly colored plume that's brushing against my friend Eliseo's ear. How I love Eliseo — truly the last genuine

Chiantigiano (but I've assigned this title to others, haven't I? . . . Well, each of them deserves it). He's 87 or thereabouts, and spends his days lovingly tending his vegetable garden. Only recently did I learn that he is totally blind. He fooled me for *years*. I discovered his secret when once I saw him walking the village; I stopped in front of him and without saying a word opened my arms to embrace him; but instead of returning the greeting he collided with me and knocked us both to the ground. I blurted out some apologies, then as I helped him back to his feet he said, if nothing had happened, "You know the old saying, Dario?"

"Which saying is that, Eliseo?"

"In Chianti, you either stumble on a rock or upon a fool," and he let loose a raucous laugh while lighting a Tuscan cigar.

I then spot Valentino (God bless him!) and his daughter, who's now in her early 80s. Valentino himself is a spry 103. I've often tried to engage him in conversation, even just to exchange a few words, but he's never had time for me; he's a busy, busy man. His most recent hobby is carving statues out of wood. Despite his age he smokes and drinks wine every day, and whenever I try to chat with him he tells me to come back in a few weeks, as though he has all the time in the world still before him.

My eyes now fall on Emanuele; but I don't let them rest there, immediately looking beyond him to where Giulio rests on his walking stick. I imagine he's envying the priest, who's about to drink the consecrated wine from the chalice. Orazio is there too, scratching his head and releasing a blizzard of dandruff onto his shoulders, and I also see Becchini, who I imagine is amusing himself by mentally translating Don Aldo's sermon into some exotic language. Dino is snoozing in a dark corner just like he does at the *polisportiva*, with his wife nudging him with her elbow every time he snores. Iuzzolino is in the front pew, wearing his *carabinieri* uniform for his last official occasion, since he is due to receive a pension soon; he twitches the tips of his now snow-white moustache as if anticipating it.

The younger generation is here at mass, too — the teenagers exchanging furtive, flirting looks and then blushing each time their crossed glances endure for more than a few seconds.

At the end of the service the entire village files into the local bar for an espresso or aperitivo, and *Dottor* Becchini sidles up beside me with a friendly countenance.

"Dario, you look extremely serene. You even came to mass today!"

"*Sì dottore, grazie.* And I had friends over for dinner last night, and I'm going to my *contrada* tonight. Do you need me at the *polisportiva* these days?"

"Sure; how about serving dinner to the seniors on New Year's Eve?"

"Count on me, *dottore.*"

"Glad to hear it! Let me buy you a drink."

"Just water for me, *dottore.*"

He waves a hand at me in dismissal and says, *"Dio non ha fatto che l'acqua, ma l'uomo ha fatto il vino"* ("God made only water but man invented wine").

"*Dottore*, what will I do without you?" I murmur with a touch of sincere sadness, "You're not really intent on leaving us, are you?"

"*Sì*, Dario; but my door will always be open for you." He orders us some wine and asks if I prefer mine with water or without.

"This time with water, *dottore.*"

"Il vino ha due difetti se ci aggiungi l'acqua lo rovini, se non aggiungi acqua, ti rovini" ("Wine has two defects: if you add water you'll ruin it; if you don't, you'll ruin yourself"). How I love this man!

"I'll opt for the second possibility this morning, *dottore.*" He shrugs and passes me my watered wine. "So when is *Dottor* Bevilacqua taking possession of the ambulatory?"

"Next week, as a matter of fact. Care to join me for lunch today?"

"*Grazie, dottore*, but I have an appointment with an American girl." I pause, then add, "She's called Mia, and I think I love her."

"I'm happy to hear it! Will you promise to introduce her to me?"

"*Promesso, dottore.*" Then, to change the subject and to gather material for my book, I ask him for five reasons why one should drink wine.

"Facile a ben riflettere: primo per fare festa, poi per colmare la sete, poi per evitare di avere sete dopo, poi per fare onore al buon vino ed infine per ogni motivo" ("Easily done, on reflection: first, to have a good time; then to quench your thirst; then to avoid being thirsty; then to honor good wine; and lastly, for any good reason").

I laugh, and after Becchini turns to speak to someone else I spend a few moments committing these reasons to memory. When I've finished my wine I turn to head for the door, but feel compelled to return to the counter and interrupt Becchini, who is in deep conference with a young mother. I overhear just his last words, which are *"Il vino uccide i vermi e salva il fanciullo"* ("Wine will kill the disease and heal the toddler").

"Excuse me, *dottore*," I say, but with a graver expression than before, "but I think I need a sixth reason."

He stares a me questioningly for a moment, then says, "Then let me quote Cardinal Richelieu: *Se Dio avesse proibito il vino perché mai l'avrebbe fatto così buono"* ("If God had wanted to prohibit wine he would have never made it taste so good").

I nod in appreciation. "I'll miss you, *dottore*."

"And I you, Dario. Look after your Mia. And remember that *il vino fa allegria e l'acqua fa malinconia"* ("Wine produces joy, water only melancholy").

"I will, Giovanni," I say, for the first time using his Christian name; and I embrace him with sadness clutching my heart. He exchanges the hold and whispers in my ears *"l'acqua divide gli uomini; il vino li unisce".* ('Water divides men; wine unites them') "It's by Libero Bovio *from Don Liberato si spassa"* he boasts proudly.

I return home as if I really am expecting Mia, while thinking how much I'll miss Becchini when he retires to Rome for good.

At home I return to reality, and it is desolate. I fill the pot with water and prepare a simple *penne* with tomato sauce, then open a bottle of Chianti Classico Fattoria La Mandria and propose a *brindisi* to *La felicità, che come un vino pregiato, deve essere assaporato sorso a sorso* ("Happiness, that like a prestigious wine must be enjoyed gulp by gulp").

Now it's time to check email. I find hundreds of messages but none from Mia, and I get worried. "Where are you, *piccola?"* I whisper to the computer.

Despite her unusual silence I decided to send her the "Madre of Them All" chapter, but first I give it a careful rereading. Later, still feeling somewhat abandoned by her, I don my Caterpillar scarf and drive to Siena.

I park outside the Ovile gate and walk to the headquarters of my *contrada*. The tables have been laid and I can hear the kids singing the Caterpillar anthem: *"Si sa che non lo volete il nostro bel brucone, per forza o per amore lo dovete rispettar!"* ("We all know that you don't want our fine Caterpillar, but with strength or with love we will make you respect it!")

I enter the halls of the Noble *contrada* and Danilo and the other members all greet me. I choose to sit at a table with Ennio, Macario and a character known as Roccia (the Rock) who are discussing the 1989 Palio, the one in which we drew the legendary horse Pytheos and yet managed to lose anyway; the race was won by Lupa (She-Wolf) with a riderless horse.

I remain silent, listening to their experiences of that Palio, and how our jockey, so sure of the victory, had raised his arm in triumph just before the She-Wolf overtook him on the very last yard. Then the subject turns to the 1951 Palio, which was won by Panther; we had drawn a horse named Niduzza, and the jockey we hired was nicknamed Rompighiaccio (Ice-breaker). Roccia and Ennio have trouble remembering the name of the horse drawn by the Shell (Nicchio); this takes the entire first course and part of the second, during which they toss out some few hundreds of horses' names until they finally settle on the Fox (Volpe). Then as the main course arrives Macario introduces a new subject: the 1913 race. I decide to return home. I'm just not in the right mood; it's too much for me.

I head towards the exit but am blocked by Duccio, who offers me a glass of red at the bar. I make up an excuse but am polite enough to toast with him. *"Chi beve vino rosso beve felicità"* ("He who drinks red drinks happiness"), he says, raising the cup towards the effigy of the Caterpillar (Bruco). After this I return to the car.

On the way back home I feel somewhat weird again. The stars glitter above me and I try to imagine Mia's eyes in them. I wish that she were here next to me. "Where are you, Mia?" I repeat to myself.

I go to bed frustrated; and the next morning jump up to check e-mail. I hold my breath as the mailbox opens . . . but there it is! The one to lighten my heart. Curiously, it's blank; there's no text! . . . Then I notice the attachment. I double-click on the paperclip symbol, and suddenly it opens before me: a letter — a real one. This is the very first time I've received such a long message from her.

From: Mia Lane
To: Dario Castagno
Subject: Summer 1982

Dear Dario,
Please excuse my absence; I've had lots to think about over

the past few days, and I've decided it's time you read the following. All I ask is that you have patience and read attentively.

In 1982 my parents sent me to Rome to study at a prestigious institute for exchange students, because they wanted me to learn Italian as well as to experience life in a foreign country. The plan was that at the end of the semester they would join me and we'd spend a vacation together before returning home to California. Well, that summer an extraordinary happening happened: Italy was in the world football cup finals, and the whole nation seemed to go crazy. Whenever the azzurri played, the country came to a halt; heavy traffic dissolved before your eyes, shopkeepers pulled down their shutters, offices stopped answering the phones, and the squares were transformed into a sort of surreal De Chirico painting. Everyone was tuned into RAI UNO, and at the end of each game a collective cry of joy preceded the mob spilling back into the piazzas, waving the Italian tricolor flag and embracing each other wildly, diving into the ancient fountains, parading and carousing and honking their car horns until sunrise. When the azzurri finally won the title, in Spain, the whole country exploded into pure rapture; it was just as you say, Dario, another Italy. Even the terrorists, left and right wing, must have been soccer fans (now you understand my curiosity for that era) because not one single attack took place that month. Through it all, I remained mesmerized by Rome, its friendly people, the exquisite cuisine, the typical Italian disorder where nobody seems to work but things somehow get done anyway. Rome was a big city but it had a charmingly provincial aura that I doubt has survived today.

It was my very first visit to Europe, and as often happens when you're a teenager, it instilled in me some very intense sensations. My parents eventually arrived and rented a large Mercedes, and after having spent some days in the eternal city we drove up to Tuscany, our destination a small village somewhere deep in Chianti. I remember leaving Rome reluctantly because I had a life there now, and was conscious that I was spending my final days in Italy far from its lovely chaos and the sort of amusements that attracted a girl of my age. Instead, I was with my parents, in a car, in the country. You can imagine my mood.

We were guests of a well-off family who produced and distributed Chianti Classico in the U.S., and who gave us a magnificently warm welcome. Their farmhouse had been recently restored and enjoyed an envious position perched atop a hill, surrounded by luxurious vineyards loaded with copious juicy grapes. I recall the optimism of the owners that year; they predicted a five-star vintage, and if I'm not mistaken 1982 is remembered as one of the best of the century.

Tourism had not reached these latitudes yet, and when Mom and I went to purchase groceries the villagers stared at us as though we were space aliens fresh off our rocket ship. Inevitably the news spread around Castellina in Chianti, and soon everybody seemed to know who we were and where we were staying. It seemed as if our presence was the main subject for gossip and chat. Everyone was mawkishly friendly and forthcoming with us, in particular the owner of the drug store, who insisted we taste his homemade cheeses and salamis until my mother felt obliged to buy the entire stock, more out of kindness than desire. The inhabitants enjoyed stopping us and asking questions about America, which evidently still existed mainly as a myth in the collective imagination.

I used to walk past the local bar in the evenings; there were always dozens of Vespas parked in front and boys sitting on the wall smoking and drinking wine, and whistling to get our attention.

One morning, after a breakfast of fig jam spread on Tuscan bread, I asked Mom for permission to go for a walk; I was feeling a little restless, and everyone else had decided to spend the day sitting around the pool in company of a bottle of Chianti. I left by way of the manicured garden, which on that day was soaked in the perfume of rosemary and lavender, and strolled down to the well of the valley, bordered by chuffs of wild fennel that in the boiling summer air gave off a strong licorice scent. Despite the heat, at those altitudes the air was dry and pleasant. I was amused to note that my flowery dress attracted a myriad of multicolored butterflies, which circled my head and tried to land on me.

When I reached the end of the vine that bordered my route, the path took me into a chestnut forest; the air instantly became more humid and the surface was covered by soft moss. I slipped off my sandals and walked barefooted on that green carpet, gathering a small bunch of wildflowers for my mother and binding it with lace I took from my hair.

I was unconsciously attracted by the sound of the water somewhere below, a sound that grew more distinct as I wended my way down to it.

When I reached the stream I realized I wasn't alone.

I noticed a light blue Vespa (azzurro, like the shirts of the recent world champs) with a white seat, resting on an oak tree, and I could hear faint strains of music wafting through the thick bramble bushes and skittering over the clamor of the running water. I ducked behind the bush and I peered out at a boy with long hair wearing a pair of tiny cutoff jeans; his gaze was lowered because he was absorbed in a book, which rested in his lap while he sat cross-legged on a rock in the center of the river. There was a towel and a leather rucksack on the riverbank, as well as the stereo whose music I now recognized as being that of Lucio Battisti, who was extremely popular in those years.

I furtively studied the expression of that young boy; he seemed enchanted. He was smoking something, occasionally parting his lips to release a tissue of thick smoke that seconds later evaporated in the sky. I could tell that he was from these hills; he was completely at ease in this rustic context, his gestures were so easy and natural it was like they were an integral part of the landscape, like the swaying of grass in the breeze. Suddenly he stood up and with an energetic swoop tossed the book onto the riverbank, then dove headlong into the water, so confidently he must have known its depth would accommodate him. I pulled farther back into the bushes so that he couldn't see me, but I continued spying on him from my secret vantage point: a lithe young man swimming against current, sending up sprays of water at every stroke.

Then he disappeared from sight and I felt alone again. I cautiously crept out of the bushes and sat on the pebbled beach, contemplating the limpid water that ran before of me. This place was so full of life; a variety of fireflies and other insects were whirring through the air, and I was surprised and delighted when a gray crab climbed on a rock, and instants later clambered away again, as if it were startled by my presence. I remained there gazing at the light dancing on the water; then I recognized some words from the song now playing in the stereo: acqua azzurra acqua chiara (blue water, clear water). It was so incredibly appropriate to the situation. Then I went back behind my bush and hid again in case the boy returned.

I remained there for a long time, until I felt something tickling me on my nape. I whirled around and saw the boy from the rock, right there behind me, holding a long blade of grass and smiling at me.

He was alarmingly thin but had well sculpted muscles, and despite his fair hair his skin was deeply tan. He said "Ciao," and narrowed his eyes, which were the same blue as the sky; then he flicked the grass to the ground and twisted the water out of his long hair, tightening it in his hands until the gravel below was spattered with moisture.

I remained mute with embarrassment while he towered over me. He went and fetched his leather rucksack, then produced a flask of wine and offered it to me with a friendly gesture. I tentatively took it from him, but still couldn't say a word.

"Bevi," he said, entreating me to drink, and despite never before having done so I took a swig; but the contents lodged in my throat and I coughed them up onto the riverbank. The boy laughed. Instantly I felt the urge to run and hide; I was so mortified. I could feel my eyes redden, and as your friend Giulio would say, my face was probably the spitting image of a sore ass.

Then he stopped laughing and handed me a sunflower that he had hidden behind the bush, and which he had probably just plucked from a nearby field. My arm trembled as I accepted it..

Then he laid the towel on the riverbank and sat down, and invited me to sit next to him. He said, "My name is Dario. And yours?" . . . Yes. It was you, Dario.

I said that my name was Mimì (that's what they called me in Rome), and when I told you that I lived in L.A. you switched to English, which you spoke with a very distinct (and may I say charming) British accent. I told you that I was taking my vacation at the farm on top of the valley. "I know," you said with an impish smile.

Pearls of river water trickled down your body, and your face remained dreamily facing the sun. Then you turned and looked at me for what was probably a nanosecond, but which seemed to me a small infinity; and suddenly you leaned over and pressed your lips to mine, catching me by surprise. I had never kissed a boy before, and the sensation was utterly amazing. I felt your biceps become hard while you squeezed me, and your damp torso became dry against my flowery dress. My heartbeat went wild.

Then you released your grip and started talking about Chianti, about that enchanted place you came to daily, to bathe in glorious solitude. You changed music and inserted a Pink Floyd cassette — I believe it was "More" — and again you kissed me. I was captivated by every word you said; it all blended together with the running water and the sweet essence in the atmosphere.

But the spell was broken when I heard my mother's voice echo down the valley, calling me for lunch. I had to leave you because if I didn't she would come looking for me; and if she found me in your company, well — she certainly wouldn't have been pleased.

You didn't seem to be upset, you lay down with your hands under your head and said that you would pick me up "stasera." I tried to explain that my parents never allowed me out with a local boy, even though it that was my last night and we had to leave early the following morning to catch a plane.

You remained unperturbed as I said all this; you merely watched a stray white cloud as it crossed then sky above our heads. Then you said, "Mimì, I desire that you should wear the same dress tonight." And with that you leapt up, donned a long white shirt that look more like a tunic, grabbed your things, hopped astride your Vespa, kick-started the engine, and went zooming away on the steep rubble road. I stood motionless, watching your figure recede into the distance; and when I could no longer hear the rumble of the motor I felt suddenly alone again, the silence broken only by the ceaseless sound of running water, the buzz of the insects, and every now and then the chant of a cuckoo. I could still smell the aroma of fresh river water and musk that you had left on me, and taste your intense masculine flavor (with hints of wine and tobacco) on my lips.

I returned home with the sunflower in my hand and a thousand thoughts in my head, and the words to Acqua azzurra playing over and over in my memory. Of course I didn't tell my mother about either the encounter or the invitation, but I was subdued and thoughtful all afternoon around the pool, focussing my attention on the swallows diving in to quench their thirst and the industrious bees swarming about a hive inside an old linden tree.

Dinner was served by our hosts, and despite it being a splendid multi-course meal prepared in our honor I didn't eat much; I couldn't. It was our final night in Chianti; my last night in Italy. I gave the banal excuse of a headache and excused myself early, then went to my room and lay on the bed. The windows were wide open and the sounds of the evening reminded me of you; I couldn't seem to get you off my mind. I imagined your sunny expression and the smile that lit up when you talked about how intensely you loved these hills — which, curiously, started feeling more familiar to me now. How I longed to see you again! I wanted it so intensely, that if a genie had granted me any wish at that very moment, that's what I would have chosen.

A faint breeze stirred the branches of the mulberry outside the window. Suddenly I felt a gentle swoosh and a shadow appeared on the window ledge. I was terrified and was about to scream — but then I realized it must be you. My heart started clanging inside my chest. The next moment an intense scent of roses filled the room, and you followed it — jumping over the sill in the same shirt, and a pair of worn jeans ripped open at both knees. You handed me the roses and quickly adjusted your long hair; but all you said was, "Mimì vieni!" I didn't have to be told twice.

I was only wearing my panties — not even a bra — but I felt no shame; it was as if I had known you forever. You went over to the sofa where I'd draped the flower-print dress I wore that morning, and you tossed it to me. I slipped it on, then you grabbed my hand and helped me out the window and onto the mulberry tree. The crickets were our unknowing accomplices, their shrill chirping covering the rustle and snap of our escape as we climbed down. I wasn't at all concerned about what I was doing; I was just happy —I'd never felt such intensely wonderful sensations in all my young life.

Once we reached the ground you told me your Vespa was on the other side of the woods, and you led me there, holding my hand. I felt so free, leaving behind my strict parents and my over-regulated existence, even though I was knew it would only be for a few hours.

Before we reached the scooter we crossed a cypress forest, where you told me researchers had dug up ancient Etruscan tombs; did I want to see them? To be honest, I had no idea who the Etruscans were, but you were so enthusiastic I eagerly said yes. As we made our way there you patiently put in plain words the background of that noble, lost race, who ruled those lands hundreds of years before Christ. Your eyes sparkled, you were so taken by these "ancestors" of yours as you called them, and when we entered the main tomb I felt as if history was oozing from those walls built on lava bricks. The moon reflected on the entry of the central tomb, which you thought probably belonged to a noble family. You also showed me where the

Etruscans would have placed the funerary urns containing the ashes of the deceased, and shared a number of anecdotes regarding them; then you crouched down and picked up some tiny fragments that you placed in my hand. You told me it was bucchero — a material they used to make ancient vases and other ornamental objects.

It was obvious you were going to become a tour guide, Dario; you had the capacity to make these dead things come alive, and to seem so powerfully important and beautiful. When I read your books, years later, I laughed at how much the man who wrote them reminded me of the boy I had known (and I laughed even harder over your experiences with zany, demanding tourists and their bizarre questions and observations). I was disappointed to learn that you no longer escort groups, because, trust me, you were a natural born guide.

You had a small flashlight that you used to illuminate those ancient stones, but it wasn't necessary because the moon was so bright and even the swarms of fireflies contributed their glow, making the light seem soft and magical. You stroked my hair and caressed my face and kissed me, right there within that ancient enclosure. You hunted for my tongue and I felt your taste buds; I felt I needed to bite them one by one. My nipples grew turgid, I had no idea what was going on — what was coming over me? Then you took my hand and we continued along the path. When I heard some frightful grunts in the bushes, you calmly explained they were emitted by wild boars and told me not to be afraid, because these beasts were normally innocuous.

Then we reached a clearing and I followed you towards your Vespa. You straddled the seat and I climbed on after you, clutching your pelvis, and as we rode the wind filled my face with the aroma of your hair, which was flowing behind you. I raised my head and saw a sky that seemed a carpet of stars, and grew dizzy as they seemed to fly by me.

Minutes later you turned onto an avenue bordered by an elegant line of cypress tress that led to a castle. I didn't know that castles still existed; I thought that was only in fairy tales. But I was now living in one, Dario, so it seemed almost natural. You parked close to a small door and I could hear strains of music through a partially opened window. Everything was so still and lovely, like a rare, sweet dream.

You put your arm around my shoulder and guided me into

a large, white hall adorned by very old paintings. The only light came from the candles placed all around the room, in the middle of which a group of teenagers reclined on pillows strewn about the floor, listening raptly to a young man with jet-black hair and green eyes who was playing a grand piano.

As soon as they noticed us, the others quietly got up and came to greet us. To my surprise, I recognized some of them; they were the boys who hung out by the bar and had whistled at me so many times. I was shocked that they now kissed me on the cheek so informally, as though I had always been part of the group.

Dario, the hour or so we spent in that hall, listening to your friend Matteo and drinking wine — which, incidentally, I was quite beginning to appreciate — was simply stupefying. Then you whispered in my ear that you wanted to show me the entire castle, and I followed you away from the others.

In one hand you held a brass chandelier, and with the other you squeezed my waist. We kept climbing flights of stairs, trailed by the ever fainter sound of the music we'd left behind. We opened door after door, passing from hall to hall; the place seemed never to end. And when we finally returned to ground level you showed me the garden, where the moonlight spilled over the lush trees and shrubs like golden honey. I felt as if I were a princess, and you my prince.

There were a number of statues; we sat on the bench below one that was a small marble putto and we kissed again. You raised the base of the statue and scratched on its mossy base Mimì/Dario. At that very moment I realized what it meant to be happy, and knew that for the rest of my life I would measure any new joy or pleasure by comparing it to this moment with you in the castle garden.

You told me that as soon as Matteo ended his performance we were all going to the Belvedere, which was an abandoned house you and your friends had taken possession of; it had become your secret refuge. We went back inside and you introduced me to Matteo, who was no longer playing and who was refreshing himself with a glass of red. He was so handsome; and now that I was face-to-face with him, his green eyes seemed even more intense, and his hair shone in the light of the candles. His posture was so elegant and he was so warmly cordial; not at all a typical teenager. It seemed right that he lived in a castle.

Then you doused all the candles and the whole group filed

outside, climbed aboard their scooters, and zipped away, shrouding the wrought-iron gate in a cloud of dust.

I clug to you as you took one side road, then another and another; the turns got tighter and the road rougher, until we were literally on a cross-country track — and then at last we reached the abandoned house, deep within an old oak forest.

Inside, the boys, who all had very long hair, lit the fire and I started to chat with the girls, who asked me many questions about California. I tried to tell them everything they wished to know, but alas my Italian wasn't very good. Then they invited me to sit before the hearth, which was now ablaze, and as I observed the carefree faces of these young Chiantigiani, lit up as much by joy as by the fire, I fantasized that you were all descendents of the Etruscans.

Flasks of wine appeared like magic, and so did sausages, which you roasted in the glowing embers. Then you all started to sing and I recognized Acqua azzurra acqua chiara — I even managed to join in.

We stayed in that house for many hours, and I wasn't the least bit worried about my parents. I didn't really want to torment myself by thinking about them, because everything was so ridiculously beautiful; to bring them into it would spoil it.

But at a certain point you stood up and announced that it was time to take me back home. My heart sank, because I thought you'd had enough of me. I reluctantly said goodbye to your kind and generous friends, and moments later was back on your Vespa, thinking this wonderful night had ended.

But the surprises were far from over, because instead of going straight back you took another side road and kept going for many miles, until suddenly you stopped the scooter and leaned it against a tree. In the air there was a foul odor of rotten eggs; I had no idea what it could be, but didn't say anything. I trusted you so much I think I would have followed you anywhere in that moment. Then you told me there was a hot sulfur spring nearby, and that I would soon get used to the terrible stench. Nobody else was there, and you took off your clothes and invited me to do the same.

It was a small pool of bubbling water fed by a tiny waterfall that spouted from a rock, and which overflowed into an ice-cold creek. The water felt boiling when we lowered ourselves into it;

then you picked up some mud and applied it to my shoulders, and started to massage me delicately while I gazed up at the sky, again marveling at all those glittering stars. The only sounds were the soothing bubbling of the water and the tender words you whispered in my ear. The atmosphere was simply surreal.

We talked deep into the night, and promised to write and to meet again one day, but probably subconsciously we knew it was very unlikely. Our worlds were too far apart. The next day I would fly home, go back to my high school and to the frenetic rhythms of my chaotic city, and you would stay here leading your lovely, simple life. We kissed, completely naked, until we were literally steamed by the water; our skin was wrinkled and we suddenly looked eighty years old. Even so, Dario, I could have stayed in that pool with you for an eternity.

Without drying ourselves, we put our clothes back on. You suggested that as soon as I got home I should take a shower and scrub my skin with a sponge before going to bed.

You left the Vespa far from the farmhouse and walked me all the way back to the mulberry tree outside my room. I can't help thinking now, as I write this, that a perfect ending would have been coming back to find my parents and our hosts frantic with alarm, and Iuzzolino on the scene in response to their summons; but in fact all was quiet. No one had noticed my absence.

You helped me scramble up the tree trunk, and once I was through the window I turned and watched as you strode away. Just before you vanished, you turned and blew me a kiss, punctuated by a hearty wave; and then you were swallowed by the darkness. I had never even thanked you for that magical night, Dario: I will do so now. Grazie!

My life in California continued along its predictable path. I finished high school, then continued my studies at a prestigious college on the East coast and became a lawyer. I got married very young and had a beautiful son who is almost eighteen now; he's older than we were when we met, don't you find that weird? I got divorced after only a few years of marriage, and then three years ago I learned that I had contracted a terminal disease. You can imagine the shock; for a while I was almost unable to function. Then, perhaps inevitably, I began to accept that I was to share my body with this terrible monster that is inexorably consuming me. I quit my job and began to rediscover myself; I started reading again, went to museums and art galleries and, within the limits allowed, even traveled a bit. I realize this may sound paradoxical but in a way I feel privileged; the simple fact is, by most accounts I shouldn't even be here. After my diagnosis I was optimistically given a few months to live, and instead I've been holding on for over two years. Waking up each day and realizing I'm still alive, is an amazing gift.

One day, quite by chance, I picked up your book Too Much Tuscan Sun here in a bookshop in L.A., and I was so surprised. Then I bought your second, A Day in Tuscany. I would have recognized you as their author even if they'd hidden your name. I could tell you were still the same innocent renegade I met that summer on the river bank, and as I read the stories I imagined that you were reading them aloud to me.

When I read about Matteo's fate I wept, thinking that he must have left us just weeks after I met him. In the same way, I cried just recently when you sent me your new chapter about the Belvedere, and how you spent a day there recalling your teenage years. I feel so privileged to have been part of that world, even briefly. It was then that I seriously considered revealing myself, but I decided to hold off because I wanted you to finish the book.

Forgive me, Dario, but I felt so strong a need to relive the sensations of those places you shared with me, and that I've preserved in my heart ever since. You see, recently my condition worsened, and I decided to send you an e-mail pretending that I worked for a book pulblisher; I didn't know if you would reply to me otherwise, I guess. And once you did reply, I felt I had to keep up the pretense. But I knew I had to end it sometime; and now is that time. I'm happy, Dario, even if outside my window I don't have anything like the vistas you enjoy, just another austere wing of this hospital, and instead of the loamy-scented air of Chianti I'm breathing in the sharp aroma of disinfectant.

Dear Dario, the time has come for me to close the imaginary window you opened for me on your amazing world. I hope you don't feel that I've betrayed you by all the lies I made up; I simply wanted to read one more book by you before I go, and now my desire has been fulfilled. Please do accept my apologies, they come from the bottom of my heart.

I feel extremely weak and yet very serene, and much of that is due to you and the friendship you've given me over these last months. I ask you one more favor: conclude the book right here. By all means reply, but let's not get too maudlin or downbeat; I want this story to end on a note of rediscovery and redemption. Also, as to a title . . . ? I came up with Too Much Tuscan Wine. What do you think?

Mimì

I finish reading, and am both incredulous and devastated. The first thing to pass through my mind is, why hadn't I ever suspected it was her? . . . On second thought, she hadn't really given me cause for suspicion; she'd been very consistent with her "publisher's representative" pose, even to the point of contacting my manager.

Inevitably my thoughts return to that night I spent with her, and I realize that the keyboard of the computer is spattered with my tears. *Piangevo come una vite tagliata* — "I cried like a pruned vine." In all the intervening years I have never forgotten Mia and our brief but blissful encounter. In fact, for months afterwards I berated myself for not having asked for her address; I had no way to contact my sweet little Mimì. I could never forget the day I caught her spying on me from behind that bush, and recognized the young girl who often swept into the village like a jasmine-scented breeze to shop for groceries with her mother. She was so petite, so slender. When she passed before the bar she caused such an excited stir among my friends; in fact we used to fantasize about ways to get her attention and invite her to the Belvedere. So when I spotted her crouching behind that bush, I only pretended to read; in fact I was working out a plan to surprise her from behind. I dove into the river and swam away, then when I was well out of sight I climbed out and crossed a sunflower field to double back — and while I was at it, I plucked one from the ground to give to her.

I've always been extremely shy and my heart was pounding like a sledgehammer. But when I gazed into her dreamy eyes I realized that she was even more timid than I; and also I was playing on my home ground. From there everything just happened so naturally. I believe I first fell in love with her when she spat out the wine on the beach and blushed. She seemed so defenseless and had such an air of trust about her. I particularly liked it when she spoke in Italian with her marked American accent. When the time finally came for us to part, my heart sank like lead. I actually remained a long while on the grounds of her house with my eyes glued to her window; and when I saw the light go out I realized that I would never see her again.

Now, almost a quarter of a century later, she suddenly reappears and confides in me about her terrible fate. I desperately want to do something, but the only thing I can do right now is reply. My hands are shaking but somehow I manage.

My Sweet Mimì,
Of course it's you! How did I not realize before? You've been very smart about keeping up your alter ego, but there was still something about you that showed through; it's been nagging at me for some time.

I thought about you for years after our meeting; then, inevitably, you became a memory — a memory I treasured, certainly, but still confined to the past. Now I find myself writing these words with difficulty, because I'm trembling and tears are blotting my keyboard. My only desire now is to be next to you and hold you tight and kiss you as we did that magical day fate threw us together on the river bank. My sweet little Mimì, the girl in the flowery dress, whose hazel eyes could have lit up the entire planet. Now I realize why nobody is out there waiting for me; because that place belongs to you. You are the woman with whom I should have shared the sunrises and sunsets on the Chianti hills, the one who should have brightened my lonely life, Mimì. You ask me to forgive you . . . what for? You've been so close to me these past months, keeping me company in my solitude, returning my friendship and affection. You've also prodded me to write an entire book — and when it's published I'll come and promote it in the U.S. You'll accompany me, won't you, Mimì? And then you'll come and stay with me in Tuscany, and I'll take you back to those enchanting places that so captivated you all those years ago and that still nourish your soul.

In the meantime I respect your wishes and will conclude the book right here, right now (anyway, I'm running out of wine quotes!). And to celebrate I will open a very special Brunello Riserva that I've been saving for just the right occasion. For *this* occasion, whether I knew it or not.

Now I will go and light the fire because winter has arrived, and I expect to find the hills covered in frost tomorrow. Allow me raise the goblet to us, and to our book, *Too Much Tuscan Wine*.

Thank you, my sweet Mimì!

Love
Dario

Dedicated to MIA LANE
December 31, 1966 – April 24, 2007

Mia Lane Mimì as I remembered her

279

RINGRAZIAMENTI

How can I not begin by mentioning Mimì Lane; alas, she is no longer among us, but it is *only* thanks to her that I now have a third book on the shelves. I know somewhere she is smiling with pride and joy that she has achieved her final objective.

Also, if you will bear with me, I must once more pay tribute to the Chianti hills among which I live, and which continue to inspire me daily.

Thanks are also due to Robert Rodi and his partner Jeffrey Smith. Robert has played a fundamental role in creating this work and I invite my readers to discover his own books, which are the fruit of a truly talented literary *genio*.

An exceptionally special thanks to James Swift for the proof reading he volunteers doing and that he does so well

A partcular appreciation to my manager Laura and to her daughter Esther Rose who are both so patient and generous to me.

Thanks to Barbara, Riccardo, Arianna, and Tommy and his girlfriend Cristina of Moviement, with whom I have produced a number of DVDs on themes similar to my books.

Loving gratitude goes out to my *sorellina* Agnese and her boyfriend Giacomo, even if they no longer come visit me; also to my *socio* Stefano and his wife Elisa; and to my *special* agents Alan and Mindy. To Laura Strom and Deb and Bob. *Grazie mille* to Andrea/Luca (and his newly born son Aldo) and to Leo; I hereby invite them to partake in one more final Truss. *Grazie* to my team of guides: Annalisa, Alessandro, Alessandra, Elena, Franco and Leonardo.

Thanks to everyone in my village, and to the bars that I have helped make rich. Thanks to Carolina, because the day the book was completed she joined me in my celebrations.

Grazie to my parents, who worry too much about me: Mamma Biancastella & Poch Giovanni (both of whom I'm sure will be shocked when they read certain chapters), my brother Cristiano the winemaker who supplies me with "inspiration" (i.e. cases of wine), his wife Danda; and their children Anastasia, Sebastiano and Nicky.

Warmest thanks to all the members of my *contrada*, especially Ennio who is sadly no longer with us, and who had a dream that I will try to realize for him. Also Francesco the archivist and *Rettore* Fabio, and *Capitano* Giovanni Falciani for our recent victories.

Thanks to Paolo Nascimbeni and the seven thousand people on my mailing list who regularly endure my updates. Thanks to Borgo Scopeto, in particular Alessandro, Patrizia, Giuseppe, Michaela,Eliana and the chef.

Thanks to Gina, Oriano, Clara, and Paola and Massimo, of course. *Grazie* to Eliseo, Fabio, Bianca, Paolo and Rosanna's family. Another particular thanks to Orazio, Giulio (who has shrunk recently), *Dottor* Becchini, Michele, Manola, the late Umberto, Pietro, Alessio, Clara, and even Emanuele, because they make such wonderful characters, even if they aren't aware of it. *Grazie* to Mauro and Emilia and their noble dog Loris. *Grazie infinite* to all those who host me when I come to the U.S. on my book tours, and who go to so much trouble organizing events for me. Thanks to Laura C. and to all those who deserve to be thanked but who I have inevitably forgotten. Thank you Stephanie (Go LSU!)

And finally — thanks to the Chianti Classico, an endless source of comfort, inspiration, sublimity and joy.

Grazie nuovamente dolce Mimì.

CHECK OUT MY NEW DVD's!

I have produced together with Video Professional Studio three DVD's and am excited to share them with you! All DVD's are narrated in English language (with my voice) and are available in Pal or NTSC (for US only) versions.

MY CHIANTI:

A Day in the Life of Tuscan Author Dario Castagno

"My Chianti," loosely based on the book *A Day in Tuscany*, features author Dario Castagno as himself, and his real-life neighbors that he encounters in the small Chianti village of Vagliagli. Filmed in only 3 days, most of the scenes are impromptu and unscripted, and even captures scenes in which the "actors" were unaware that the cameras were still rolling! The documentary-style movie illustrates a "day in the life" of the author after having just returned from a 3-month long book tour in the U.S. It introduces viewers to a colorful array of local characters, each with their own unique stories to tell, breathtaking panoramas from the author's real-life home, and an intimate "walking tour" through the memories and locations dearest to Castagno's heart. Spend A *Day in Tuscany* and experience the simple life in the enchanting hills of Chianti. Narrated in English by Castagno himself with excerpts from his second book. The film also features authentic Italian dialog (subtitled) and includes some passages from his new book, *Too Much Tuscan Wine*, due out in April 2008.

Feature length approx. 120 min. Language: English. Widescreen, High-Definition, Color, Dolby Digital Surround Sound, NTSC version

THE DAYS OF THE PALIO

The Days of the Palio is a brief history of our unique medieval tradition that is held twice a year in Siena. By viewing this video you will experience not only the race but also the celebrations of the victors and the intense emotions the Sienese live on the days proceeding the Palio.

SIENA: A WORLD APART

The newly released DVD "Siena- A World Apart" is a documentary filmed in high definition by Video Professional Studio motion picture company in Siena. The film reveals the motives that make a small town like Siena appeal to thousands of tourists and the reasons why so many sociologists worldwide choose to study the bizarre character of its inhabitants whose roots go as far back to the Etruscan period. The movie has been conceived together with Emilio Ravel a national celebrity deeply in love with his city and is narrated by best selling British born Sienese author Dario Castagno in his typical "signorile" voice. Be prepared to enjoy over an hour of emotions that reach its peak when you will experience the passions lived by the Sienese during the days of the Palio horse race through amazing unforgettable touching scenes.

DVD'S CAN BE ORDERED ON WWW.DARIOCASTAGNO.COM

A Day in Tuscany

CHIANTI SENSATIONS COLLECTED ON A ONE-MILE WALK

by **Dario Castagno**
with **Robert Rodi**

In the same series available

Too Much Tuscan Sun
CONFESSIONS OF A CHIANTI TOUR GUIDE

by **Dario Castagno**
with **Robert Rodi**

Printed in Italy
May 2008